# Chemistry for You

BOOK TWO

# *Acknowledgements*

Acknowledgements are due to the following for permission to reproduce photographs:
C. Ashall p.127; BP Oil Ltd pp.6, 85; British Airways p.14; British Alcan Aluminium Ltd pp.136, 149; British Gas Corporation p.84; British Steel Corporation pp.136, 154, 155; The British Sulphur Corporation Ltd p.10; The Boots Company PLC p.60; J. Allen Cash Ltd pp.67, 126; Copper Development Association p.38; Crompton Parkinson Ltd p.31; The Distiller's Co. PLC p.92; FAO pp.61, 127; Fison's Pest Control Ltd p.45; The Flour Advisory Bureau p.93; Grants of St James's pp.90, 92; Griffin and George p.75; *The Guardian* p.30; ICI Agricultural Division p.127; ICI Corporate Slide Bank pp.30, 54, 61, 103, 104, 105, 115, 119; *Industrial Diamond Review* p.86; Institute of Dermatology p.60; Institute of Geological Sciences p.86; Mary Quant p.101; Metropolitan Police p.93; National Coal Board pp.6, 84; Nuffield-Chelsea Curriculum Trust p.8; Nuffield Foundation (from *Revised Nuffield Chemistry Handbook for Pupils*, Longman 1978) p.9; G.E.C. Overton pp.18, 26, 51, 99; Portsmouth and Sunderland Newspapers Ltd p.30; Space Frontiers Ltd p.67; St Mary's Hospital Medical School p.60; Tungstone Batteries Ltd p.31; UK Atomic Energy Authority pp.45, 85; Wella p.101; Zinc Development Association p.38.

Hutchinson & Co. (Publishers) Ltd
An imprint of the Hutchinson Publishing Group
17–21 Conway Street, London W1P 6JD

Hutchinson Group (Australia) Pty Ltd
30–32 Cremorne Street, Richmond South, Victoria 3121
PO Box 151, Broadway, New South Wales 2007

Hutchinson Group (NZ) Ltd
32–34 View Road, PO Box 40-086, Glenfield, Auckland 10

Hutchinson Group (SA) (Pty) Ltd
PO Box 337, Bergvlei 2012, South Africa

First published 1983


Designed by The New Book Factory, London
Phototypesetting by Parkway Illustrated Press, London and Abingdon
Illustrations by M. J. Latchem
Cartoons by Dave Parkin

Printed and bound in Great Britain by
Anchor Brendon Ltd,
Tiptree, Essex

**British Library Cataloguing in Publication Data**

Latchem, W. E.
Chemistry for you. Bk. 2
1. Chemistry—Examinations, questions, etc.
I. Title
540'.76 QD42

ISBN 0 09 144511 6

# Chemistry for You

## BOOK TWO

W E Latchem

Hutchinson

London Melbourne Sydney Auckland Johannesburg

# Safety

In Science we find out about ourselves and our world. To do this we ask questions. Those in Chemistry are about substances. Sometimes we can answer them just by looking. Using eyes (and ears) is called observation.

To answer other questions we need to do tests. A test in which we do something is called an experiment. It must be carefully planned. Even then it may be dangerous. So may the substances we use in doing it. We need to make Science safe for ourselves and others.

## Safety rules

**Experiments marked * should only be done by a teacher.**
Keep working areas clear of cases, books etc.
Listen carefully to instructions.
Work with care and watch results.
Remember that clothes and hair will burn.
Point test tubes away from yourself and others.
**Wear eyeshields if there is any risk to eyes.** (To be quite safe wear them all the time.)
**Report any accident, however small, at once.**

DO NOT run, push or be silly in a laboratory.
DO NOT taste anything without permission.
DO NOT smell a gas except with great care.
DO NOT try your own experiments without permission.

The drawings shown are labels. They are used for dangerous substances. Each picture explains what the danger is. They appear on bottles and containers. Look for them on tankers and trucks.

Willie, Grace and George appear in this book too.

*Willie, for everyone's protection,*
*Points test tubes in a safe direction.*
*Grace, when stuff from test tubes flies,*
*Has eyeshields to protect her eyes.*
*George treats the bunsen flame with care,*
*He wouldn't like to lose his hair.*
*In all experiments we do in schools,*
*We must obey the Safety rules.*

explosive

toxic (poisonous)

corrosive

oxidizing agent (oxidant)

flammable (will burn)

harmful or irritating

# Contents

This book is made up of units, usually of two pages, which deal with one topic. Several related topics make up a section. Experiments are numbered with the section number. Suitable questions are included in each section.

**Important note**
**Experiments marked * should only be done by a teacher.**

# What is chemistry? Tell me again!

Chemistry is part of Science. In Science we find out and explain. We find out about ourselves and our world. To do this we have to ask questions.

Our world is made of 'stuff'. It has earth, air, rocks, sand, water. . . . We are made of bones, teeth, hair, skin. . . . All this 'stuff' is called matter.

A particular kind of matter is called a substance. Iron is a substance. So is chalk. Water is a substance too. A substance can be a solid, a liquid or a gas. Solid, liquid and gas are the three states of matter.

Most matter is a mixture of substances. Air is a mixture of gases. Soil is a mixture of solids and water. Water has other substances dissolved in it.

In Chemistry we find out about substances. To do this we first ask three kinds of question.

1. How can we get a substance on its own? This means taking other substances away from it. In Chemistry we first need to make substances pure.

2. How can we recognize a substance? Suppose you have a white powder. How do you know whether it is chalk, salt, sugar, aspirin or . . .?

3. How can we use a substance to make new ones? A change which gives a new substance is called a chemical change. If no new substance is formed the change is a physical one. We make the changes. We also explain them. Many questions begin with 'Why'.

In Science we find out about our world.

Drilling for oil in the North Sea.

## Where do we get substances?

They come from the earth. For example, coal is mined. Oil is found underground. Rocks in the earth are mixtures of substances. These substances are all minerals.

The sea is a liquid, water. It has many substances dissolved in it. Salt is only one of these. Air can provide substances which are gases.

Plants give us food. They provide fibres such as cotton and linen. We use these to make clothing.

Plants provide sugar and starch. They give plant oils. Plants are the source of substances like rubber.

Opencast mining for coal.

Our world provides mixtures. From mixtures we make single substances. We make substances as pure as possible. From them we find ways of making useful new ones.

Sulphur is a substance which comes from the earth. We buy it in lumps called roll sulphur. We shall use it to remind ourselves of some important ideas.

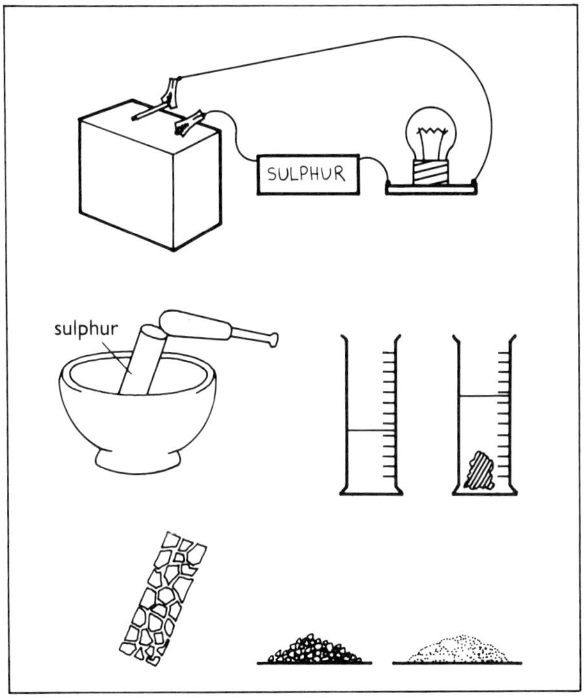


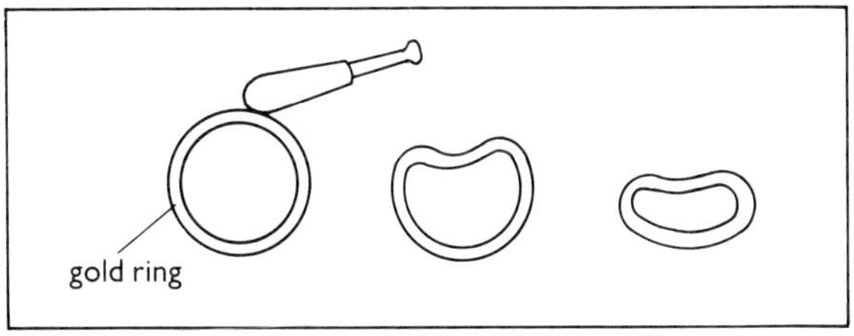


## Experiment 1.1 The properties of sulphur

**Take a lump of roll sulphur. Find out if it is a conductor. Put it in a mortar. Hit it with a pestle.**

**Use one piece to find its density. Measure its mass on a balance. Drop it into a measuring cylinder containing water. Note how much the level rises.**

**This rise is its volume.**

$$\text{density} = \frac{\text{mass}}{\text{volume}} \ (\text{g/cm}^3)$$

**Grind the rest of the sulphur into a fine powder.**

What colour is sulphur?
Does it break into pieces easily?
Does it conduct an electric current?
Is its density high or low?
Could you mistake sulphur for gold?

The lump of sulphur splits up into smaller pieces. It can be ground into a fine powder. But no one has split sulphur up into different substances. Sulphur is an element.

Sulphur is a shiny yellow solid. So is gold. Both are elements. But no one mistakes sulphur for gold. Sulphur is brittle. It breaks up when it is hit. Gold is not brittle. It changes shape when hit.

Both elements are shiny. Gold is shiny in a different way. All metals have this shine. It is called metallic lustre. Gold is a conductor. Sulphur is not. The density of gold is much higher than the density of sulphur.

Gold and sulphur differ in appearance. We can tell one from the other. They also behave in different ways. What a substance looks like and what it does are its **properties**. **Appearance and behaviour are properties**. Behaviour is the most important.

# More properties of sulphur

## Experiment 1.2 The action of heat on sulphur

Use the powdered sulphur from Experiment 1.1. Nearly fill a test tube with it. Heat it gently. Shake the tube. Heat and shake the tube until the sulphur has melted. The colour should still be pale yellow.

Pour the liquid into a filter paper cone. Wait until the top is solid. Slowly open the cone.

Is gentle heating enough to melt the sulphur?
Are the crystals on the paper a form of sulphur?

As liquid sulphur cools crystals form. They are needle shaped. They are one form of sulphur. Gentle heating melts sulphur. Sulphur is a non-metal element. Most non-metals have low melting points.

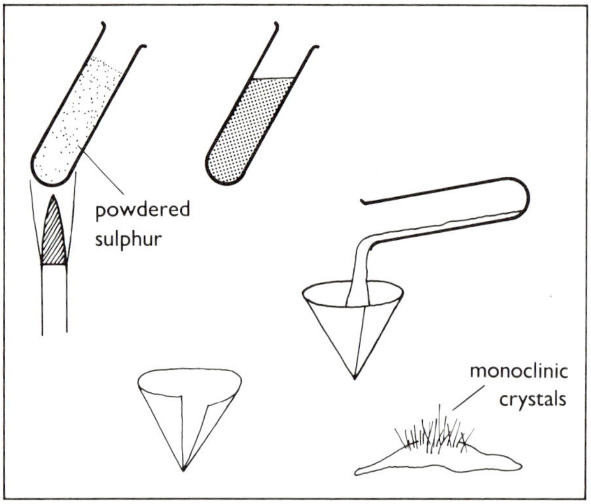


## Experiment 1.3 Other crystals of sulphur

Put powdered sulphur in a test tube. Add warm olive oil. Stopper the tube and shake it. Put drops of filtrate on a glass slide. Put the rest in a shallow dish. Leave these to stand. Observe the crystals.

Are they like those in Experiment 1.2?

These crystals are also sulphur. They are not needle shaped. These double pyramid crystals are **rhombic sulphur**. We can prove that they are both sulphur.

Rhombic sulphur crystals.

## Experiment 1.4 To burn sulphur in oxygen

Put rhombic sulphur in a combustion spoon. Set it alight. Hold it in a gas jar of oxygen, or air. Take out the spoon. Add a dry blue litmus paper.

Add water to the jar. Replace the lid. Shake the jar. Add Universal Indicator in drops. Burn the needle shaped crystals from Experiment 1.2 in the same way. Use the same tests. Compare the results.

Do both crystal forms burn in the same way?
Do the tests give the same results with both?
What happens to the dry litmus paper?
Do the indicators show an acid in the water?
Does the gas formed by burning react with water?

The needle shaped crystals are **monoclinic sulphur**.

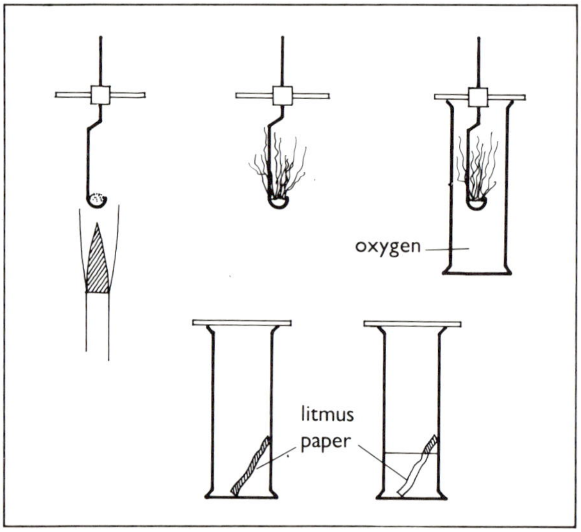

Burning is a chemical change. A new substance is formed. It is the gas sulphur dioxide. It has little effect on dry litmus. Indicators show an acid in the water.

Sulphur + oxygen → sulphur dioxide
Sulphur dioxide + water → sulphurous acid

Word equations sum up chemical reactions.

Both crystals behave in the same way. Both contain sulphur. We can prove by experiment that they contain only sulphur. They are forms of the same element.

**Different forms of the same element are called allotropes.** Rhombic and monoclinic sulphur are allotropes of sulphur. Their chemical properties are alike. They differ in appearance.

### Experiment 1.5 The melting point of sulphur

Rotate a piece of glass tubing in the flame. When the glass is soft, take it out. Draw it out. Let it cool. Cut off a 3 cm length of the narrow tubing.

Seal one end in a bunsen flame. Fill the tube with powdered rhombic crystals. Tie it to a 200 °C thermometer. Hold it upright in medicinal paraffin.

Gently heat the paraffin. Stir it steadily. When the sulphur melts note the temperature. Take out the thermometer. As soon as the sulphur becomes solid put it back. Determine the melting point.

What is the first melting point of sulphur?
Will boiling water be hot enough to melt sulphur?
Is the second melting point different?

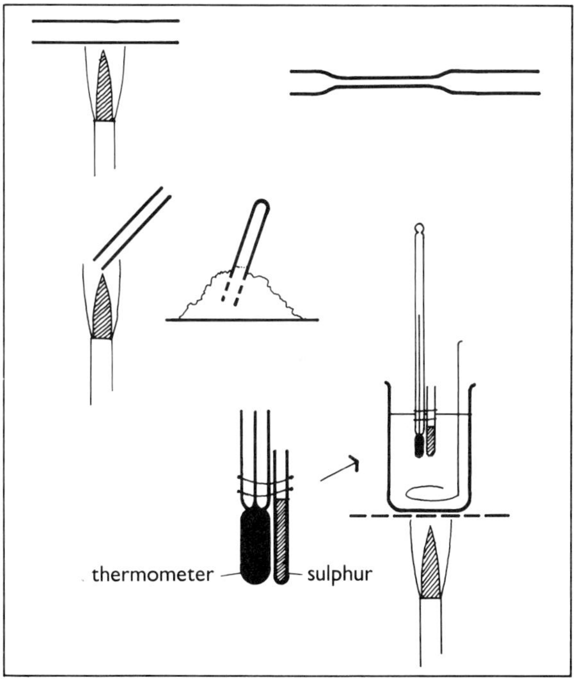


The melting point of sulphur is 113 °C. Most metals melt at much higher temperatures. Liquid sulphur forms monoclinic crystals on cooling. The second temperature is the melting point of these. It is about 119 °C. Allotropes differ in physical properties.

Monoclinic crystals form at temperatures above 96 °C. Rhombic crystals form below 96 °C. Each form changes to the other at this temperature. It is called the **transition temperature**.

*Willie's teacher got quite stroppy*
*When Willie called it allo – tropy.*
*'The name for crystal forms' said he,*
*'Must be pronounced al-ot-ro-pee.*
*But if you mean just one, I hope*
*You will pronounce it allo-trope.'*

Monoclinic sulphur crystals.

# *Where does sulphur come from?*

Sulphur occurs 'native'. This means that the element itself is found in nature. Most of the world's sulphur comes from the USA. It is found in the southern states. People drilling for oil found it by accident. It was thirty years before it was mined.

The sulphur is in a layer of limestone. This is about 150 metres down underground. The problem is quicksand. There is a layer of it between the surface and the sulphur. This prevents normal mining.

In 1890 a man named Frasch solved the problem. Under normal pressure water boils at 100 °C. It is not hot enough to melt sulphur. An increase in pressure will raise the boiling point.

Frasch heated water at fifteen times normal pressure. Water is still liquid at 170 °C. It is called superheated water. It can melt sulphur.

A hole is bored down to the limestone. Three steel pipes are fed into it. They are placed one inside the other. Superheated water is forced down the outer pipe. It spreads through the limestone. At 170 °C it melts the sulphur.

Compressed air is blown down the inner pipe. The liquid sulphur is forced up the middle one. It is kept hot by the superheated water going down. The liquid runs out into huge tanks.

At 170 °C only the sulphur melts. Other substances are left behind. So the sulphur which reaches the surface is pure. It cools and turns to a solid.

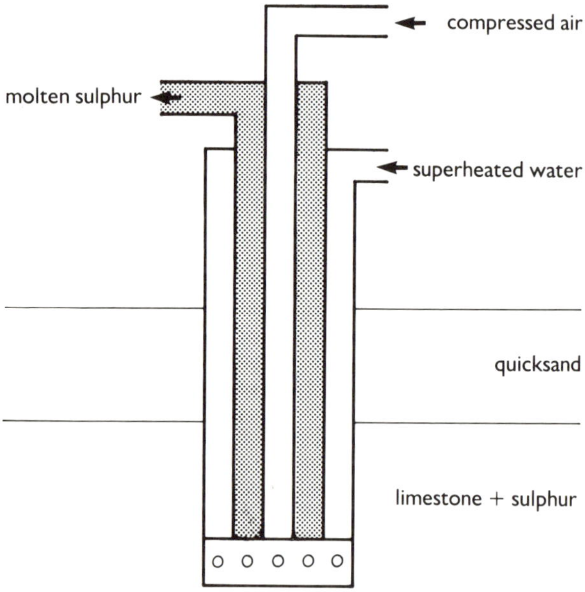


### What makes sulphur important?

Huge amounts of sulphur are used to manufacture sulphuric acid. We shall deal with this acid soon. Sulphur is also used to make other sulphur compounds. It is used in making matches and fireworks.

Rubber comes from the sap of the rubber tree. It can also be made from petroleum gases. In both cases it is soft. Sulphur added to the rubber makes it harder and more elastic. This is called vulcanization.

The Frasch process is used to mine sulphur. The photograph shows liquid sulphur pouring into a tank where it will become solid.

## Summary

We and the world are made of 'stuff'. This 'stuff' is called matter. It can be solid or liquid or gas. Solid, liquid and gas are the three states of matter.

A particular kind of matter is a substance. Gold is a substance. So is sulphur. So is sulphur dioxide. We recognize a substance by its properties. These are what it looks like and what it does.

An element is a substance. It cannot be split up into other substances. Most elements fall into one of two classes. They are either metals or non-metals. Sulphur is a non-metal. Gold is a metal.

Elements combine. When sulphur burns it combines with the element oxygen. A new substance is formed called sulphur dioxide. Sulphur dioxide is a compound. It can be split up into other substances.

In some changes new substances are formed. They are chemical changes or chemical reactions. The reactions of a substance are its chemical properties.

Melting is a physical change. No new substance is formed. Molten sulphur is still sulphur. So its melting point is a physical property of sulphur.

Some elements exist in more than one form. Each form is the pure element. Different crystal forms of an element are allotropes. They have the same chemical properties. Their physical properties differ. Rhombic and monoclinic crystals are allotropes of sulphur. Allotropy is the existence of allotropes.

*A clever young fellow named Frasch*
*Mined sulphur to make some hard cash.*
*Steel pipes through the quicksand*
*Took an air-water mix and*
*Molten sulphur came up in a flash.*

## Questions

1. Copy this out, filling in the blanks.

   Sulphur is found in the earth. It occurs ______. Most of the world's sulphur comes from ______. It is in a layer of ______. This is about ______ metres down. A layer of ______ prevents ordinary mining of sulphur.

   Sulphur melts at ______°C. It is not melted by ______ water. It needs ______ water. This is water heated under greater ______. It is still liquid at ______°C.

   Label the drawing of the Frasch method. Explain why the sulphur it gives is very pure.

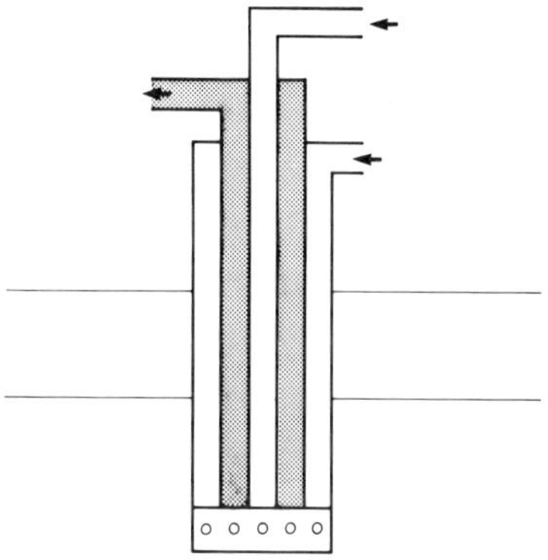

2. Explain what each of the following is. Use two short sentences for each.
   a) an element,
   b) a compound,
   c) an allotrope,
   d) the transition temperature of sulphur,
   e) a chemical reaction,
   f) a physical property.

3. Elements fall into two main classes. Name them. In which class would you put
   a) sulphur,
   b) gold?

   In what ways do gold and sulphur differ in
   c) behaviour,
   d) appearance. What are appearance and behaviour called?

   Write word equations for
   e) burning sulphur in oxygen,
   f) dissolving sulphur dioxide in water.

   What colour is litmus in the solution? What could be used in place of litmus?

# Atoms and molecules

In Chemistry we ask questions about substances. Many of them begin with 'What'.

What crystals form in molten sulphur?
What happens when sulphur burns?

We can plan an experiment to answer them.

Many questions begin with 'How' or 'Why'.

How do sulphur and oxygen combine?
Why are allotropes so different?

We ask 'What' questions every day.
An L–driver may ask:

'What happens when I turn on the ignition?'
'What happens if I press the starter?'

Some L–drivers go on to ask 'How' and 'Why':

'Why does the ignition light come on?'
'How does the engine work?'

We need answers to 'How' and 'Why' questions in Science. One answer to them is often 'Particles'. All matter is made up of particles. They are called atoms and molecules.

### Experiment 2.1 Particles

**1. Put a gas jar of carbon dioxide over a gas jar of air. Slide the lids out from between them. Count up to five. Put the lids back. Separate the jars. Test each of them for carbon dioxide.**

What test did you use for carbon dioxide?
In which of the jars is it found?
Can you explain *how* it gets there?

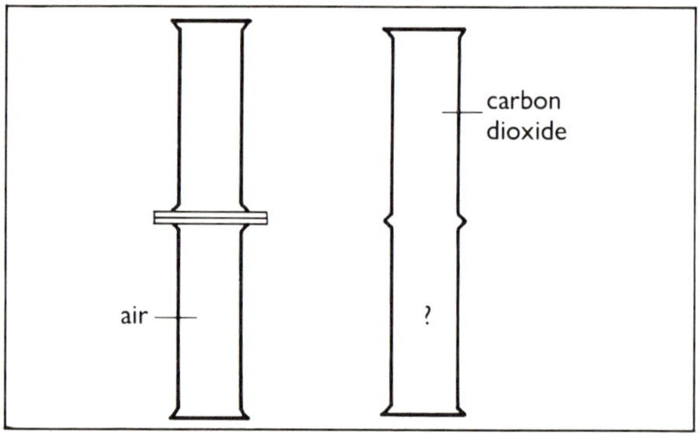


**2. Do this again with the air gas jar on top.**

Is there carbon dioxide in the top jar?
If so, how did it get there?

**3. Grease round the edge of a gas jar lid. In a fume cupboard put three drops of bromine on the lid. Cover it at once with a gas jar. Let it stand with a white screen behind it.**

What happens to the liquid bromine?
What other changes can you see?
Can you explain how and why they happen?

**4. Turn the gas jar from test 3 the right way up. Invert another gas jar over it. Take away the lid. Let the gas jars stand for some time.**

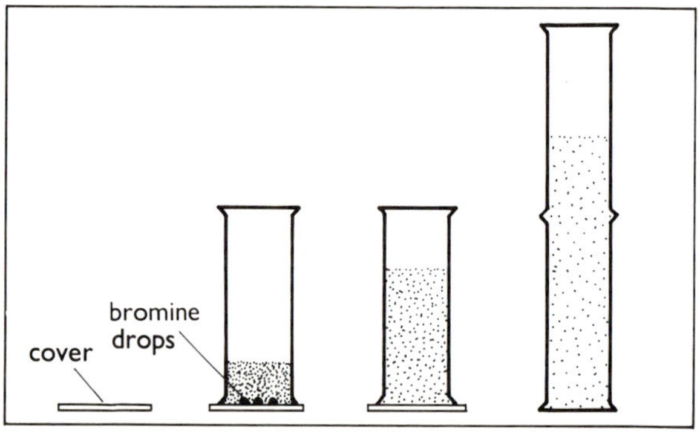

Carbon dioxide is 'heavier' than air. $CO_2$ is more dense. We expect it to fall out of the top jar in test 1. Lime water proves that it does. When we add lime water to the bottom jar it turns 'milky'.

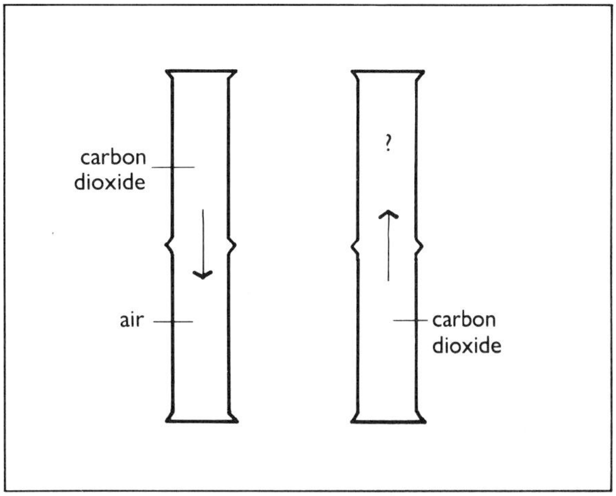


In test 2 lime water shows carbon dioxide in the top jar. It rose into this jar in five seconds. How does a 'heavier' gas manage to rise?

In test 3 the liquid bromine evaporates. Brown vapour slowly spreads up the jar. It fills it. In test 4 it goes on slowly to fill a second jar.

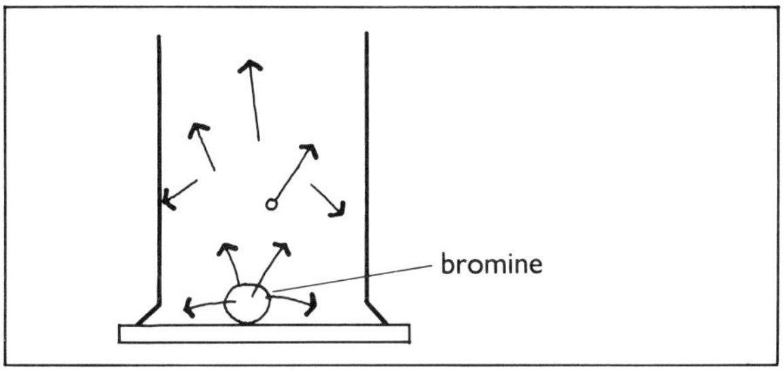


Do liquids and gases stretch like elastic?
Or do they slowly grow upwards like plants?
Or are they made up of tiny moving particles?

I expect you chose the right answer. All matter is made up of particles. They are atoms and molecules. They move. This movement explains the results.

Particles in solids are in fixed positions. They move very little. This explains why solids have a definite shape. Experiments show some movement.

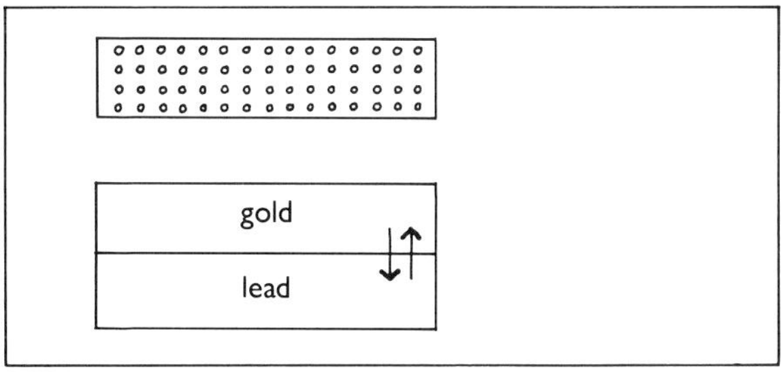


A gold block stands on a lead block. They are left for a long time. The gold next to the lead is tested. It contains some lead. The top surface of the lead contains some gold. Traces of each metal have moved into the other one.

Substances spread by particles moving. This movement is called **diffusion**.

## Atoms and molecules

We hit a lump of roll sulphur. It broke into small pieces. Suppose we go on splitting up these pieces. The bits will get smaller and smaller. Suppose that we reach the smallest possible piece. Because sulphur is an element, this piece is an atom. The word atom means 'not cuttable'.

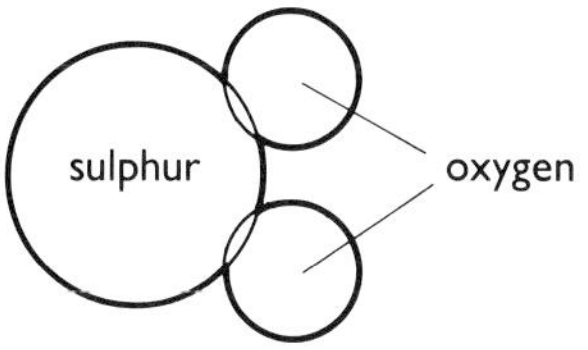


Oxygen is an element. Sulphur burns in it. Their atoms meet. They join up to form larger particles. Each of these is a molecule. It has one sulphur atom bonded to two oxygen atoms.

An **atom** is the smallest piece of an element.
A **molecule** consists of two or more atoms bonded together.

# *Atoms – are they really there?*

The idea that matter is made of atoms is not new. It was first suggested in about 400 BC. The idea is called the Atomic Theory. It was revived by John Dalton in 1803. He added extra ideas as well.

Atoms are too small to be seen. Why do we believe that they exist?

Vapour trails tell us that a plane is high in the sky.

**First:** We can see their effects. What they do shows. We may not *see* a high flying jet plane. Its vapour trail tells us it is there. We may never see a mole under the lawn. Its mole hills show us that it has been there. The effects of atoms can be seen.

**Second:** The Atomic Theory answers 'How' and 'Why' questions very well. It can explain all our results in Science. Some results can *only* be explained by the existence of atoms.

### Experiment 2.2 The Brownian motion

**Set up a small glass cell. Focus a beam of light through it. Puff some smoke into the cell. Look at it through a microscope. Describe what you see.**

What is it which is actually moving?
What makes this movement happen?

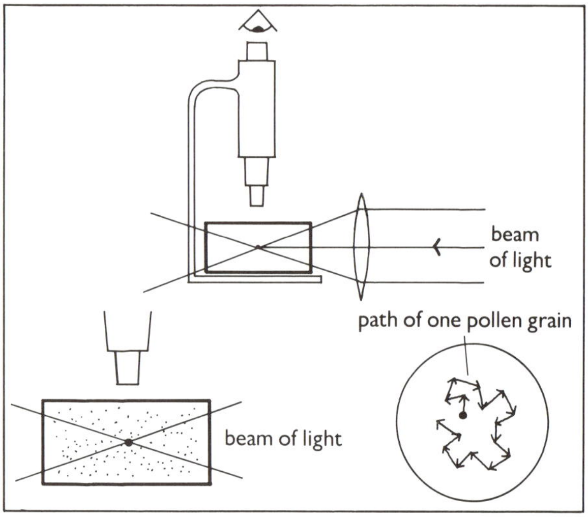


Smoke consists of tiny bits of solid. The beam of light acts as a searchlight. The solid bits of smoke are lit up. They look like tiny points of light. We can see them through the microscope.

They are always moving. This effect was noticed in 1827 by Robert Brown. He floated grains of pollen on water. He looked at them through a microscope. They moved in all directions. They never stopped. This was called Brownian motion.

A pollen grain cannot move on its own. Neither can a particle of smoke dust. Something must make them move. There are air and water molecules around them.

Imagine millions of people round a balloon. They throw tennis balls at it. Suppose more balls hit it on the left hand side. Which way will it move? A second later more hit it on the right. What happens?

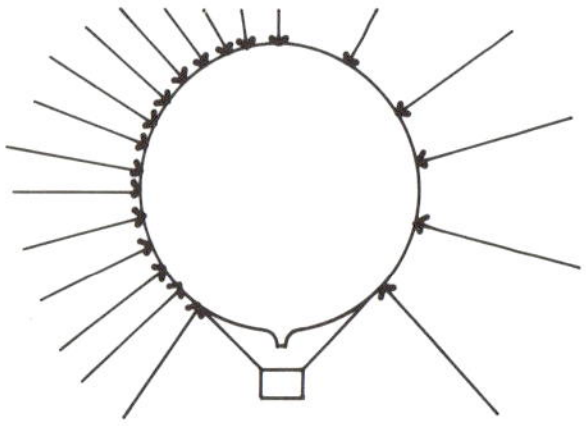

A smoke particle is like the balloon. Air molecules are like the tennis balls. They hit the smoke particle from all sides. If more hit it on one side, it moves. An instant later more hit it on a different side. It moves again.

Only moving particles explain Brownian motion.

We can use the idea of atoms and molecules. They explain many of our results. Here are some examples.

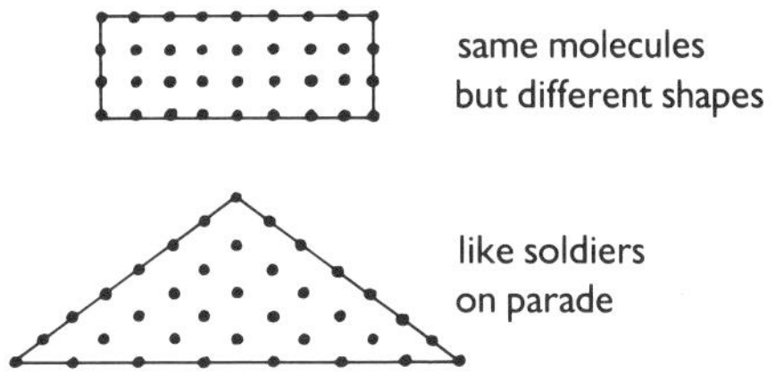


Any solid contains atoms and molecules. They are in fixed positions. They move very little. This explains why a solid keeps its shape. It explains why **allotropes** differ in shape. They have the same atoms. The atoms are arranged in different patterns.

Ice is a solid. We know ice melts to a liquid. How does it do this? Heat provides energy. This makes the molecules in ice move faster. They break out of their fixed positions. This is why ice **melts**. 0 °C is hot enough to make the change happen.

In a liquid the molecules move freely. They can move in all directions. This is why a liquid takes the shape of the vessel. Take water as an example.

Its molecules move inside the liquid. Some of them hit the surface. Fast moving ones will go through. This explains why liquids evaporate away in air. Heat makes the water molecules move faster. More of them are able to escape. **Evaporation** becomes faster. At 100 °C huge numbers of them escape. We see them as rising bubbles. These tell us that the water is boiling. The gas steam is given off.

Vapour is gas coming from a liquid below its boiling point.

The air above the water contains molecules. Water molecules escape. Some collide with air molecules. This may put them back into the water. Raising the pressure puts in more air molecules. Fewer water molecules escape. It needs a higher temperature to make the water boil. This is **superheated** water.

Put a soluble solid into a liquid. Molecules leave the solid. They pass into the liquid. They move freely. So they spread evenly through the liquid. A soluble solid is called a solute.

The molecules in the surface make it harder for liquid molecules to escape. The liquid must be heated more strongly. Its boiling point will be higher. A solute makes the **boiling point** of a solvent higher.

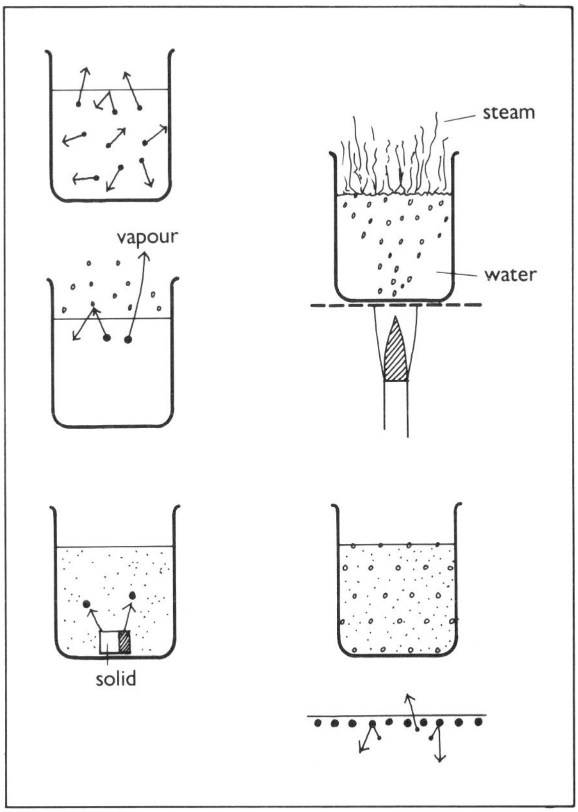


Gas and **vapour** molecules move anywhere. This explains why bromine vapour fills the jar. Cooling makes the molecules move more slowly. The gas turns back to a liquid. Further cooling almost stops them. The liquid turns back into a solid.

# *Atoms and molecules – how big are they?*

In Book 1 we tried to answer this question. We did two experiments. One tried to measure the mass of a molecule. In the other we tried to measure its thickness or diameter. Revise or repeat those experiments.

## Experiment 2.3 The mass of a particle or molecule

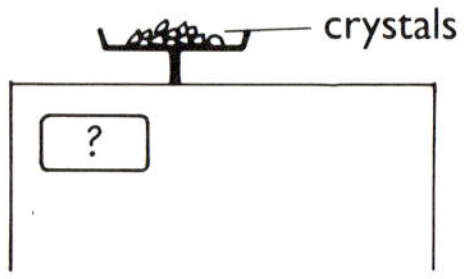


**Fill a 1000 cm$^3$ beaker with water. Measure the mass of four or five potassium manganate(VII) crystals. Drop them into the water. Let the crystals dissolve. Find out how many drops are needed to make 1 cm$^3$ of solution. Look at one drop through a microscope.**

Do the crystals colour the whole solution?
How much potassium manganate(VII) is there in one drop?
How much in one hundredth of a drop of solution?

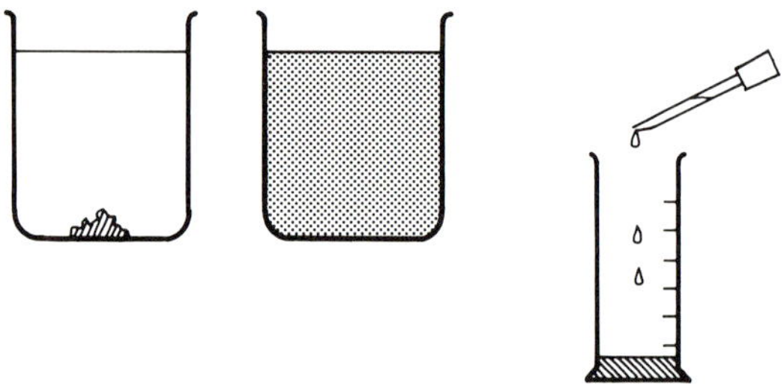

Purple solution forms round the crystals. It spreads. The whole solution becomes pink. A drop is seen to be pink through a microscope. Every drop has some potassium manganate(VII) in it. So has one hundredth of a drop.

Suppose the mass of the crystals is 0.2 g.
1000 cm$^3$ of solution contain 0.2 g. 1 cm$^3$ contains 0.000 02 g.

1 cm$^3$ is about twenty drops. One drop of solution contains 0.000 001 g.
One hundredth of a drop contains 0.000 001 g divided by 100.
The solution is pink. It contains at least one molecule of manganate(VII).
One molecule has a mass of less than 0.000 000 01 grams.

An atom or molecule has a very, very, very small mass.

In Book 1 we floated oil on water. We kept the oil inside a circle of cotton. We tried to make the oil layer one molecule thick. We compared the oil molecules with tennis balls on a pond.

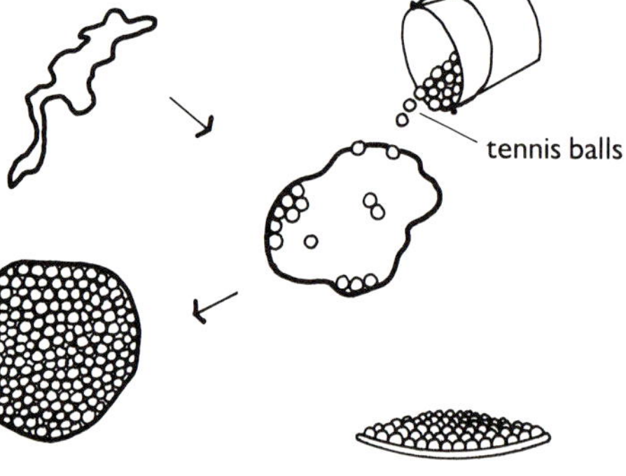


The oil used is stearic acid. It dissolves in some liquids. We used petroleum ether. The solution contained 0.1 cm$^3$ of oil in 1000 cm$^3$ of solution. Each drop contains oil molecules. The drop is like a bag or bucket of tennis balls.

Imagine a rope loop floating on water. Pour into it a bucket of tennis balls. Add a second bucket full. Go on until the loop is full. It then becomes a circle. The layer of tennis balls is one ball thick.

## Experiment 2.4 The diameter of a molecule

Fill a large funnel with water. Tie a 30 cm length of cotton into a loop. Grease it slightly. Drop it on to the water. Put one drop of oil solution into the loop. Add more drops, one at a time. Stop when the loop is just full. Test this by tapping it.

Count the number of drops used. Measure across the loop in centimetres. Find out how many drops make 1 $cm^3$ of solution. Work out the area of the circle.

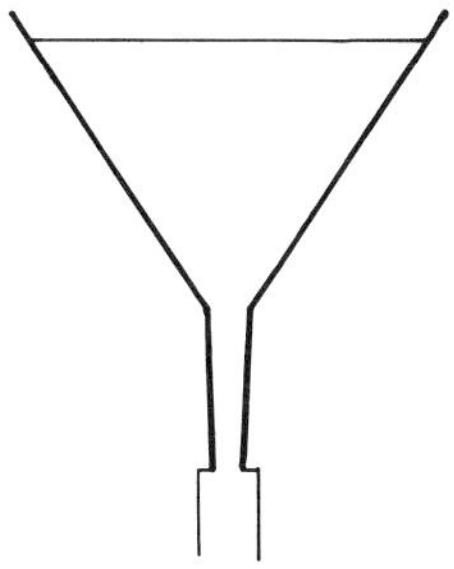

In Book 1 we put on watch glasses i) a drop of oil, ii) a drop of solution, iii) a drop of the solvent. The drop of oil did not evaporate. The solvent and solution did so very rapidly. This happens on water.

The ether in each drop of solution evaporates. The oil in it is left on the water. The oil molecules are moving. They spread over the water. Enough of them will fill the cotton loop. The oil layer is one molecule thick.

<u>My results</u>

Distance across cotton loop = 10 cm

Area of cotton loop
$= 3 \times 5^2 cm^2 = 75 cm^2$

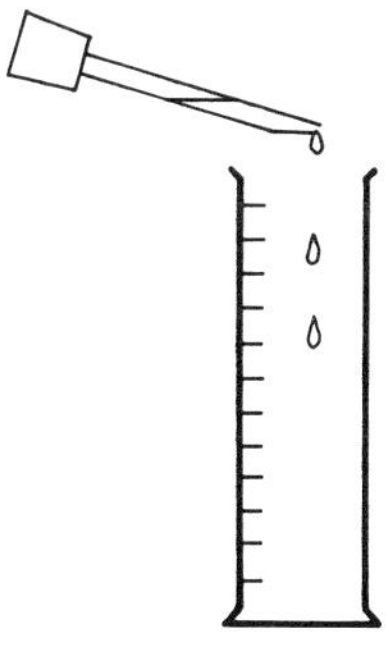

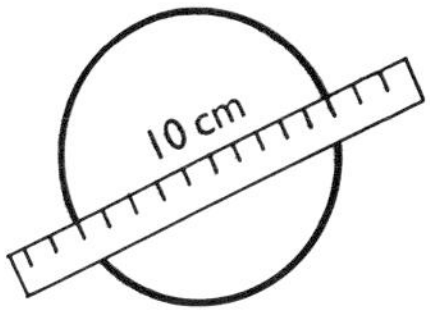


area $= \pi r^2 \simeq 3 \times 5^2$

1000 $cm^3$ of solution contains 0.1 $cm^3$ of oil
1 $cm^3$ of solution contains 0.0001 $cm^3$ of oil

There were 20 drops in 1 $cm^3$ of oil solution
1 drop contains $0.0001 \div 20$ $cm^3$ of oil

3 drops were needed to fill the loop with oil.
They contain $3 \times 0.000\,005 cm^3 = 0.000\,015 cm^3$.
This is the volume of oil in the loop. Its area is 75 $cm^2$. Volume is area × thickness.
The thickness of the loop = diameter of one molecule = 0.000 000 2 cm.
The result is about one ten millionth of a centimetre.
This is one thousand millionth of a metre.
Atoms and molecules are very, very, very small.

# More about atoms

Dalton revived old ideas about atoms. He added new ones. These ideas were the result of experiments. Much more has been done since then. Compare Dalton's ideas with the modern ones.

| Dalton's Atomic Theory | Modern ideas |
| --- | --- |
| Every element is made of atoms. They are small and indivisible. | Every element is made of atoms. Atoms are made of even smaller particles. |
| Atoms of the same element are exactly alike in mass and size. | Atoms of the same element are alike. They may not all have the same mass. |
| Atoms of one element are different from the atoms of others. They differ in mass and behaviour. | Atoms of different elements are not alike. They contain different numbers of the smaller particles. |

Atoms join together. The result is called a molecule. The smallest part of a compound is a molecule. It contains different atoms.

## Symbols

It is difficult to show an atom on paper. Dalton used a different picture for each kind.

a sulphur atom ⊕
an oxygen atom ○

Now we often use the first letter of the name of the element. O stands for an atom of oxygen. O is the **symbol** for oxygen. Choose symbols for hydrogen, sulphur and nitrogen. What would you use for the elements carbon, calcium and copper?

The symbol for carbon is C. For calcium and copper an extra letter is added. The symbol for calcium is Ca. For copper it is Cu from its Latin name cuprum.

Modern methods can measure the actual masses of atoms. They are too small to be useful. Instead, like Dalton, we compare the masses of atoms.

Do you remember this picture? The mass of the marble is 5 g. The mass of the golf ball is 45 g. This is nine times the mass of the marble. A cricket ball has a mass of 155 g. This is thirty-one times the mass of the marble. The relative masses are 1 to 9 to 31.

The hydrogen atom is like the marble. It is smallest. The mass of an oxygen atom is sixteen times as big. A sulphur atom has thirty-two times the mass of a hydrogen atom. The numbers 1, 16, 32 compare the masses of the atoms. They are called **relative atomic masses**.

We write relative atomic masses as H = 1, O = 16 etc.
1 gram of hydrogen contains a huge number of atoms.
It is roughly 602 000 000 000 000 000 000 000.
(Six hundred and two thousand million million million.)
We use L to stand for this number. It is called a mole.

L oxygen atoms make up a mole. Their mass will be 16 g. Each O atom has sixteen times the mass of an H atom. How many grams of sulphur will give us a mole of atoms?

Sulphur burns in oxygen. One S atom joins to two O atoms. A molecule of sulphur dioxide is written $SO_2$. Its mass is sixty-four times the mass of a hydrogen atom. L molecules of sulphur dioxide make up a mole. Its mass will be 64 g. 128 g of it will be two moles. $SO_2$ is the formula of sulphur dioxide.

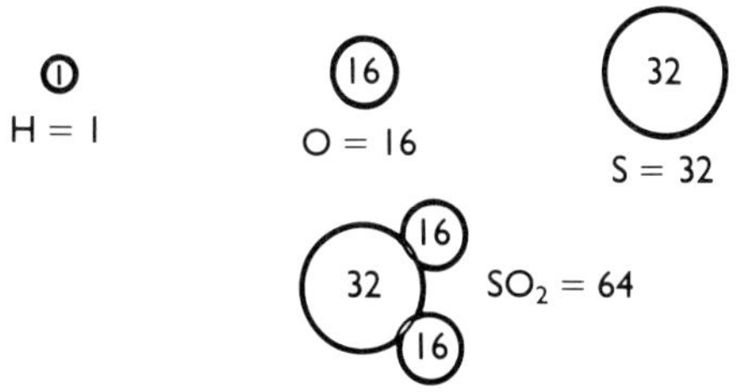


## *Experiment 2.5 The formula of tin oxide

**Gently heat a clean dry test tube. Let it cool. Measure its mass. Put into it about two grams of tin foil. Measure the mass of test tube and tin.**

**Support the tube in a fume cupboard. Add drops of concentrated nitric acid. When reaction has almost stopped, add more drops. Repeat this until no tin is left. Gently boil the liquid away.**

**Heat the solid. Stop when it gives no more brown gas. Let it cool. The white solid is tin oxide. Find the mass of tube and oxide. Use the results to work out the formula of the oxide. Sn = 119; O = 16.**

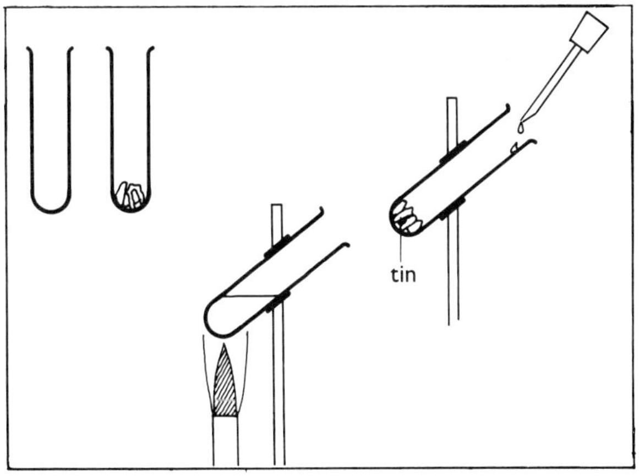


My results

Mass of test tube and oxide = 28.17 g
Mass of test tube and tin = 27.63 g
Mass of test tube = 25.62 g

Mass of tin oxide = 2.55 g
Mass of tin = 2.01 g
Mass of oxygen in the oxide = 0.54 g

2.01 g of tin combine with 0.54 g of oxygen
1 g of tin would combine with $\frac{0.54}{2.01}$ g of oxygen
119 g of tin would combine with $119 \times \frac{0.54}{2.01}$ g
119 g of tin [combine with] 31.9 g of oxygen
one mole of tin atoms ↕ Two moles of oxygen atoms
Sn 2O atoms
[Formula $SnO_2$]

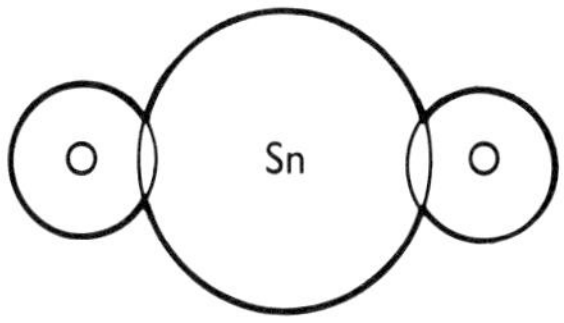

# Formula and equation

Chemistry deals with reactions. The substances we start with are reactants. The new substances formed are the products. Tests will tell us what they are. Then we can write a word equation.

reactants → products

It is the atoms and molecules which react. We find out how many moles of each take part. From this we can work out a formula equation for the reaction.

Moles of solid and liquid are easy to measure. We simply measure their masses. We use many of them in solution. We measure these by using molar solutions. A **molar solution** contains one mole of solute. It is present in 1000 $cm^3$ of solution.

Sodium carbonate reacts with dilute hydrochloric acid. We shall work out an equation for the reaction.

### Experiment 2.6 The equation for a reaction

**a) Put sodium carbonate into a test tube. Add the dilute acid. Test any gas given off. Evaporate some of the solution. Examine the crystals formed.**

**b) Measure 1 g of the anhydrous carbonate. Put it into a conical flask. Add drops of methyl orange indicator. Fill a burette with a molar solution of the acid. Note the reading on the burette.**

**Run a little acid into the flask. Swirl the mixture around. When reaction is nearly over, add a little more. Add acid until the indicator just changes colour. Note the burette reading at the end.**

What gas is given off?
What substance are the crystals likely to be?
What volume of acid reacts with the sodium carbonate?

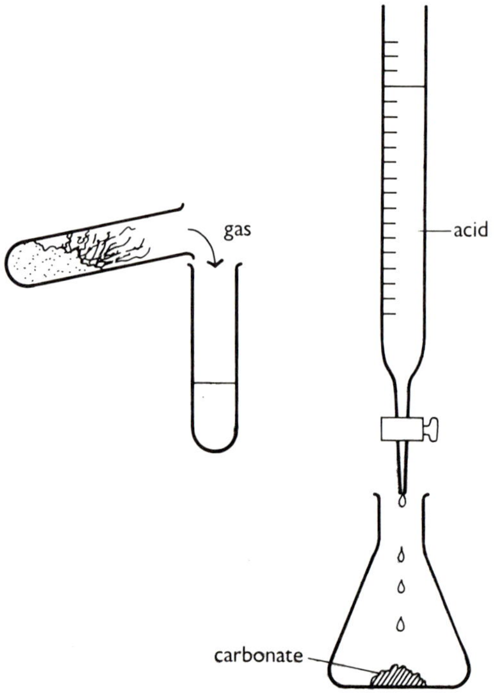


The formula of sodium carbonate is written $Na_2CO_3$. $Na_2CO_3$ has 106 times the mass of a hydrogen atom. One mole of it is 106 grams.

Relative atomic masses
Na = 23, C = 12, O = 16
Na + Na + C + O + O + O
23 + 23 + 12 + 16 + 16 + 16 = 106

The M solution contains 1 mole of acid in 1000 $cm^3$. Its formula is HCl. We know the volume of acid solution used. This reacts with 1 g of sodium carbonate.

The gas puts out a lighted splint. It makes lime water milky. One product is carbon dioxide. The solution gives cube-shaped crystals. This product is likely to be salt, sodium chloride.

The word equation starts as

sodium carbonate + hydrochloric acid → sodium chloride + carbon dioxide

Suppose 1 g of carbonate reacts with 19 $cm^3$ of M acid.
106 g of carbonate would need 106 × 19 cm = 2014 $cm^3$.
One mole of carbonate needs two moles of acid.

$Na_2CO_3 + 2HCl$

$Na_2CO_3$ will give $CO_2$. $Na_2$ will form 2NaCl. We still have one O atom and two H atoms. Together these make $H_2O$. Water is a third product.
The formula equation is

$$Na_2CO_3(s) + 2HCl(aq) \rightarrow 2NaCl(aq) + CO_2(g) + H_2O(l)$$

The states of the substances are shown. (s) stands for solid, (aq) stands for 'in water'. What do (g) and (l) mean?

## Summary

All matter is made up of atoms. An atom is shown by a symbol. It is usually the first letter of the name of the element. A second letter is added if needed. Some symbols come from Latin names. Sulphur is S, so silicon is Si and silver Ag (Latin name argentum).

The hydrogen atom is the smallest. Any other atom has a bigger mass. The number of times bigger is its relative atomic mass. If H = 1, then C = 12, O = 16 etc. These are relative atomic masses. 1 g of hydrogen, 12 g of carbon etc. contain the same number of atoms, L. L particles are called a mole.

Atoms combine to form molecules. A molecule of an element has only one kind of atom. A compound molecule contains different atoms. A formula shows which atoms a molecule contains. Many contain two atoms. They are called diatomic molecules.

Atoms and molecules are always moving. Those in a solid move only slightly. They are in fixed positions. Molecules move freely inside a liquid. A liquid evaporates because its molecules escape through the surface. Vapour passes into the air.

Gas molecules move freely in the vessel holding it. Heat makes all molecules move faster. This explains melting and boiling and other properties of matter.

A word equation shows the reactants and products. A formula equation shows how many moles of each react. The states of substances can be shown, e.g. (s) = solid.

## Questions

1. Which of these symbols come from Latin names? sulphur S; zinc Zn; lead Pb; calcium Ca; gold Au; sodium Na; potassium K; tin Sn; silver Ag.
2. Ice, water and steam contain only $H_2O$ molecules. What happens to them when
   a) ice melts,
   b) water evaporates,
   c) water boils,
   d) water freezes?
3. Say what each statement means
   a) the formula of water is $H_2O$,
   b) O = 16,
   c) the relative atomic mass of carbon is 12,
   d) smoke shows Brownian motion.
4. H = 1; O = 16; Br = 80; C = 12; S = 32; Fe = 56; Mg = 24; N = 14; Pb = 207; Cu=64.
   Which of these atoms has the greatest mass?
   Which has four times the mass of a nitrogen atom?
   Which has five times the mass of an oxygen atom?
   Which atom has half the mass of a copper atom?
   How many grams of magnesium make one mole?
5. 1.6 g of copper oxide is heated in hydrogen. Water and 1.28 g of copper are formed. Work out the formula of copper oxide. Cu = 64; O = 16.

# Sulphur dioxide and sulphuric acid

## Experiment 3.1 Properties of sulphur dioxide

**Fill four gas jars with sulphur dioxide. Use the method of Experiment 1.4 or a syphon of liquified gas. Shake the gas in each jar with water. Put in a neutral litmus paper.**

**Jar 1. Add potassium manganate(VII) solution.**
**Jar 2. Add potassium dichromate(VI) solution.**
**Jar 3. Add hydrogen peroxide solution.**

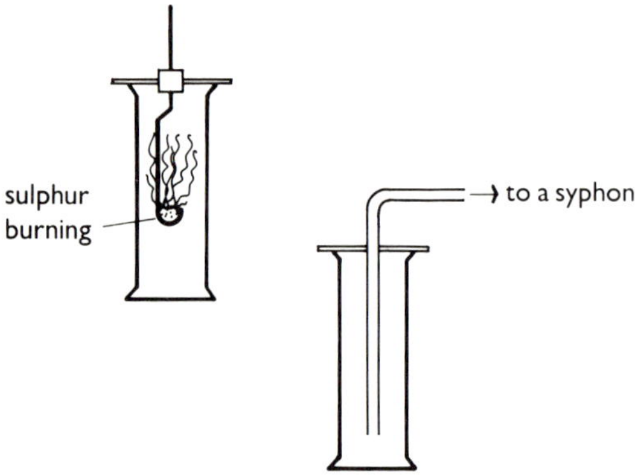


What does the litmus paper prove?
What happens to the potassium manganate(VII) solution?
What happens to the potassium dichromate(VI) solution?

In water litmus is neutral. The liquid in the jars turns litmus red. It must be an acid solution.

sulphur dioxide + water → sulphurous acid
$SO_2(g) + H_2O(l) \rightarrow H_2SO_3(aq)$

(g) stands for gas
(l) stands for liquid
(aq) means dissolved in water

The purple potassium manganate(VII) solution loses its colour. This may be a chemical change. The litmus is still red. There is still acid there. It is sulphuric acid. Its formula is $H_2SO_4$.

To convert $H_2SO_3$ to $H_2SO_4$ needs oxygen. It comes from the substances added. Losing oxygen turns them into new substances. The new substances are different in colour. Those from potassium manganate(VII) are colourless. Those from potassium dichromate(VI) are green. The colour changes show that they are giving oxygen.

$H_2SO_3(aq)$ + oxygen from potassium manganate(VII) → $H_2SO_4(aq)$

Gas jar 3 contains an acid solution. Which one?

## Experiment 3.2 Sulphurous acid or sulphuric acid?

**Gas jar 4 contains sulphurous acid solution. Add barium chloride solution. Pour in dilute hydrochloric acid. Do the same to gas jar 3.**

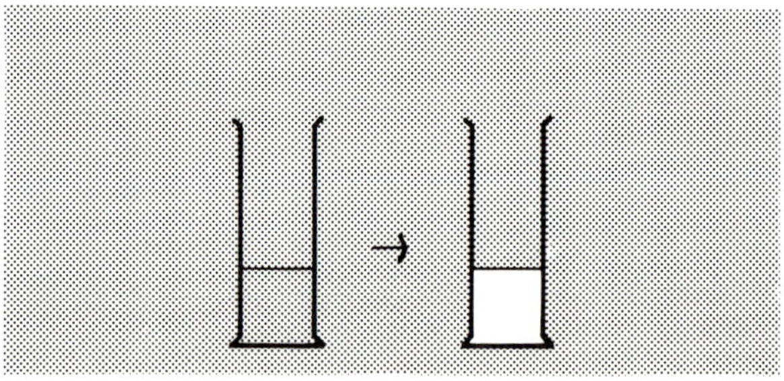

Are the results in the two jars the same?
Do both jars contain the same acid?

Hydrogen peroxide is $H_2O_2$. It loses oxygen to sulphurous acid. Loss of oxygen is reduction. Hydrogen peroxide is reduced. Sulphurous acid gains oxygen. Gain of oxygen is oxidation.

reduction ($H_2O_2 \rightarrow H_2O$)

$$H_2SO_3(aq) + H_2O_2(aq) \rightarrow H_2SO_4(aq) + H_2O(l)$$

oxidation ($H_2SO_3 \rightarrow H_2SO_4$)

The two changes always happen at the same time.

With barium chloride both solutions become 'milky'. White solids are formed. Neither dissolves in water. Solids formed in this way are called precipitates.

With barium chloride solution

- sulphurous acid → a white precipitate which dissolves in dilute hydrochloric acid
- sulphuric acid → a white precipitate which does *not* dissolve in dilute hydrochloric acid.

## The manufacture of sulphuric acid

This acid is very important. Huge amounts of it are used. It was first made by burning sulphur.

It was burnt in a spoon. The spoon was pushed into a large bottle. The bottle contained water. This dissolved the sulphur dioxide. Sulphurous acid was formed. Oxygen from the air slowly oxidized it.

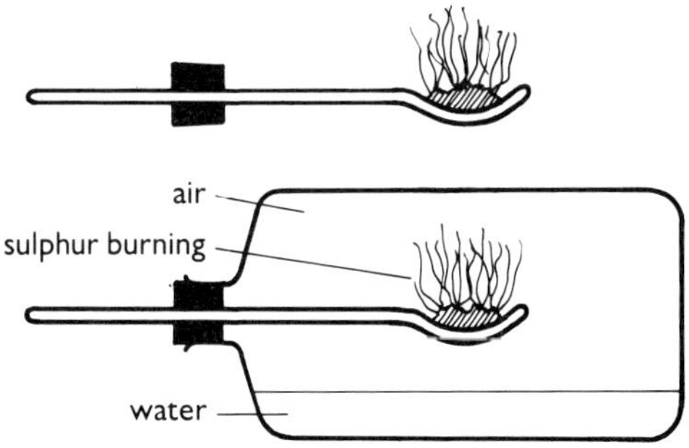


This gave sulphuric acid solution. The process was very slow. Later a substance giving oxygen was mixed with the sulphur. Oxidation was speeded up. Sulphuric acid was formed much faster.

The modern method also uses oxidation. Sulphur dioxide is oxidized, not sulphurous acid. $SO_2$ in water forms $H_2SO_3$. What substance in water will give $H_2SO_4$? What is its formula and name?

$SO_2 + H_2O \rightarrow H_2SO_3$

$? + H_2O \rightarrow H_2SO_4$

The answer is sulphur trioxide, $SO_3$. It is the result of sulphur dioxide combining with oxygen. These gases do not easily combine. If they did, sulphur dioxide would react with air. What can we use to speed up a reaction?

1. We can use heat.
2. We can use a **catalyst**.

Both make reaction faster. The catalyst does so by just being there. It is still there at the end.

# Sulphur trioxide and sulphuric acid

### *Experiment 3.3 To make sulphur trioxide

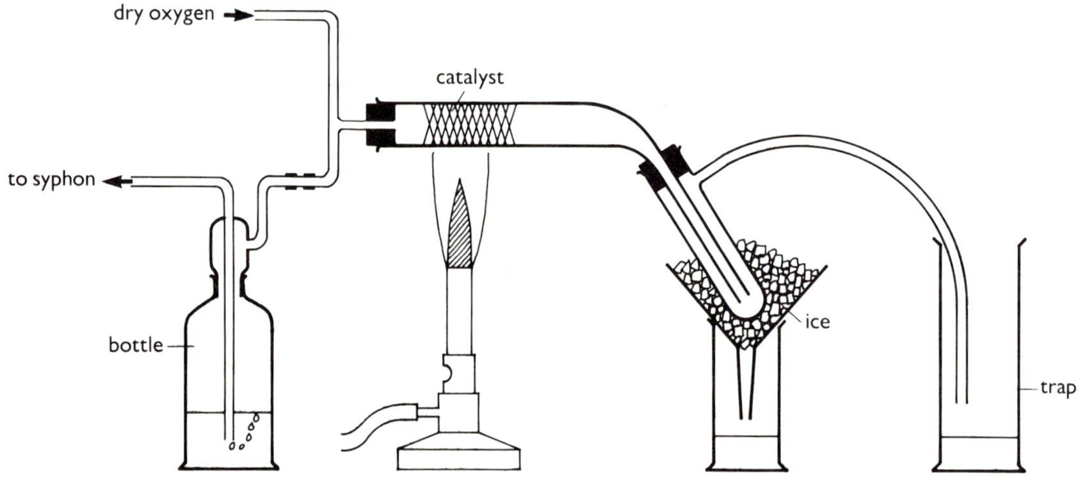


The drawing shows a suitable apparatus. Set it up in a fume cupboard. Use oxygen from a cylinder. Use sulphur dioxide from a syphon. Bubble each gas through concentrated sulphuric acid. This dries them. It also shows how fast they pass through.

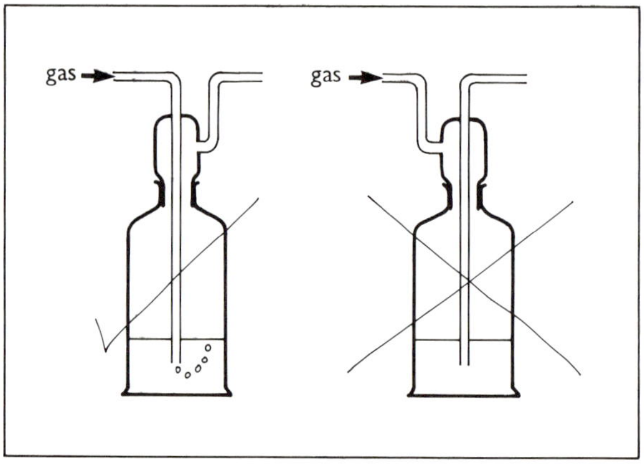


Cool the test tube with ice. Put aqueous ammonia into the gas jar. This traps unused gases. The catalyst is fibre coated with platinum. Heat it fairly strongly. Check that the bottles are connected correctly. Start the gases bubbling through. Oxygen should be at one bubble per second. Sulphur dioxide should be twice as fast.

What does the product look like?

Hold a little of it on a spatula in air. Drop small amounts of it into water in a test tube. Divide this solution into four parts.

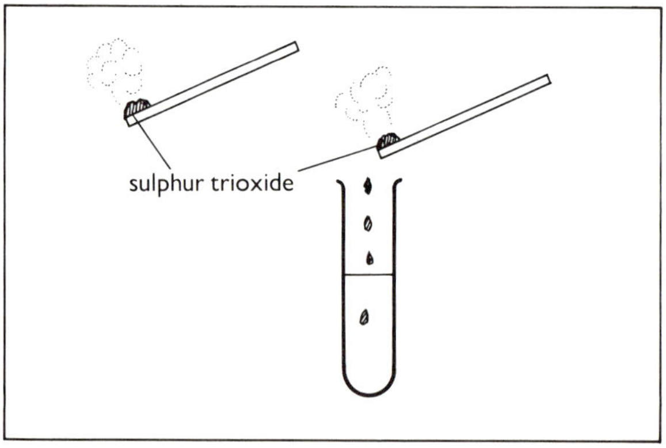


Add litmus to one part.
Add Universal indicator to a second part.
Add barium chloride solution to the third. Then pour in dilute hydrochloric acid.
Put a strip of magnesium in the fourth portion. Test any gas given off with a lighted splint.

What do the tests tell us about the solution?

Reaction happens in the catalyst tube. Work out word and formula equations for it.

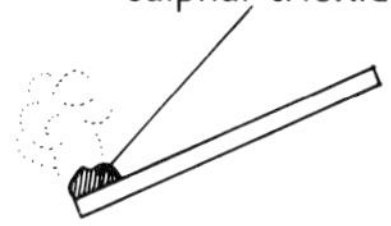


Solid white crystals form in the cold test tube. They are crystals of sulphur trioxide. They evaporate in air giving smoky white fumes. In water they make a hissing, spitting noise. They do not dissolve and react easily.

The solution is an acid. It gives a white precipitate with barium chloride solution. This does not dissolve in hydrochloric acid. The solution contains sulphuric acid, $H_2SO_4$.

Word equation:
sulphur dioxide + oxygen → sulphur trioxide
oxygen is diatomic, $O_2$

One oxygen molecule can oxidize two sulphur dioxide molecules. The formula equation will be

$$2SO_2(g) + O_2(g) \rightarrow 2SO_3(g)$$
$$SO_3(s) + H_2O(l) \rightarrow H_2SO_4(aq)$$

## The manufacture of sulphuric acid

reactants

Sulphur dioxide is made by burning sulphur in a stream of air. Excess of air is used. This provides oxygen. Sulphur ores are also used in place of sulphur.

conditions

The mixed gases are freed from dust. They are cooled to 450 °C. They are compressed to three times air pressure.

catalyst

The gas mixture passes over the hot catalyst. Vanadium(V) oxide is used. It is cheaper than platinum.

making the acid

Sulphur trioxide is formed. It does not react smoothly with water, so it is passed into concentrated sulphuric acid. The liquid formed is called oleum, $H_2S_2O_7$.

oleum

$$SO_3 + H_2SO_4 \rightarrow H_2S_2O_7$$

With water it gives sulphuric acid.

$$H_2S_2O_7 + H_2O \rightarrow 2H_2SO_4$$

**The Contact Process**

This is the Contact Process. Reaction between sulphur dioxide and oxygen produces heat. It is exothermic. It is also reversible. Conditions are chosen to give as much sulphur trioxide as possible.

A catalyst alters the speed of reaction. It usually speeds it up. The catalyst is still there at the end.

# Concentrated sulphuric acid

Pure sulphuric acid has no colour. It is a dense, oily liquid. Treat it with great care. Keep it off your clothes, your skin and the bench. Wear eyeshields. If you have to wash it off, use a large amount of water.

corrosive

### *Experiment 3.4 The properties of sulphuric acid

1. Half fill a 100 $cm^3$ beaker with water. Take its temperature. Pour in a little concentrated acid. Stir the mixture with a glass rod. Take the temperature again.

2. Fill a 100 $cm^3$ beaker one third full with the acid. Stick a label on it. Mark the acid level on the label. Let it stand in air for a few days. Note the level again.

3. Put crystals of blue copper sulphate in a beaker. Add concentrated acid. Stir with a glass rod. Note any change. Pour off the acid into another beaker. Add drops of water to the solid left behind.

4. Dip a paper spill into the acid. Take it out. Hold it over the sink.

5. Put a layer of sugar in a tall 100 $cm^3$ beaker. Make it damp by adding drops of water. Pour in some concentrated acid.

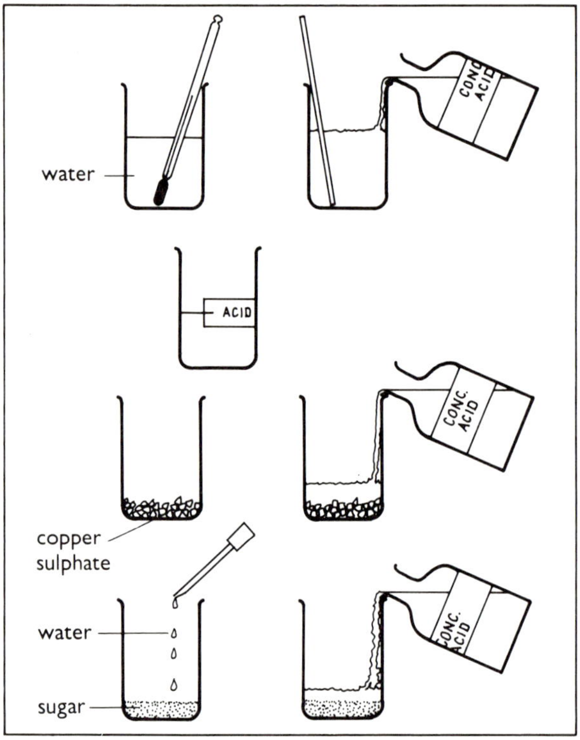


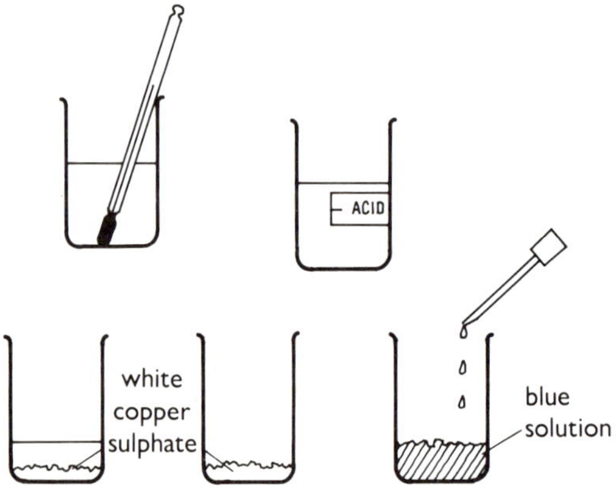


What happens to the temperature in test 1?
Why does the volume increase in test 2?
What happens to the copper sulphate?
How does water affect the white solid?
What is the black substance in tests 4 and 5?

The mixture of water and acid becomes very hot. It may even boil with enough acid. After a few days the volume in test 2 is bigger. The acid takes water vapour from the air. Sulphuric acid has a 'liking' for water.

Blue copper sulphate crystals contain water. It is water of crystallization. The formula is written $CuSO_4 . 5H_2O$. Concentrated sulphuric acid removes it. White anhydrous copper sulphate is formed. Adding water gives the blue form again. This is a test for water.

Sugar turns into black carbon. It rises out of the beaker. Smoke and steam pour out of it.

A molecule of sugar is $C_{12}H_{22}O_{11}$. There is no water in it. It does contain hydrogen and oxygen. It has twice as many hydrogen atoms as oxygen. So has water, $H_2O$. The acid takes away this hydrogen and oxygen as though they were water. Carbon remains.

$$C_{12}H_{22}O_{11} + \text{sulphuric acid} \rightarrow 12C + 11H_2O$$

Some water turns into steam. This blows the carbon out of the beaker. The acid does the same thing to paper. It can also do it to skin, clothes and wood. Heat is also produced.

**Taking water from a substance is dehydration**. Some compounds contain two H atoms for every O atom. Taking away hydrogen and oxygen is also dehydration. Concentrated sulphuric acid dehydrates.

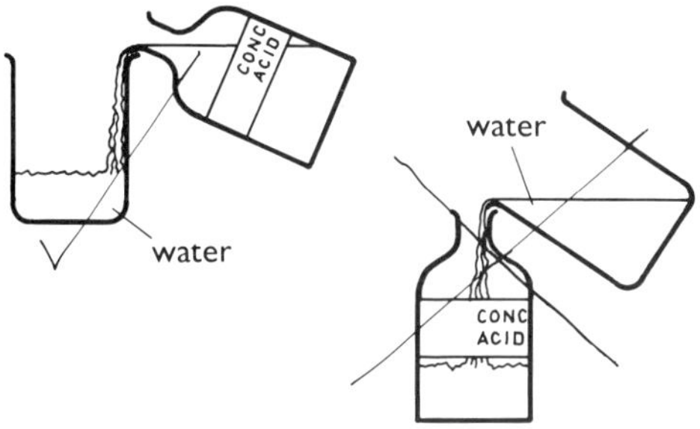


Never add water to concentrated sulphuric acid. Heat is formed. It turns the first water added to steam. This may blow acid into the air. If acid is to be diluted, add acid to water. Wear eyeshields.

## Summary

Sulphur dioxide is a gas. Pressure turns it into a liquid. This can be stored in a syphon. The gas dissolves in water. The solution contains sulphurous acid.

$$SO_2(g) + H_2O(l) \rightarrow H_2SO_3(aq)$$

This acid takes oxygen from other substances. Removal of oxygen is reduction. Sulphuric acid is formed. Adding oxygen to a substance is oxidation.

$$H_2SO_3(aq) + \text{oxygen} \rightarrow H_2SO_4(aq)$$

Purple potassium manganate(VII) solution gives oxygen. It needs sulphuric acid as well. The products are colourless. The colour change shows that oxidation is happening.

Sulphuric acid is manufactured by the Contact Process. Sulphur dioxide and air are mixed. They pass over a catalyst. It is vanadium(V) oxide at 450 °C. Sulphur trioxide is formed. It is dissolved in concentrated sulphuric acid. Oleum, $H_2S_2O_7$, is formed. It can be diluted with water to give the pure acid.

$$2SO_2(g) + O_2(g) \rightarrow 2SO_3(g)$$
$$SO_3(s) + H_2SO_4(l) \rightarrow H_2S_2O_7(l)$$

Sulphuric acid takes up water. It becomes dilute. It takes water from the air. It removes water of crystallization. It takes hydrogen and oxygen from substances. These are examples of dehydration. Heat is formed. This makes adding water to concentrated acid dangerous. Always add acid to water.

$$CuSO_4.5H_2O \rightarrow CuSO_4 + 5H_2O$$
$$C_{12}H_{22}O_{11} \rightarrow 12C + 11H_2O$$

## Questions

1. What is dehydration?
   Explain how concentrated sulphuric acid dehydrates
   a) blue copper sulphate crystals,
   b) sugar.
   Are the changes exothermic?

2. Sulphuric acid is made by the Contact Process. Explain two ways in which sulphur dioxide is made for this Process.
   What is sulphur dioxide mixed with?
   What catalyst is used?
   What temperature is it at?
   The sulphur trioxide formed is dissolved in concentrated acid.
   What substance is formed?
   Why is the oxide not dissolved in water?

3. The two oxides of sulphur are acidic. Write an equation for the reaction of each of them with water. Name the two acids. What test is used to show which is which? Give one use of sulphur dioxide.

4. Write an equation for each of these changes
   a) sulphur burning in air,
   b the reaction between sulphur dioxide and oxygen,
   c) sulphur trioxide dissolving in sulphuric acid.

# *Dilute sulphuric acid*

Dilute sulphuric acid is a typical acid solution. We shall use it to revise what we know about acids.

### Experiment 3.5 The properties of the dilute acid

Fill test tubes about a quarter full of the dilute acid. To each tube add one substance. Use those listed below. If nothing happens heat the tube gently. Identify any gases. Use a lighted splint and any other test needed.

**Metals**: pieces of magnesium, zinc and copper.

**Oxides**: use small amounts of zinc oxide and copper(II) oxide. Copper(II) is pronounced copper two. We shall find out later why we use this name.

**Carbonates**: use a few crystals of sodium carbonate; a pinch of copper(II) carbonate; two small lumps of marble, calcium carbonate.

Add a drop of Universal Indicator. With a dropper add sodium hydroxide solution. This is an **alkali**.

Write your results in the form of a table.

| Substance used | Does it react? | Is a gas given off? | Effect on a lighted splint | Other results |
|---|---|---|---|---|
| magnesium | yes, very vigorously | yes | flame goes out with 'squeaky pop' | mixture is hot |

The 'squeaky pop' shows that the gas is hydrogen. The reaction gives heat. Zinc reacts more slowly. It gives less heat. Both metals dissolve. Reaction stops when acid or metal is used up.

The symbol for magnesium is Mg. We can write the acid formula as $H_2SO_4$. Hydrogen is diatomic. Its molecule has two atoms, $H_2$.

So $Mg(s) + H_2SO_4(aq) \rightarrow ? + H_2$

The solution contains magnesium sulphate.

$$Mg(s) + H_2SO_4(aq) \rightarrow MgSO_4 + H_2$$

Copper does not react even when heated. It is not an active metal. Reaction with acid puts the metals in order. Work out an equation for zinc and acid reacting.

Copper(II) oxide dissolves in the acid. It gives a blue solution. This must be copper(II) sulphate. The formula of the oxide is CuO.
Thus

$$CuO(s) + H_2SO_4(aq) \text{ must give } CuSO_4(aq) + H_2O.$$

Work out an equation using zinc oxide.

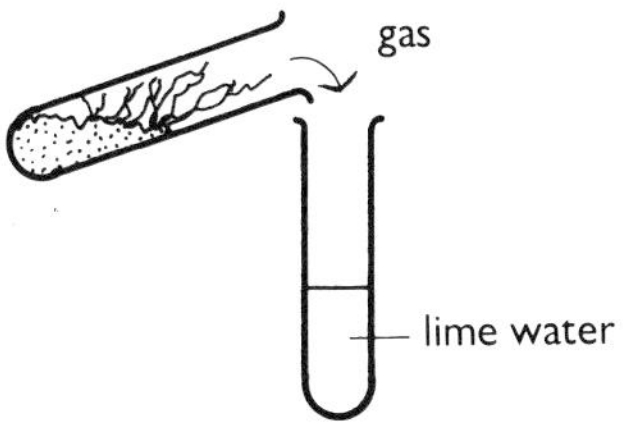


All the carbonates effervesce. That is, they give off a gas. The gas puts out a lighted splint. It is probably carbon dioxide. Confirm this. 'Pour' the gas into lime water. The reaction with marble soon stops.

Copper(II) carbonate can be written $CuCO_3$. With acid it gives a blue solution. This must be copper(II) sulphate. The gas is carbon dioxide. No other product shows itself. We can write a word equation.

| | | | | | | | | |
|---|---|---|---|---|---|---|---|---|
| copper(II) carbonate | + | sulphuric acid | | copper(II) sulphate | + | carbon dioxide | + ? |
| $CuCO_3$ | + | $H_2SO_4$ | → | $CuSO_4$ | + | $CO_2$ | + ? |

~~Cu~~ ~~C~~ ~~O~~ ~~O~~ O
H H ~~$SO_4$~~

This leaves two H atoms and one O atom. $? = H_2O$

In acid, Universal Indicator is red. Adding enough alkali changes it to violet. You saw other colours too. The full range is

| red | orange | yellow | green | blue | dark blue | violet |
|---|---|---|---|---|---|---|
| acidic | | | neutral | alkaline | | |

Acid and alkali react. The right amount of each gives a neutral solution. This contains a salt. Every solution from these tests contains a salt.

The salts of sulphuric acid are sulphates.
The salts of sulphurous acid are sulphites.

A salt is formed by replacing the hydrogen of an acid by a metal.

Acids react with

1. metals → a salt + hydrogen ( in most cases)
2. metal oxides → a salt + water
3. metal hydroxides → a salt + water
4. metal carbonates → a salt + carbon dioxide + water

Oxides and hydroxides are bases. Hydroxides which dissolve in water are called alkalis.

*Willie's sister's teacher taught her*
*Acid + base gives salt + water*

# The uses of sulphuric acid

Nearly four million tonnes of sulphuric acid are made in Britain every year.

1. It is used in making sulphates. Many of these important salts are used in industry. *Farmers* and other *food producers* use them too.

For example, aluminium sulphate is used in making *paper*. It is needed to make *dyes* cling to cloth. It is also used in *sewage* treatment. Plants such as *potatoes* and *vines* suffer from blight. This is a fungus disease. Bordeaux mixture kills or prevents blight. It is a solution of copper sulphate mixed with lime. Copper sulphate also prevents *timber* rotting.

Sulphuric acid is used to make fertilizers. This is a sulphate of ammonia silo.

2. The acid is used in making *fertilizers*. One of these is ammonium sulphate (sulphate of ammonia). Another is 'superphosphate'. Making these uses about one third of the acid manufactured.

3. Sulphuric acid is used in making many other substances. These include *man-made fibres* such as rayon. This is used in clothes, carpets and tyres. The acid is used in making *soap*. With plant oils the acid forms *detergents*.

*Explosives*, *dyes* and many medical *drugs* need the acid in their manufacture. It is used in refining crude oil, or *petroleum*.

The acid is also used in making explosives.

4. Many *metals* corrode in air. A layer of oxide forms on them. To prevent this the metal may be painted. It can also be plated with a layer of less active metal. The layer of oxide must first be taken off. It is dissolved in acid. This is called 'pickling'. The clean surface is washed free of acid before *plating*.

5. About one sixth of the acid made is used in the *paint* industry. Barium sulphate and titanium dioxide are solids made for paints.

6. About eighteen million *cars* and *lorries* use the roads in Britain. Most of them run on a *'wet battery'*. The liquid in it is sulphuric acid. So millions of litres of sulphuric acid travel on Britain's roads every day.

Cars use batteries containing sulphuric acid.

Look again at the words in italic on the opposite page. They show how much we depend on the sulphuric acid. The more prosperous the country the more acid it uses.

A wet battery contains fairly concentrated acid. It is made up of a number of cells. Each cell consists of two plates, or poles. They dip into the acid. The negative pole of one cell is joined to the positive pole of the next.

A dry battery is also a series of cells. But each cell has a moist paste instead of a liquid. Electric current passes through paste and acid. Both must be conductors.

Wet batteries.

Dry batteries.

## Experiment 3.6 Is sulphuric acid a conductor?

**Set up the apparatus using a dry battery. Any source giving six volts will do. Connect its positive pole to a switch. Connect this to a carbon rod. Connect the negative pole to a bulb. Connect this to a carbon rod. Switch on. Touch one carbon rod with the other.**

**Take three 100 cm$^3$ beakers. In one put a little pure sulphuric acid. In the next put dilute sulphuric acid and in the third, distilled water.**

*** 1. Hold the rods in the pure acid as far apart as possible. Switch on the current. Move the rods closer together. Do not let them touch. Take them out of the acid. Wash them several times with distilled water.**

**2. Dip the rods in the dilute acid. Repeat the same tests as in the pure acid. Again wash the rods with distilled water. Dip them in the distilled water and do the same tests as before.**

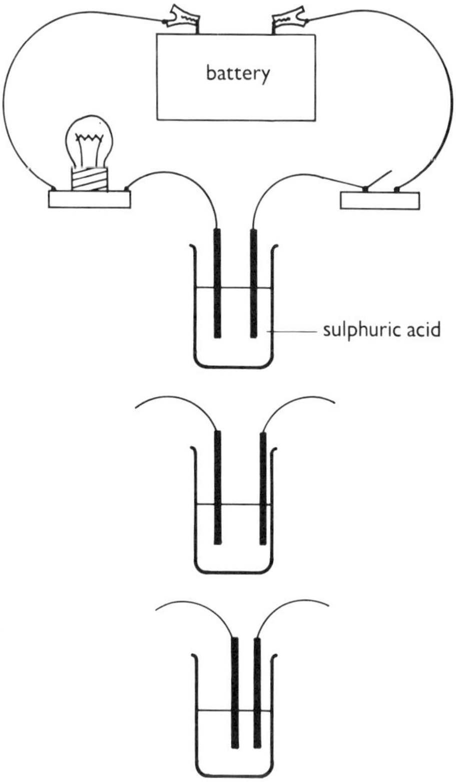


When the carbon rods touch in air the bulb lights up. Why does this happen?

The rods are then separated by three different liquids. Which of the three liquids can conduct a current?

In these tests we have used a very small voltage.

# Electrolysis

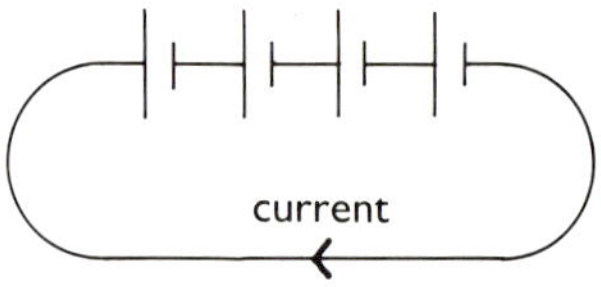


A battery supplies electric current. It flows from one pole of the battery to the other. It must have something to flow through. The poles must be joined by a conductor. A current always produces heat.

We connected the poles to carbon rods. A bulb was included. It has a thin wire, or filament. A current makes the filament very hot. It glows. The bulb lights up. This proves that a current is flowing.

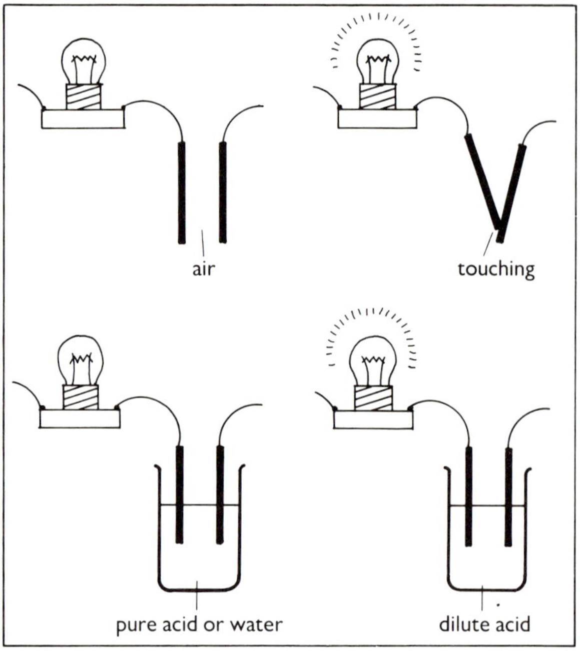


In the 'OFF' position a switch has an air gap. Switching on puts a conductor across the gap. With air between the rods the bulb does not light. Current is not flowing. Air must be a non-conductor. If the rods touch, current passes. The bulb lights.

We dipped the rods in a liquid. The liquid is between them. If the bulb lights, the liquid must be a conductor. The bulb does not light with pure acid. Distilled water gives the same result. Both are poor conductors. With the rods in dilute acid the bulb lights. Dilute acid is a conductor.

Can you see why we washed the carbon rods? Did you notice any other result with dilute acid?

Current passes into the dilute acid through one rod. It leaves through the other. The rods are electrodes. Bubbles of gas form on both rods. They start when the current is switched on. They stop when it is switched off. The gases formed are new substances.

The change is called **electrolysis** (el-ec-trol-iss-iss). It is the passage of a current through a liquid, forming new substances.

The liquid is called the **electrolyte**. The electrode joined to the positive pole is called the **anode**. The one joined to the negative pole is the **cathode**. The new substances appear at the **electrodes**.

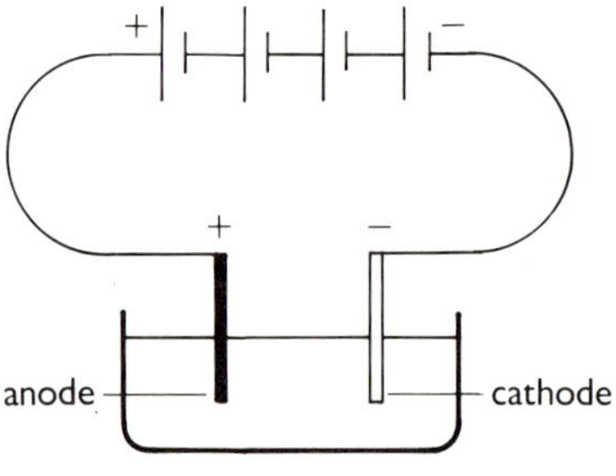


High voltages make air, water and other substances become conductors. Lightning is a current in air.

## Experiment 4.1 To find out what the gases are

Set up the apparatus. Fill the vessel with dilute sulphuric acid. Fill two test tubes with the acid. Invert them in the vessel. Hold one over each electrode. Switch on. Collect the gases. Test both with a lighted splint. Try any other test you need.

What gas is formed at each electrode?
Which of the gases has the bigger volume?
Can you guess how much bigger its volume is?

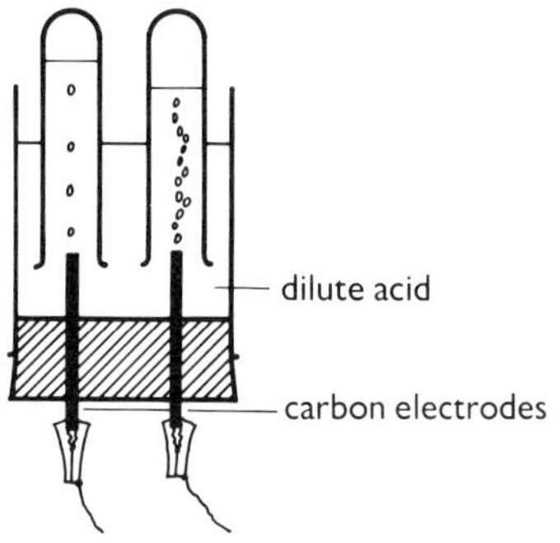


## Experiment 4.2 To compare the volumes of the gases

The apparatus is called a voltameter. Pour dilute sulphuric acid into it. Open the taps on the side tubes. Let the acid fill these tubes. Close the two taps.

The electrodes are pieces of platinum foil. Each is welded to a platinum wire. This is sealed into glass tubing. The tubing passes through the stopper.

Switch on. Switch off when the gas formed is enough to test. Hold a test tube over each tap. Open the taps. Let the side tubes fill up. Close each test tube with your finger. Test the gases in them.

Switch on again. When one side tube is nearly full of gas, switch off. Read off the volume of each gas.

Why does a voltameter have a centre tube?
What are the two gases which form at the electrodes?
How do their volumes compare?
Which gas appears at the cathode?
Where do these gases come from?

**At the anode** (+): oxygen appears. A splint burns brighter in it. It relights a glowing splint.

**At the cathode** (−): hydrogen forms. Its volume is twice the volume of oxygen. It gives a squeaky pop with a lighted splint.

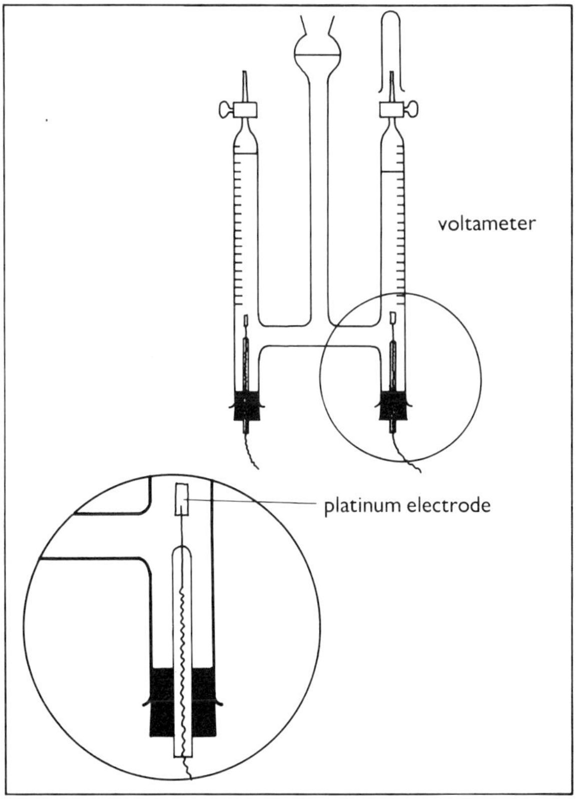


## Summary

Water is a poor conductor. So is pure sulphuric acid. The dilute acid is a mixture of the two. It is a good conductor. It can be electrolysed.

At the cathode: hydrogen is set free.
At the anode: oxygen is set free.
The volume of hydrogen is twice the volume of oxygen.

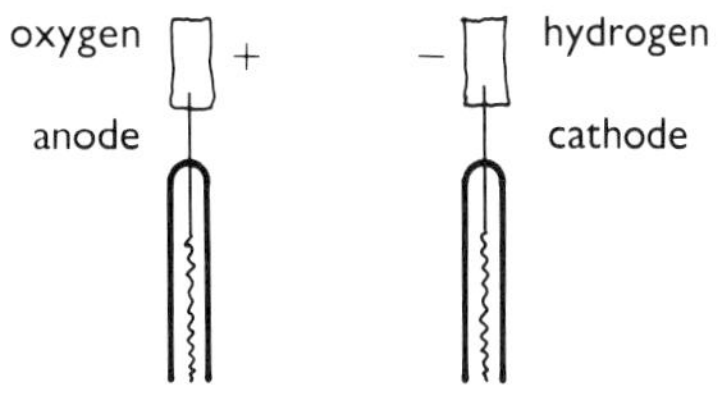


Our results so far leave questions to be answered.

# *How does electrolysis work?*

Three questions to answer are:

1. Where do the gases come from?
2. Why does hydrogen appear at the cathode, not the anode?
3. Why do we get a good conductor by mixing two poor conductors?

We shall try to answer question 1 first.

Can the gases come out of the electrodes?
Carbon and platinum are elements. Elements cannot be split up into other substances. Neither can provide hydrogen or oxygen. Yet both do this in electrolysis.

Do the electrodes react with the acid?
The gases could be products of reaction. If so, the electrodes would be used up. Anode and cathode are the same element. It could not give *different* gases by reacting with the *same* acid. Gases appear *when the current is switched on.* They stop *as soon as it is switched off.*

Gas molecules must reach the electrodes from somewhere. Testing other liquids may give helpful results.

### Experiment 4.3 Electrolysis of other liquids

**Use the apparatus of Experiment 4.1. Put a bulb in the circuit. Collect and test any gas. Look for any other changes. Check the electrodes for changes.**

**Use ethanol (meths), dilute hydrochloric acid, salt solution, oil, copper(II) sulphate solution, zinc sulphate solution and *mercury.**

**Write your results in the form of a table.**

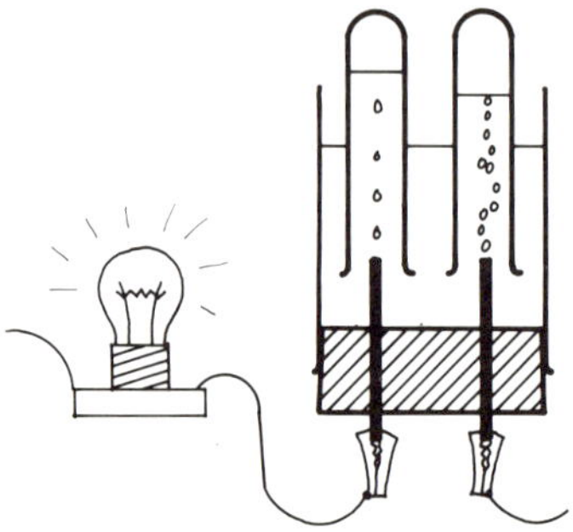

| Liquid used | Conductor or not | Result at the cathode | Result at the anode | Any other result |
|---|---|---|---|---|
| copper(II) sulphate solution | conductor | a red-brown solid forms | oxygen appears | the blue solution becomes paler |

Ethanol and oil do not conduct. The bulb does not light up.
Mercury is a metal. It conducts. No new substances are formed.
The others are conductors. In each of them new substances form.

# The substances set free – how much?

Metals and hydrogen form at the cathode.
Non-metals are the products at the anode.

Take the results for copper(II) sulphate solution. A red-brown solid forms on the cathode. This must be copper. The copper sulphate solution becomes paler. Copper sulphate is being used up. The copper must come from the copper(II) sulphate electrolyte.

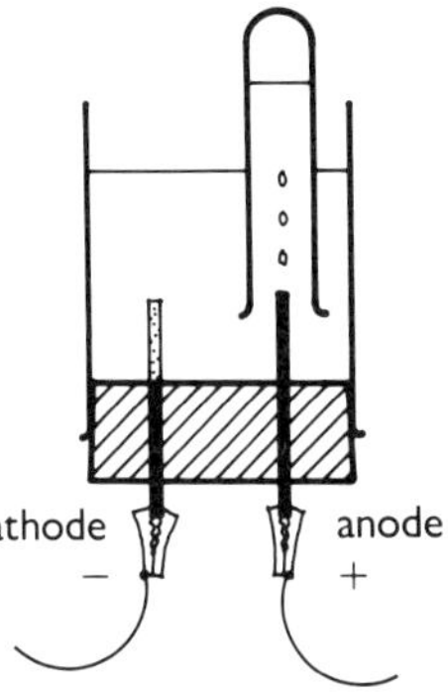


**The products of electrolysis come from the electrolyte.**

What makes hydrogen and copper move to the cathode? And how much?

### *Experiment 4.4 What masses are formed?

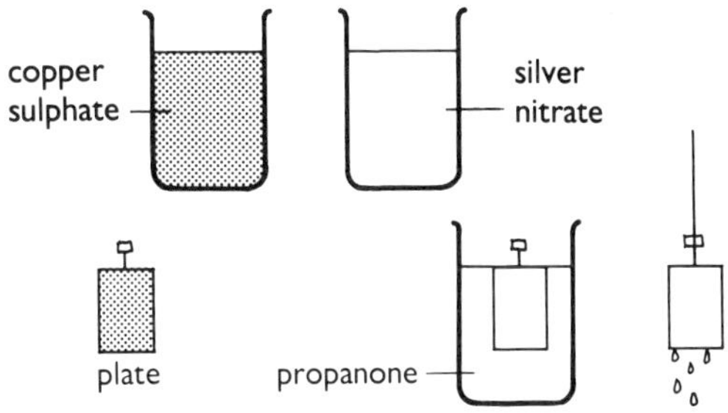


Almost fill a 100 $cm^3$ beaker with 0.5 M copper(II) sulphate solution. Almost fill another with 0.05 M silver nitrate solution. Clean two copper plates with fine emery paper. Clean silver electrodes.

Wash the metals with water. Let them drain. Wash them with meths. Let them drain. Dip them in propanone. Take them out and let them dry. Measure the mass of each electrode.

Support the copper electrodes in the copper sulphate solution. Connect them up as shown. Note which of them is the anode. Support the silver electrodes in the silver nitrate solution. Label the cathode.

The milliammeter is to measure the current. Adjust the rheostat to get a current of 0.1 ampere. Start a stop clock. Use the rheostat to keep the current constant. Let it pass for about one hour.

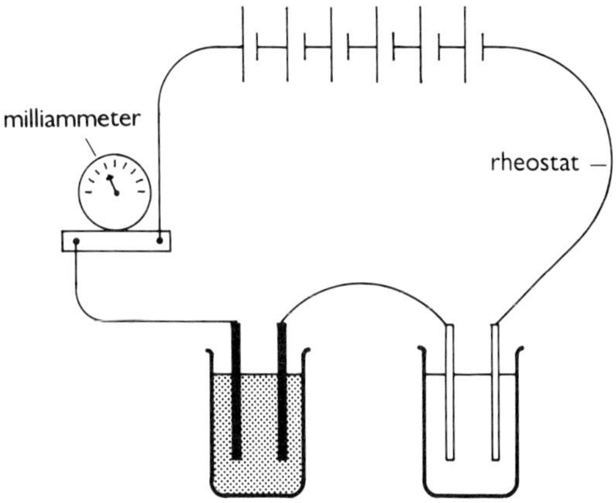


Switch off. Measure the time accurately. Take out each electrode with care. Wash them with distilled water, meths and propanone as before. Let them dry. Measure the mass of each of them again.

What happens to the copper cathode?
Does the mass of the silver cathode change?
What happens to the two anodes?
Does the copper(II) sulphate solution become paler?

Each cathode gains in mass. Copper is deposited on the copper cathode. Silver forms on the silver cathode. The cathode also gains in mass. The mass of each anode gets less. They are losing metal.

gain of mass of cathode = loss of mass of anode

The copper(II) sulphate does not become paler. It loses copper to the cathode. The copper (II) sulphate must gain copper from the anode. The two balance.

# Ions and electrolysis

We have answered question 1.
The electrolyte provides the products of electrolysis.
How do they get to the electrodes? The answer is ions.

We know that electrical charges of the same sign repel
unlike charges attract each other.

+ repels +
− repels −
+ attracts −

Copper is deposited on the cathode. Then copper particles must move towards it. The cathode is negatively charged. The copper particles must be positively charged. Negative attracts positive.

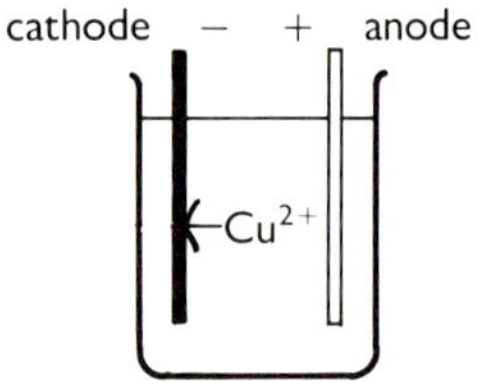


These particles are called copper **ions**. Each ion is a copper atom with two units of positive charge. It is written $Cu^{++}$ or $Cu^{2+}$. The 2 explains why they are copper(II) compounds.

At the cathode the ions lose their charge. They become neutral copper atoms. They join on to the cathode. A layer of copper metal is formed on it.

Copper(II) sulphate, $CuSO_4$ has no over-all charge. If the copper ion is $Cu^{2+}$, $SO_4$ must have an equal negative charge. It is the sulphate ion, $SO_4^{2-}$.

$Cu^{2+}$ in $CuSO_4$?
Then $SO_4^{2-}$ is the other ion.

The positive anode attracts negative ions. They are called **anions**. Positive ions move to the cathode. They are called **cations**. The current is moving ions.

Two changes are possible at the anode. Metal ions may leave the anode. Anions may form non-metals there.

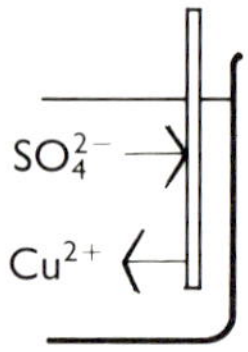


A liquid conducts if it contains ions. The moving ions are the current. Water is a poor conductor because it has few ions. Substances such as copper(II) sulphate put ions into water. Acids provide hydrogen ions. They are atoms with one unit of positive charge. We write it $H^+$. Alkalis give $OH^-$ ions.

acid gives $H^+$ ions
alkali gives $OH^-$ ions

Hydrogen ions move to the cathode. They lose their charge. They become neutral atoms. These join up in pairs to form molecules. Hydrogen gas is set free.

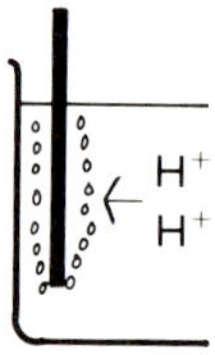


Salt crystals are made up of ions. They are $Na^+$ and $Cl^-$. The crystals do not conduct. The ions are there but they cannot move freely. When salt dissolves in water the ions separate. They can move freely in the solution. The salt becomes a conductor. Electrolysis happens.

You will learn later why metals and hydrogen have positive ions.

Heat melts crystals. Ions may be able to move in the liquid. If so, the liquid may conduct. We can test this using lead iodide. Its ions are $Pb^{2+}$ and $2I^-$.

### *Experiment 4.5 Electrolysis of a molten salt

**Connect a battery through a bulb to two carbon rods. Put lead iodide crystals into a large test tube. Dip the carbon electrodes into the crystals. Switch on the current. Heat the crystals gently.**

Does lead iodide conduct?
When?
What are the products at cathode and anode?

The bulb lights up when the salt melts. The liquid is a conductor. It must contain moving ions. Beads of shiny silvery lead form at the cathode. Violet vapour appears at the anode. The vapour is iodine.

Lead iodide is chosen because it melts easily. Its melting point is low. Other salts have high melting points.

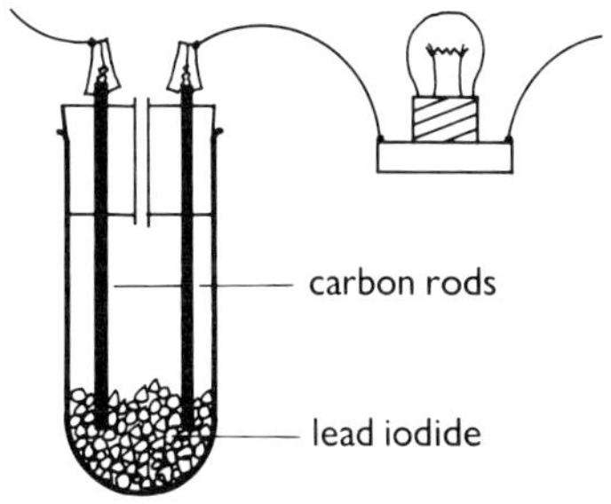


## Quantities in electrolysis

Here is a set of results for Experiment 4.4:

| | |
|---|---|
| Mass of copper deposited on the cathode | = 0.120 g |
| Mass of silver on the silver cathode | = 0.405 g |
| Current passing through both solutions | = 0.10 ampere |
| The time for which the current passed | = 3600 seconds |

Current and time can both be altered. Experiment shows that
1. doubling the current doubles the mass of product,
2. doubling the time also doubles the mass of product formed,
3. mass of product is proportional to current × time.

current (ampere) × time (second) = quantity of electricity (coulomb)

$0.1 \times 3600 = 360$ coulombs

The mass of silver is more than the mass of copper.
Why? Silver ions have a bigger mass than copper ions.
A silver ion $Ag^+$ has one unit of charge.
A copper ion $Cu^{2+}$ has twice this charge.
It needs twice as many silver ions to give the same quantity of electricity.

Cu = (64); Ag = (108)

0.405 g of silver are given by 360 coulombs

108 g would need $\dfrac{360 \times 108}{0.405}$ = 96 000 coulombs

96 000 coulombs = 1 faraday

108 g of silver = L ions or L atoms (one mole)
A mole of silver atoms needs 1 faraday. A mole of copper atoms needs 2 faradays.

$Cu^{2+}$ 2 faradays per mole set free
$Ag^+$ 1 faraday per mole set free

# The uses of electrolysis

Read through this whole section again. What substances are set free at the anode and cathode? Do the results suggest uses for electrolysis?

1. New substances form at the electrodes
Many substances are manufactured by this method. Electrolysis of salt solution (brine) produces three. They are sodium hydroxide, chlorine and hydrogen. You will learn of other substances later.

2. A layer of metal may form on the cathode
This is used to coat an object with metal. The object could be a cheap metal spoon. The spoon is used as the cathode. The coating metal is the anode. It could be silver. The solution contains silver ions. They move towards the cathode. A silver layer is deposited on it. We now have a 'silver' spoon.

The method is called electroplating. The coating layer is often used to protect a metal from corrosion.

Experiment 4.4 used copper electrodes. They stood in copper(II) sulphate solution. Copper formed on the cathode. Copper was lost from the anode.

This method is used to purify copper. The impure copper is the anode. The cathode is a thin sheet of pure copper. Copper leaves the anode. It is deposited on the cathode. Other metals in the anode are left behind.

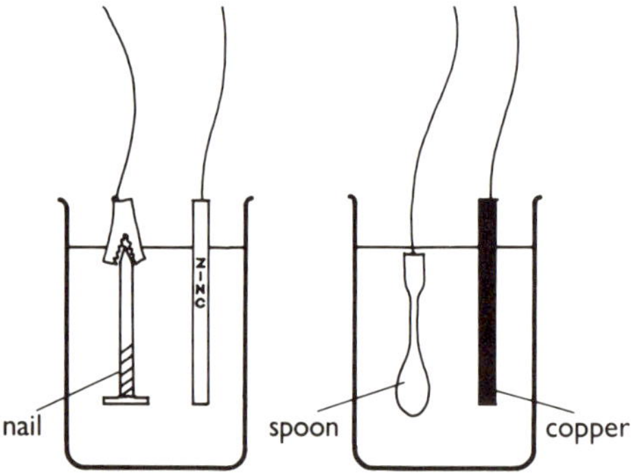

**Sea water is very corrosive. The upright post has been eaten away, but the railings, which are coated with zinc (galvanized), have not rusted at all.**

**Electrolysis is used to purify copper.**

3. Electrolysis of molten salts gives metals
Compounds of active metals are difficult to split up. These metals can be made by electrolysis. Active metals react with water. So a molten salt is used.

Sodium, calcium, magnesium and aluminium are made like this. The anode products are useful too.

### Things to do

1. Wash a new nail with detergent. Rinse in water. Use the nail as a cathode. Use a zinc anode. Put them in zinc sulphate solution. Make this acid with dilute sulphuric acid. Electrolyse the solution.

2. Put a copper anode in dilute copper sulphate solution. Use in turn as a cathode
   a) a plastic spoon,
   b) a strip of stiff paper.
   Dry them. Rub them all over with a 4B pencil. Try them again.
   What is deposited on each cathode?

## Summary

Dilute sulphuric acid is a typical acid. It reacts with metals. A salt and hydrogen are formed.

$Mg(s) + H_2SO_4(aq) \rightarrow MgSO_4(aq) + H_2(g)$

It dissolves metal oxides. A salt and water form.

$CuO(s) + H_2SO_4(aq) \rightarrow CuSO_4(aq) + H_2O(l)$

Carbonates in acid effervesce. The gas given off is carbon dioxide. This is a third method for making a salt.

$MgCO_3(s) + H_2SO_4(aq) \rightarrow MgSO_4(aq) + CO_2(g) + H_2O(l)$

Acids react with alkalis. They neutralize each other. The products are a salt and water. A salt is made by replacing the hydrogen of an acid by a metal. In all four methods the salt is in solution.

Pure sulphuric acid is a poor conductor. So is water. Mixing them gives dilute acid. This is a good conductor. We shall find out how it forms ions.

Electrolysis means passing a current through a liquid to form new substances. Conductors dip into the liquid. They are called electrodes. The negative electrode is the cathode. The positive electrode is the anode. The liquid is called the electrolyte.

Ions move through the electrolyte. An ion is an electrically charged atom. Some ions are charged groups of atoms. Positive ions move to the cathode. They are called cations. Negative ions move to the anode. They are anions.

At the electrodes they lose their charge. New substances are set free. The mass of each substance depends on a) the current, b) the time and c) the relative atomic mass. One mole of ions is set free by one, two or three faradays of electricity.

At the cathode, metals and hydrogen are set free. At the anode, non-metals form or metal is lost.

Electrolysis has many uses. Substances are manufactured by this method. Active metals are made by using as electrolyte a molten salt. Copper is made pure by electrolysis. It is used to plate metals. A layer of one metal is formed on another.

## Questions

1. Write one sentence about each word to explain what it means
   electrode; cathode; electrolyte; anode; electrolysis; positive ion; anion.
2. What is electro-plating?
   In what two ways is it useful?
   Explain how it can be done.
3. Fill in the gaps as you write this in your book:

   Current in an electrolyte is moving ______. Cations move towards the ______. Metals are set free at the ______. So is the gas called ______. Non-metals form at the ______. They have ______ charged ions. The anode may lose ______. The copper ion is written ______. A hydrogen ion is ______.

# *Inside the atom*

In 1896 Becquerel discovered radioactivity. He did it by accident. He was testing substances which glow in the dark. One of them was a uranium ore.

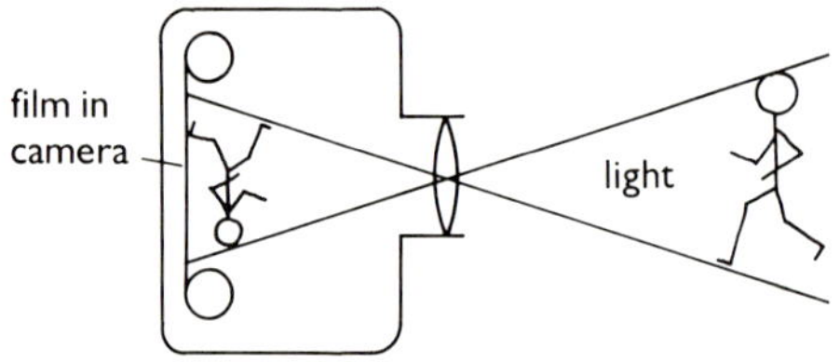


We take photographs using light. We let it strike films or plates. So they must be kept away from light before use. They are wrapped in black paper.

Becquerel had put some wrapped plates in a drawer. One had been affected. Near it was the uranium ore. Tests showed that radiation came from the ore. Like light, it had affected the plate. To do this it had to pass through black paper.

Rutherford showed that the radiation was of three types. He called them alpha, beta and gamma rays. These are the Greek letters a, b and c.

radiation: alpha $\alpha$, beta $\beta$, gamma $\gamma$

**Alpha** radiation is positively charged helium ions. **Beta** rays are also particles. They are much smaller than hydrogen atoms. They are negatively charged. They are called electrons. **Gamma** radiation consists of waves similar to X-rays.

$\alpha$-rays = $He^{2+}$
$\beta$ = electrons
$\gamma$ = waves

So far, atoms have been thought of as solid spheres. Electrons changed this picture. If they exist, atoms must contain smaller particles. How are these arranged in the atom?

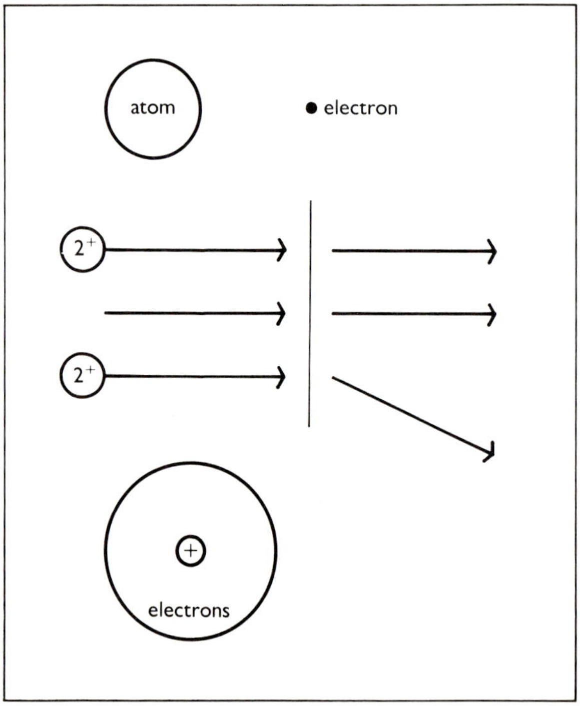


In 1909, Geiger and Marsden set up a stream of $\alpha$-particles. They aimed them at a thin sheet of gold. Most of them went straight through. They passed through gold atoms. These seemed to be mostly empty space. Atoms were far from being solid.

Some $\alpha$-particles were deflected. It suggested that they were being repelled. Some part of the atoms must be positively charged. We now believe that:

1. Every atom has a tiny centre. This is called its **nucleus**. It is positively charged.
2. Every atom contains negatively charged **electrons**. These are in groups around the nucleus. The rest of the atom is empty space. How big is the nucleus?

Imagine that we could magnify an atom. Make it as large as a sports hall. The nucleus would become as big as a pin head. An electron would be as big as a speck of dust. The rest would be empty space. You can see why $\alpha$-particles pass through gold.

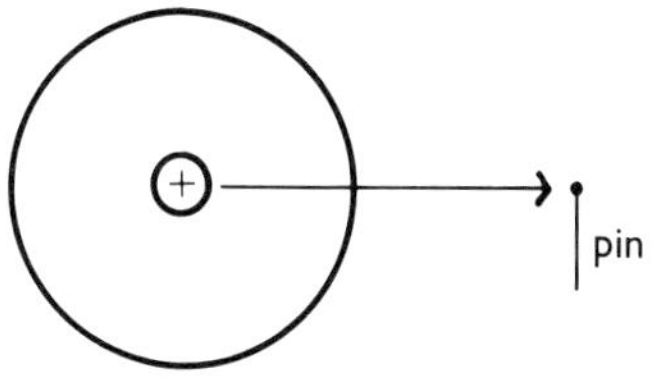


Hydrogen has the simplest atom. Its relative atomic mass is 1. It contains one electron. This has one unit of negative charge. A hydrogen atom is neutral . So its nucleus has one unit of positive charge. It contains a particle called a **proton**.

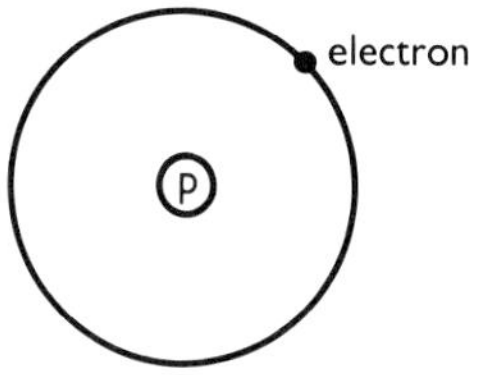


An electron has a very small mass. It is about $\frac{1}{2000}$ of the mass of a hydrogen atom. The rest of this atom is a proton. Its mass is almost equal to the mass of a hydrogen atom. If H = 1, then a proton = 1.

In 1932, Chadwick discovered a third particle. This is the **neutron**. It has no charge. Like the proton, its mass is 1 atomic mass unit.

Neutrons and protons are found in the nucleus. The nucleus contains most of the mass of the atom.

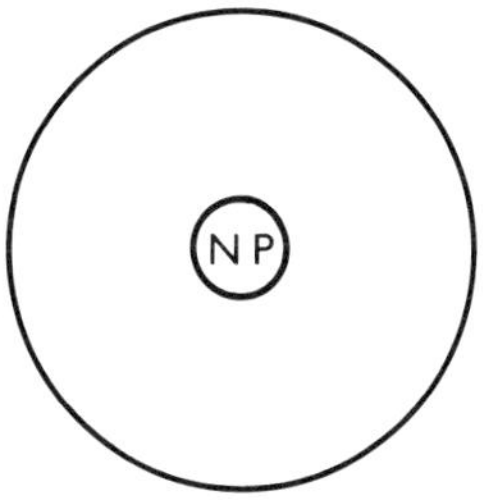


| Particle | Mass in atomic mass units | Charge | Where is it in the atom? |
|---|---|---|---|
| proton | 1 a.m.u. | + | nucleus |
| neutron | 1 a.m.u. | none | nucleus |
| electron | $\frac{1}{2000}$ a.m.u. | − | groups around the nucleus |

The next simplest atom is the helium atom, He. It has two protons in its nucleus. So it must have two electrons. He = 4. This means the mass of a helium atom is four units. Two protons provide two units. The nucleus must contain two neutrons.

nucleus = 2P + 2N
2 electrons

The lithium atom comes next. It has three protons. Li = 7. How many neutrons? Where will the protons and neutrons be? How many electrons in this atom?

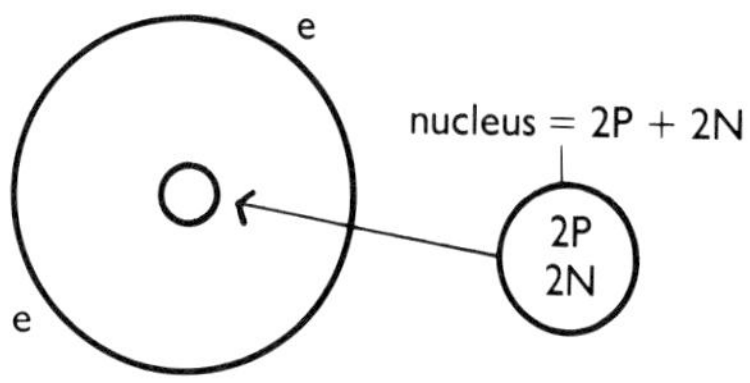


In every atom:
1. the number of protons = the number of electrons.
This number is the **atomic number** of the element.

2. The main mass of the atom is in the nucleus. It contains protons and neutrons. The number of both together is the **atomic mass number**. Electrons are in groups around the nucleus of the atom.

# Atoms and ions

Two numbers label the atom of an element. **Atomic number** is the number of protons in the atom. The atom contains the same number of electrons.

Every atom has a relative atomic mass. As a whole number this is called the **mass number**. It is the number of protons and neutrons in the atom.

The elements can be placed in order of atomic number. The table shows the first twelve of them.

| | | | | | | | | | | | | |
|---|---|---|---|---|---|---|---|---|---|---|---|---|
| Atomic number | 1 | 2 | 3 | 4 | 5 | 6 | 7 | 8 | 9 | 10 | 11 | 12 |
| Symbol | H | He | Li | Be | B | C | N | O | F | Ne | Na | Mg |
| Mass number | 1 | 4 | 7 | 9 | 10 | 12 | 14 | 16 | 19 | 20 | 23 | 24 |

Consider oxygen, symbol O. Its atomic number is 8. This means that an oxygen atom has eight protons. Then it must have eight electrons. Its mass number is 16. Protons + neutrons = 16. Its nucleus has eight protons and eight neutrons.

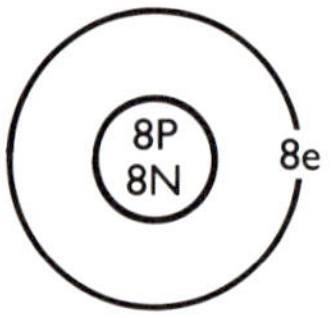


The symbol for sodium is Na. Its mass number is 23. The nucleus of its atom has twenty-three protons and neutrons. The atomic number of sodium is 11. Its atom has eleven protons. Then it must have 23 − 11 neutrons, or twelve. Because it has eleven protons it must have eleven electrons.

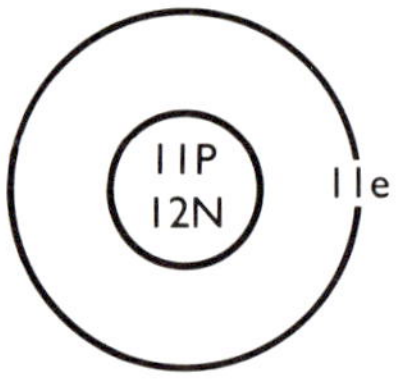


The electrons are in groups. They surround the nucleus. The groups are called **shells**. Moving atoms collide. Their electron shells will collide first.

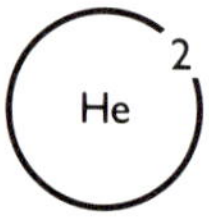


A helium atom has two electons. A neon atom, Ne, has ten. Helium and neon are noble gases. They have no simple reactions. This is why they are called noble. Their electron shells must be inactive.

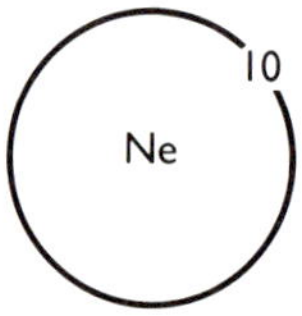


Modern theory says that other atoms become like them. They reach the same shell arrangement as a noble gas atom. To do this they gain or lose electrons.

An oxygen atom has eight electrons. This is two less than a neon atom. Neon is the nearest noble gas to oxygen. So an oxygen atom gains two electrons. It now has two extra negative charges. It is an oxygen ion, $O^{2-}$.

A sodium atom, Na, has eleven electrons. This is one more than a neon atom. The Na atom will lose an electron. Its nucleus has eleven protons (11+). It has ten electrons (10−). It has become the sodium ion, $Na^{+}$.

Hydrogen is the first element. Its atom has one electron. It can lose this. It becomes the ion $H^+$. Hydrogen and metal atoms lose electrons. They then have more protons than electrons. Their ions are positively charged. In electrolysis they move to the negative cathode. It provides electrons. These electrons turn positive ions back into atoms.

Metals and hydrogen are formed at the cathode.

Non-metal atoms gain electrons. They form negative ions. These move to the positive anode. The anode removes electrons. The ions are turned back to atoms.

Non-metals are set free at the anode in electrolysis.

## Questions

1. Write this in your book. Fill in the blank spaces.

   A radioactive substance gives off ______. There are ______ types of radiation. They are named from the first ______ letters of the ______ alphabet.

   Alpha radiation consists of helium ______, $He^{2+}$. Beta radiation consists of particles. They are called ______. They have a ______ charge. Their masses are very ______, $\frac{1}{2000}$ of the mass of a ______ atom. Gamma radiation consists of ______ similar to ______ rays.

   Every atom has a small centre called its ______. It contains ______ and ______. A proton has the same mass as a ______ atom. It is ______ charged. The number of protons in an atom is its ______ ______.

   An atom has no overall charge. Its electrons are ______ charged. Its electrons and ______ are equal in number. Electrons in an atom are in groups. They surround the ______. The groups are called ______. The number of protons and neutrons in an atom is its ______ ______.

2. The symbol for magnesium is Mg. Its atomic number is 12. Its mass number is 24. Fill in the blanks.

   A magnesium atom has a central ______. It contains protons and ______. The total number of these is ______. A magnesium atom has ______ times the mass of an H atom. It contains ______ protons. It must have ______ electrons. The neon atom has ten electrons. A magnesium atom will lose ______ electrons. It still has ______ protons but only ______ electrons. It will be ______ charged. It has become the magnesium ion, $Mg^{\_\_+}$.

3. Read the statements about each particle. Choose the ones which are correct. Write your answer as
   A if only 1, 2 and 3 are correct,
   B if only 1 and 3 are correct,
   C if only 2 and 4 are correct,
   D if only 4 is correct,
   E for any other combination of correct answers.

   a) A proton
      1 is positively charged,
      2 has the same mass as an H atom,
      3 is found in the nucleus,
      4 has the same mass as an electron.
   b) A neutron
      1 is positively charged,
      2 is found in the nucleus,
      3 has no electrical charge,
      4 has the same mass as an H atom.
   c) An electron
      1 is negatively charged,
      2 has the same mass as an H atom,
      3 is contained in a shell in the atom,
      4 is positively charged.

# *Radioactivity*

## What is it?

Becquerel discovered it by chance. He showed that uranium compounds gave off rays. The effect was named radioactivity. The compounds are radioactive. Other compounds were discovered. They contain elements with large atoms. These large atoms give the rays.

The rays are of three types. They were named alpha, beta and gamma. These are the Greek letters a, b, c. $\alpha$-rays are helium ions, $He^{2+}$. $\beta$-rays are streams of electrons. $\gamma$-rays are waves like X-rays or light.

alpha is $\alpha$
beta is $\beta$
gamma is $\gamma$

## What causes it?

A radioactive atom is unstable. Its nucleus breaks up. It does so of its own accord. 'Bits' fly out of it. We say the atom 'spontaneously disintegrates'. The nucleus alters. This is a nuclear not a chemical change.

In chemical changes atoms react. They gain, lose or share electrons. These electrons are in their outside shells. These nucleus of each atom stays the same.

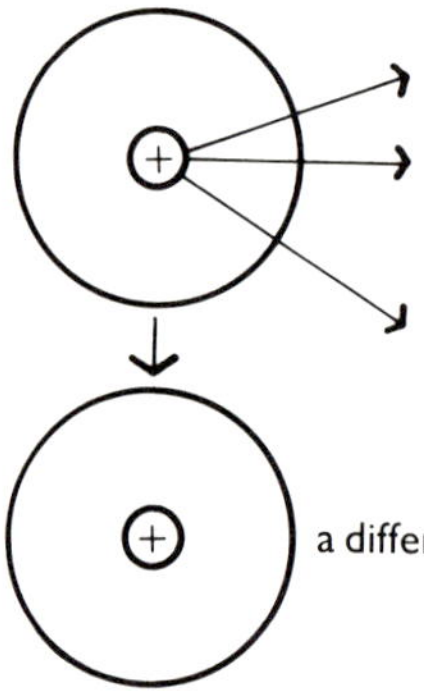


## What is the result of radioactivity?

Two quantities are enough to label an atom. They are atomic number and mass number. Each can be shown with its symbol. An atom of sodium is written as $^{23}_{11}Na$.

mass number 23
symbol Na
atomic number 11

The nucleus can 'decay' in two ways. In alpha-decay it emits a helium ion, $He^{2+}$. This has two protons and two neutrons. The mass number of the new substance is four units less. Its atomic number is two less. It becomes another element.

uranium 235 → thorium
$^{235}_{92}U \rightarrow ^{4}_{2}He + ^{231}_{90}Th$

In beta-decay the nucleus loses an electron. It comes from a neutron. It leaves an extra proton in the nucleus. Radium atoms become atoms of actinium.

neutron → proton + electron
$^{228}_{88}Ra \rightarrow ^{228}_{89}Ac$ + electron

## What does radiation do?

All three types of ray have energy. They pass through paper and metals. They affect photographic film. If they strike zinc sulphide they make it glow. They turn gas molecules into ions. In damp gas this leaves a vapour trail. These effects identify a radioactive substance. They also trace where it is.

Radioactivity is a source of energy. Power stations run on it. It damages or destroys living tissue. It can strike and alter the nuclei of other atoms.

## How long does it last?

A radioactive element emits rays. The nuclei of its atoms alter. After a time half of them will have changed. This time is the 'half-life' of the element. It can be a fraction of a second. It can be thousands of years. It is constant for any one element.

half-life 15 years
200 atoms $\rightarrow$ 100 left unchanged
Then 100 $\rightarrow$ 50 left unchanged
will also take 15 years
So will 50 $\rightarrow$ 25 unchanged.

## How can it be used?

Radioactive elements were found in nature. They can also be made. Normal compounds are hit by radiation. For example, sodium is not radioactive. A sodium compound is bombarded by neutrons. These change it.

Some sodium nuclei take in a neutron. The atoms are still sodium. The properties of the compound are not changed. But it is radioactive. It is called a radioisotope. It can be traced by the rays it gives.

$^{23}_{11}Na$ + neutron $^{1}_{0}n \rightarrow$ $^{24}_{11}Na$

For example, plants take phosphates from the soil. A radioisotope phosphate can be added. Its chemical properties are the same. The plant takes it from soil. It gives rays. These show us where it goes. We can find out how plants deal with phosphates from the soil.

Radioisotopes are used to trace living processes. They can locate tumours, cracks in metals, leaks in underground pipes, wear in car engines and many more. Their radiation destroys living cells. This gives them many medical uses. They are used against cancer.

**We can use radioactivity to find out how plants deal with phosphates from the soil.**

## Nuclear Energy

A large nucleus can be split into smaller ones. Uranium 235 splits if hit by neutrons. This is nuclear fission. The fission gives more neutrons. These hit other nuclei. A chain reaction is set up. Huge amounts of energy are released. The change can be explosive. This happened in the first atomic bomb.

Fission can be controlled by controlling the neutrons. Metals such as cadmium 'mop' them up. This slows down fission. Graphite slows neutrons down. It moderates them. This increases the rate of fission. Heat from it is converted to electrical energy. Small atoms can be built into bigger ones. This is nuclear fusion. It was used in the 'hydrogen bomb'.

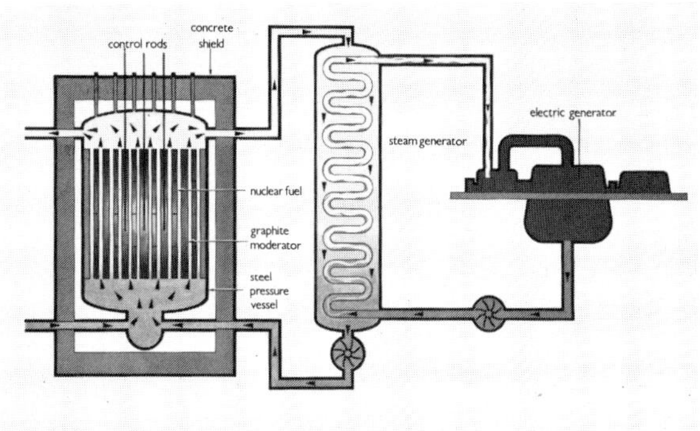

How a nuclear reactor works. Heat from the fuel makes steam which drives a generator.

# *The halogens*

We now know many properties of concentrated sulphuric acid. We shall look at one more. Be careful! It attacks skin, paper and wood.

### Experiment 6.1 Concentrated sulphuric acid and salt

**Wear eyeshields. Put salt, sodium chloride, into a test tube. Use as much as will cover a $\frac{1}{2}$p coin. Add ten drops of the acid. Use a dropper. TAKE CARE!**

**Note what happens. Hold a dry litmus paper in the tube. Then use a wet litmus paper. Put in a Universal Indicator paper and a lighted splint.**

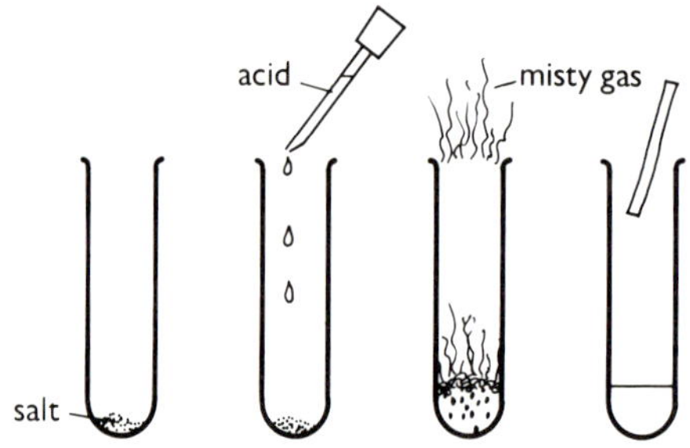


What do you see when the acid is added?
How do you know that a gas is formed?
Can you see the gas inside the tube?
Can you see it outside the tube?
What properties of the gas do the tests show?
Does it have the same effect on dry and wet litmus?

### Experiment 6.2 To find out if the gas dissolves in water

**Put three or four small pieces of rock salt in a test tube. Add ten drops of concentrated acid as before. Collect the gas in a large test tube. Cover the mouth of the tube. Turn it upside down in water. Add a litmus paper to the water in the tube.**

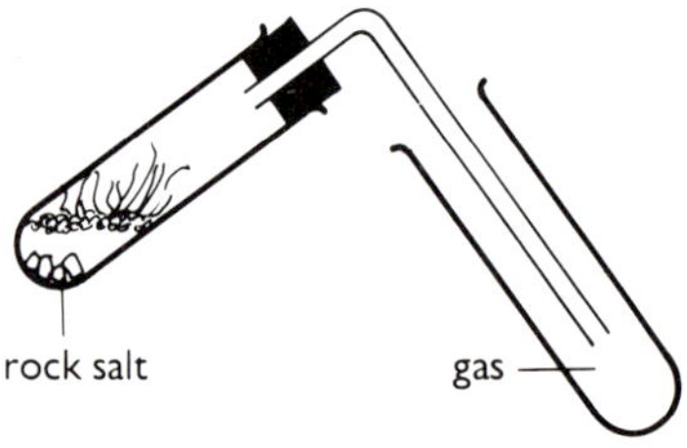


Does rock salt give a faster stream of gas?
What happens in the large test tube in the water?

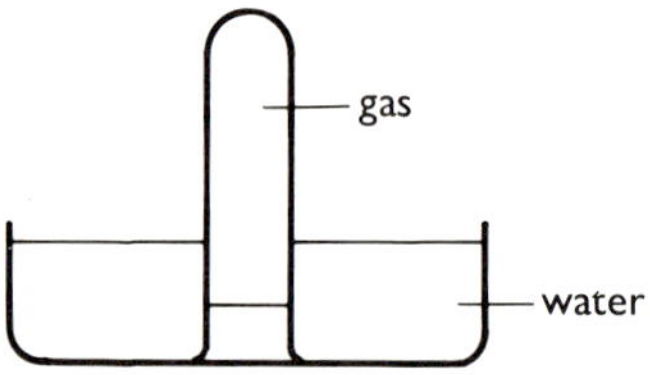


The mixture of acid and salt froths and bubbles. This is effervescence. It shows that a gas is being given off. It cannot be seen inside the tube. It becomes misty when it gets into the air.

The gas affects litmus. A dry paper changes only slowly. A wet litmus paper turns red at once. Water rises quickly in the large tube. A great deal of gas dissolves. The solution is an acid. The gas does not burn. It puts out a lighted splint.

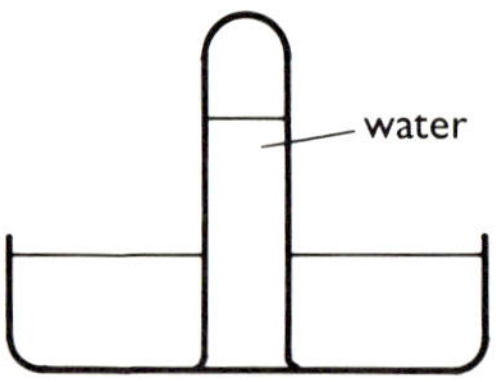


What element does every acid contain?
Acids react with metals. What is the usual product?
Acids and metals form salts. How did we define a salt?

All acids contain hydrogen. It can be replaced by a metal. The result is a salt. Hydrogen often appears as gas.

The misty gas dissolves in water. The solution contains an acid. The hydrogen of this acid may come from the gas. It may come from water. Remember that sulphur trioxide and water react. They form sulphuric acid.

$$SO_3 + H_2O \rightarrow H_2SO_4$$

The hydrogen in this acid comes from water.

### *Experiment 6.3 Does the misty gas contain hydrogen?

**Use the apparatus shown below. Put lumps of rock salt in the test tube. Add concentrated sulphuric acid. Put iron wool in the tube. Heat it gently. Collect the gas formed. Remove the delivery tube from the water.**

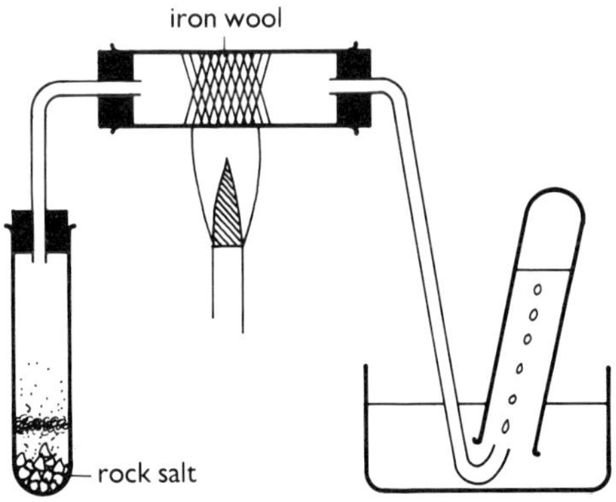


The rock salt and acid give a steady stream of gas.
What happens to the iron?
What gas is collected over the water?
Does the misty gas contain hydrogen?

Iron is an element. It contains only iron. It reacts with the misty gas. The gas formed is hydrogen. This hydrogen cannot have come from iron. Hydrogen must come from the misty gas. The misty gas is a hydrogen compound.

This compound must contain at least one other element. To find out which one we must remove the hydrogen. Oxygen from other compounds can do this by oxidation.

### Experiment 6.4 To oxidize the misty gas solution

**Wear eyeshields. Use a concentrated solution of the gas. Put it into three test tubes. Add to one a pinch of copper(II) oxide. Add a pinch of manganese(IV) oxide to the second. Drop crystals of potassium manganate(VII) into the third. If nothing happens warm the tube.**

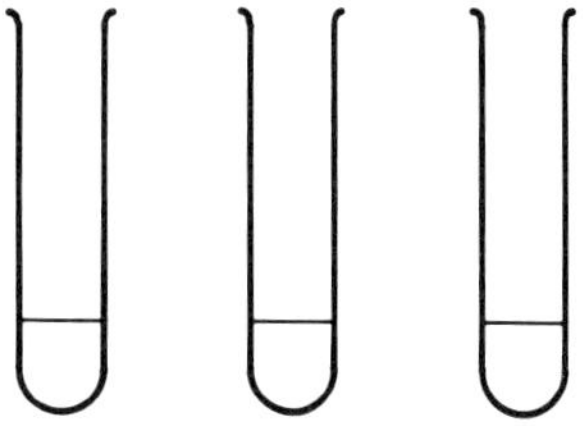

**Hold a dry blue litmus paper in the tube. Then use a wet litmus. Try a Universal Indicator paper.**

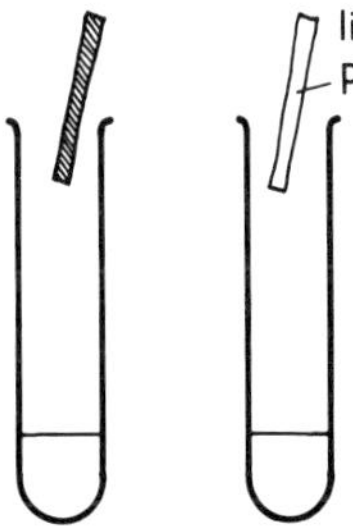


Which of the three mixtures give a gas?
Is the gas coloured?
What is its effect on dry litmus paper?
What happens to the wet litmus paper?
Do the potassium manganate(VII) crystals give a purple colour?

# Chlorine and hydrogen chloride

The misty gas in water gives an acid. We oxidized it. We used three substances. All three contain oxygen. Manganese(IV) oxide gives a gas. So does potassium manganate(VII). Copper(II) oxide gives a green solution but no gas.

The gas is pale green. It slowly turns a dry litmus paper red. It finally turns white. It is being bleached. Wet litmus is bleached at once. The name of the gas is chlorine (clor-een).

Chlorine is an element. It smells like household bleach. It is poisonous. The symbol for chlorine is Cl. It is a diatomic gas. Its molecule contains two atoms. It is written $Cl_2$.

So the misty gas is a compound of hydrogen and chlorine. It may contain other elements as well. To find out if it does we let hydrogen and chlorine react.

### *Experiment 6.5 Hydrogen and chlorine

**Make hydrogen from zinc and dilute sulphuric acid. Fill a small gas jar. Fill a second jar with chlorine.**

**Put safety screens round the jars. Invert the chlorine jar over the hydrogen jar. Remove the covers from between them. Have a lighted splint ready. After a few seconds take away the top jar.**

**Put the lighted splint into the open bottom jar. Cover the top jar. Open it after several minutes.**

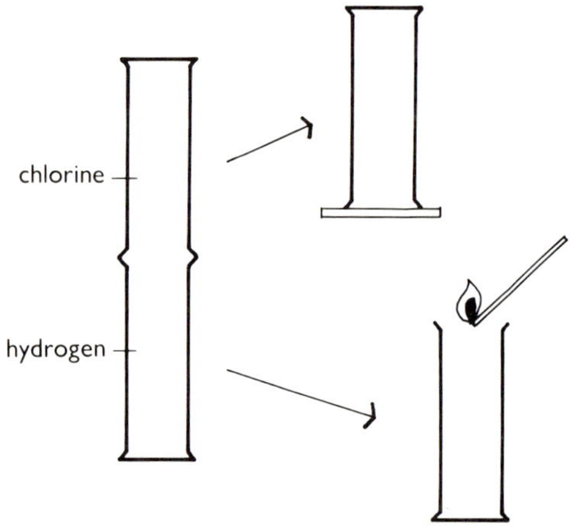


**Use hydrogen from a cylinder. Pass it through the tube. Surround the experiment with screens. Light the gas. Lower it into a gas jar of chlorine. Hold a white paper behind the gas jar.**

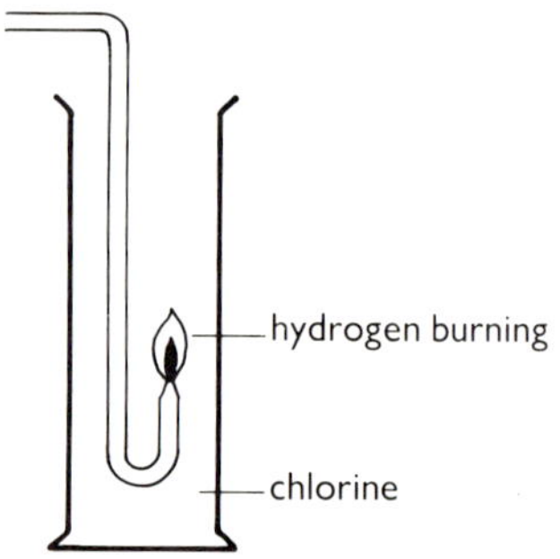


Does the lighted splint cause a change?
Do the gases hydrogen and chlorine react without it?
Is there any sign of the misty gas forming?
Does it appear when the top jar is opened?
Is chlorine used up as hydrogen burns in it?
Is one product the misty gas?

Does this experiment tell us what elements the misty gas contains?

When mixed, hydrogen and chlorine react. A lighted splint makes the reaction explosive. So does sunlight. Either gas will burn in the other. The misty gas is always formed. It must contain hydrogen and chlorine only. It is hydrogen chloride, HCl.

The names of compounds which contain only two elements end in -ide.

We used concentrated sulphuric acid and salt to make it.

$NaCl(s) + H_2SO_4(l) \rightarrow NaHSO_4(s) + HCl(g)$

In industry hydrogen is burnt in chlorine. A solution of hydrogen chloride is hydrochloric acid. It can never be 100% acid.

$H_2(g) + Cl_2(g) \rightarrow 2HCl(g)$

## *Experiment 6.6 More about hydrogen chloride

**Put small pieces of rock salt in the flask. Add concentrated sulphuric acid. Collect the gas as shown. This method is called 'downward delivery'.**

**a) Stand a gas jar of the gas over a gas jar of ammonia. Slide the lids out. Let the gases mix and stand for some time. Look at the bottom gas jar.**

**b) Fill a flask with the gas. Fit a stopper with glass tubing, narrowed at one end. Join rubber tubing to the other end. Close this with a clip.**

**Dip the narrow end of the tube in water. Put it into the flask. At the same time stopper the flask. Colour some water with Universal Indicator. Put the rubber tubing in the water. Open the clip.**

What do you see when the gases mix?
What is left in the bottom gas jar after standing?
Water rushes into the flask. Why?

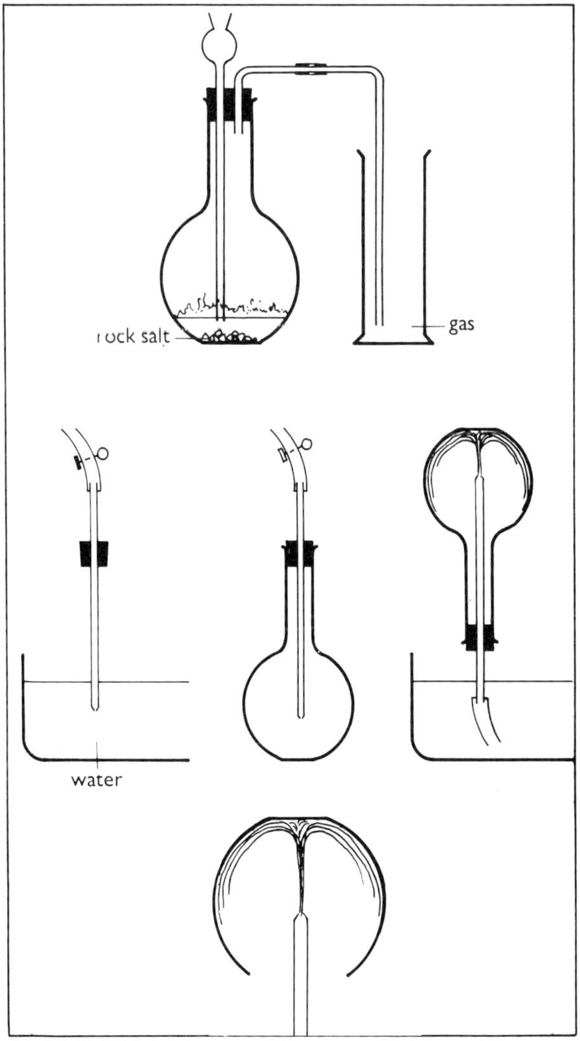


Ammonia and hydrogen chloride give dense white smoke. This settles as white crystals. They are ammonium chloride crystals. We recognize ammonia by this test.

Water rushes into the flask like a fountain. It is called the 'fountain test'. It can only do this if most of the gas has gone. It must have dissolved. The narrow tube carried only a few drops of water. Hydrogen chloride must be very soluble.

About 800 $cm^3$ of hydrogen chloride dissolve in 1 $cm^3$ of water. This gives concentrated hydrochloric acid. This explains why the gas is misty in air. The gas dissolves in the water vapour in the air. The mist is tiny drops of acid.

# Hydrochloric acid

Hydrogen chloride in water forms an acid. How does this happen. Is it an acid in other liquids?

### *Experiment 6.7 Hydrogen chloride in another liquid

**Put methylbenzene in a small flask. Add anhydrous calcium chloride. Stopper the flask. Let it stand overnight. Dry three test tubes and a litmus paper in an oven. Put the flask in a fume cupboard. TAKE CARE!**

**Pass dry hydrogen chloride into the methylbenzene. Let the gas bubble through for five minutes. Put some of this solution into each test tube. Add separately**

**a) the dry blue litmus paper,**
**b) a small lump of marble,**
**c) magnesium ribbon.**

> Hydrogen chloride dissolves in methylbenzene.
> Is the solution an acid?
> Does it affect litmus, marble or magnesium?

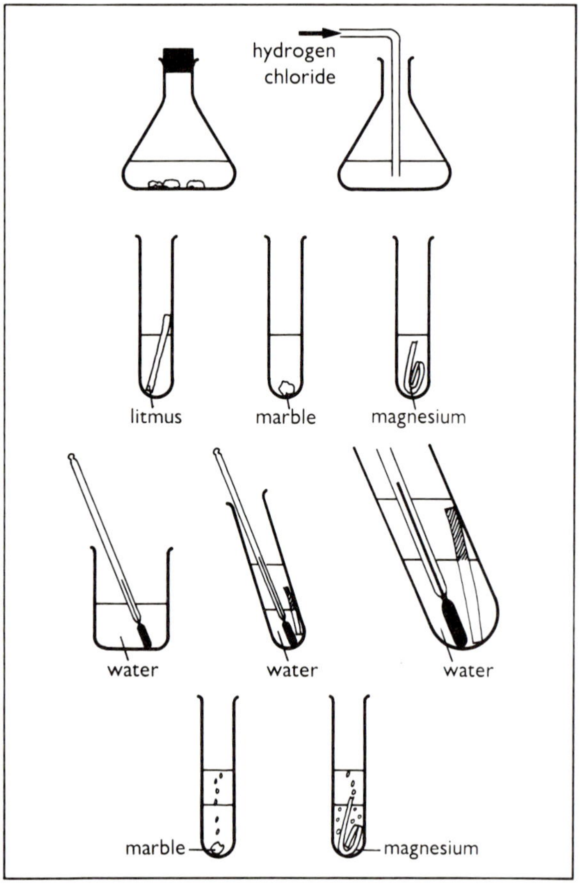


**Take the temperature of some water. Pour a little into all three test tubes. Stopper the tubes. Shake them. Take the temperature of the water in the litmus tube. Test gases formed in the other tubes.**

> The water forms a bottom layer in each tube.
> Does it become hotter or colder?
> Does it react with litmus, marble or magnesium?

The methylbenzene solution is not acid. It does not affect dry litmus. It does not react with marble or magnesium. The water dissolves some of the hydrogen chloride. This solution is acid. It affects litmus. It reacts with marble and magnesium.

> water + hydrogen chloride → acid solution + heat
> water + pure sulphuric acid → acid solution + heat

Heat suggests chemical change. Perhaps both substances *react* with water.

### *Experiment 6.8 Electrolysis of dilute hydrochloric acid

**Repeat Experiment 4.2. Use dilute hydrochloric acid in the voltameter. First colour it with litmus. Use platinum electrodes. Collect the gases formed there.**

> Check how fast the bubbles appear at each electrode. Compare them. Compare them with the volumes of gas collected. What gases are they likely to be?

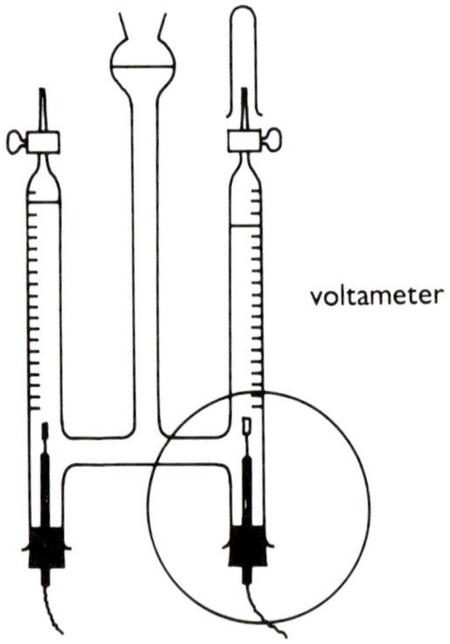

What ions give hydrogen at the cathode?
What happens to the litmus round the anode?
What gas is being set free there?
What happens to the bubbles of this gas?

Hydrogen at the cathode must come from $H^+$ ions. At the anode litmus is bleached. The gas must be chlorine. It comes off just as fast as hydrogen does. Some of it is used up in bleaching. Some dissolves. Very little of it reaches the tap.

The solution must contain $H^+$ and $Cl^-$ ions.

at the cathode (negative)
$H^+ + e \rightarrow H$
$2H \rightarrow H_2(g)$
at the anode (positive)
$Cl^- \rightarrow Cl + e$
$2Cl \rightarrow Cl_2(g)$

## Experiment 6.9 Other properties of the dilute acid

Fill test tubes one third full of dilute hydrochloric acid. Drop into each tube one of the following
a) the metals magnesium, zinc and copper,
b) small amounts of magnesium oxide, zinc oxide and copper(II) oxide,
c) copper(II) carbonate, calcium carbonate.

When reaction stops, evaporate the solutions from c). Heat the calcium chloride strongly. Drive off all the water. Leave the solid standing in air.

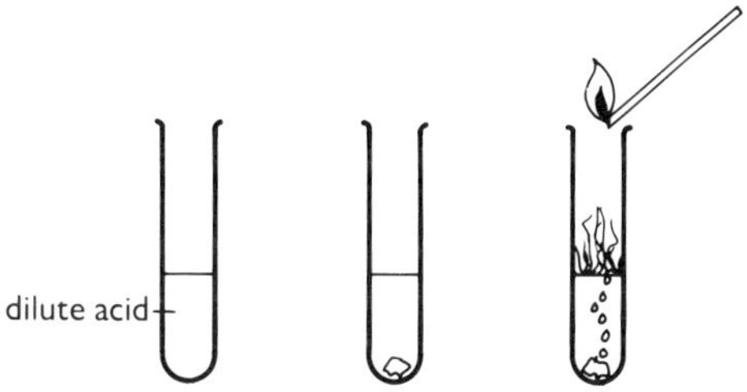


Write a word equation for each reaction. Using the formula HCl work out formula equations.
What happens to the solid in c)?

## Experiment 6.10 To make salt crystals

Fill a burette with dilute hydrochloric acid. Fill the part below the tap. Support it in a stand. Take the reading of the acid level.

Put sodium hydroxide solution into a beaker. Pick up 25 $cm^3$ of it with a pipette. Use a pipette bulb. Run the alkali into a conical flask. Add two drops of methyl orange. Run acid into the conical flask.

Swirl the mixture. When the methyl orange shows signs of changing, add acid in drops. Stop when the colour changes to pink. Read the acid level.

Wash out the flask. Put in another 25 $cm^3$ of alkali. Run in the same amount of acid as before. Evaporate the solution in a dish. Stop when a little liquid is left.

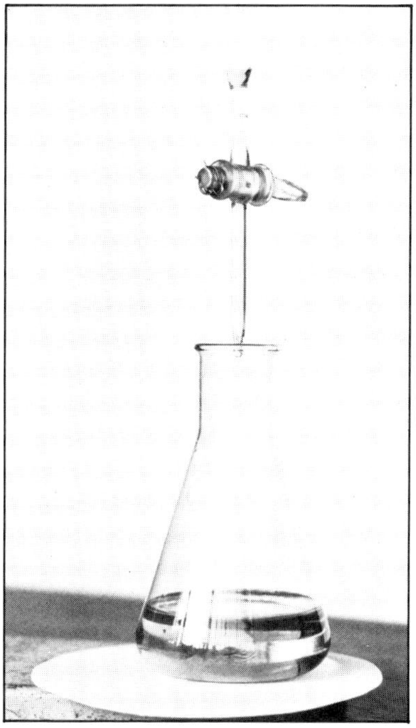

Look at the crystals. What substance are they?

# *Chlorides*

In water, hydrogen chloride turns into ions. It ionizes. In other liquids it does not ionize. The ions are $H^+$ and $Cl^-$. It is the hydrogen ions which make the solution an acid.

$HCl \rightarrow H^+ + Cl^-$
(hydrogen ion) (chloride ion)

The acid reacts with metals e.g. magnesium. The metal goes into solution as ions. Hydrogen appears, as a gas.

$Mg \rightarrow Mg^{2+} + 2e$
$2H^+ + 2e \rightarrow H_2$

$Mg^{2+}$ and $Cl^-$ ions are left in solution. Evaporating it gives magnesium chloride crystals. This is how it happens. We can sum it up by writing

$$Mg(s) + 2HCl(aq) \rightarrow MgCl_2(aq) + H_2(g)$$

$Mg + 2H^+ \; 2Cl^-$ (acid) $\rightarrow$ [$Mg^{2+} \; 2Cl^-$ salt] $+ H_2$

Sodium hydroxide solution has $Na^+$ and $OH^-$ ions. Hydrochloric acid has $H^+$ and $Cl^-$ ions. They react. Water is formed. $Na^+$ and $Cl^-$ ions are left in solution. Evaporation gives sodium chloride crystals.

$Na^+ +$ [$OH^-$ $H^+$] $+ Cl^-$
↓
$H_2O$

Most chlorides dissolve in water. A few do not.

### Experiment 6.11 An insoluble chloride

**Take solutions of sodium chloride, zinc chloride and sodium carbonate. Add drops of silver nitrate solution. Pour in dilute nitric acid.**

All three give a white precipitate (ppt).
Remember that all nitrates dissolve in water.
So do all sodium and potassium salts.

sodium chloride + silver nitrate → ? + ?

In each case, which substance is the ppt?
Does it dissolve in nitric acid?

sodium carbonate + silver nitrate → ? + ?

*All chlorides* give a white ppt of silver chloride. The ppt does not dissolve in nitric acid. *Other salts* give white ppts too. They *do* dissolve in the acid.

Chlorides have $Cl^-$ ions.
Silver nitrate solution has $Ag^+$ ions. They react.
We can use this test to recognize a chloride.

$$Cl^-(aq) + Ag^+(aq) \rightarrow AgCl(s)$$

### The uses of chlorides

Sodium chloride is common salt. We use it to preserve and flavour food. Many other substances are made from it. Potassium chloride is a fertilizer. Ammonium chloride is used in dry cells. Anhydrous calcium chloride dries substances.

## Oxidation of hydrochloric acid

Copper(II) oxide reacts with hydrochloric acid.

$CuO + 2HCl \rightarrow CuCl_2 + H_2O$

Copper chloride forms.

Manganese(IV) oxide is $MnO_2$. It has extra oxygen.

$MnO_2 = MnO + O$

$$\begin{array}{llll} MnO & + 2HCl \rightarrow MnCl_2 + & H_2O & \\ O & + 2HCl & H_2O + Cl_2 & \end{array}$$

$$MnO_2 + 4HCl \rightarrow MnCl_2 + 2H_2O + Cl_2$$

Hydrochloric acid is oxidized. The oxygen added takes away hydrogen. It gives water and chlorine.

## Questions

1. A white sodium salt has cubic crystals. With concentrated sulphuric acid it gives a fuming, misty gas. This turns a wet litmus paper red. When mixed with ammonia it gives white smoke.

   Name the sodium salt, the misty gas and the white smoke. Why does a wet litmus turn red?
   Why is the gas misty in moist air but not in dry?

2. Some white crystals are thought to be common salt. They colour a bunsen flame yellow-orange.
   What does this mean?
   Two different tests will show if the substance is a chloride. Say exactly how you would carry out one of these tests.

3. What is neutralization?
   Common salt can be made by this method.
   Name the substances you would use.
   Describe briefly how you would use them.

## Summary

All chlorides react with concentrated sulphuric acid. A misty gas is formed. Passing this gas over heated iron gives hydrogen. This proves that the misty gas is a hydrogen compound.

It is very soluble in water. The solution is an acid. All acids contain hydrogen. The misty gas must contain another element. Oxidizing the concentrated solution of it gives a green gas.

This is the element chlorine, symbol Cl. It is a diatomic gas. Its molecule contains two atoms. Hydrogen and chlorine react vigorously. The misty gas is formed. It must be a compound of hydrogen and chlorine only. It is hydrogen chloride, HCl.

Hydrogen chloride mixed with ammonia gives white smoke. It settles as solid crystals. They are the salt ammonium chloride.

Hydrochloric acid is a solution of hydrogen chloride in water. Other liquids dissolve hydrogen chloride. These solutions are not acids. They do not affect litmus, magnesium or marble.

Hydrochloric acid conducts. It can be electrolysed. Hydrogen forms at the cathode. This means that the acid contains hydrogen ions, $H^+$. An equal volume of chlorine forms at the anode. The acid must contain $Cl^-$ (chloride) ions. HCl is still a useful formula for hydrochloric acid.

Like all acids hydrochloric acid forms salts. They are called chlorides. They are made by the usual methods. Acid + metal, metal oxide, metal hydroxide or metal carbonate. Most chlorides dissolve in water.

Chloride solutions give a white ppt with silver nitrate. This does not dissolve in nitric acid. It is used as a test for chlorides in solution.

$$\text{X chloride} + \text{silver nitrate} \rightarrow \text{X nitrate} + \text{silver chloride}$$

# Chlorine

To make chlorine we oxidize hydrochloric acid. Concentrated acid is used. Manganese(IV) oxide oxidizes it.

### *Experiment 6.12 The properties of chlorine

Use the apparatus in a fume cupboard. Put some manganese(IV) oxide in the flask. Add concentrated hydrochloric acid. Heat if necessary. Bubble the gas through water. This removes hydrogen chloride.

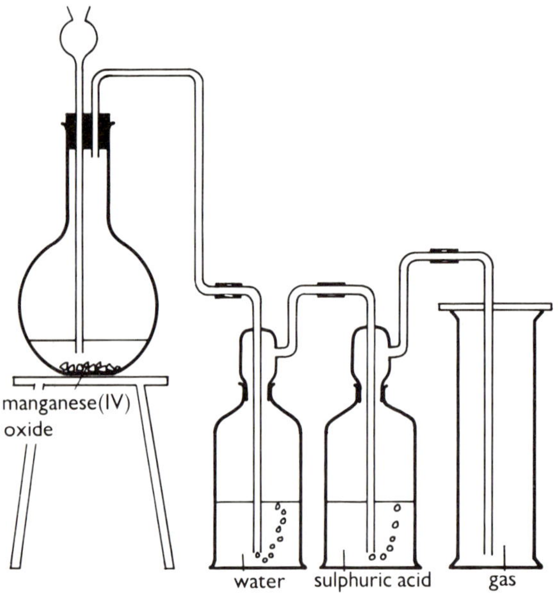


Pass the gas through concentrated sulphuric acid. This dries it. Collect the gas in gas jars as shown.

Lower into gas jars of chlorine
a) burning magnesium ribbon held in tongs;
b) sodium gently heated in a combustion spoon;
c) burning red phosphorus on a combustion spoon;
d) a burning candle on a combustion spoon.

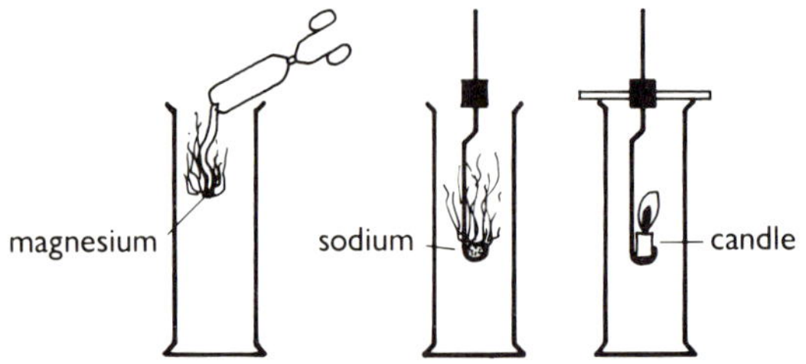


e) Stand two gas jars of chlorine in front of white paper. Add to one a few $cm^3$ of sodium hydroxide solution. Shake the mixture. Add a litmus paper.

To the second jar add newly slaked lime. Shake it in the jar. Remove the powder. Shake a little of it in water. Dip a litmus paper in the solution. Let two thirds of it get wet. Dip the other end in acid to the same depth.

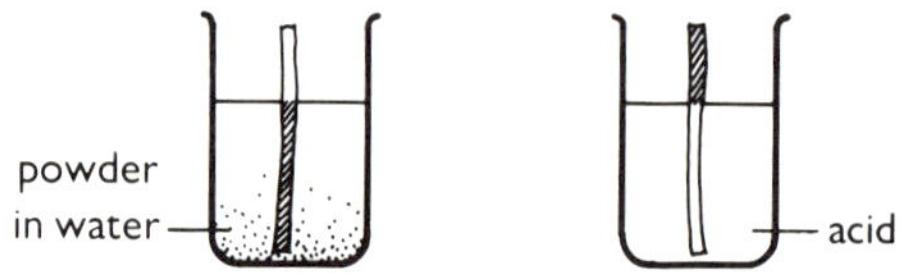


Which substances burn in chlorine?
What solid is formed when sodium burns?
Name two substances formed by the candle flame.
Does chlorine disappear when alkali is added?
Do the two react to form new substances?
What happens to the litmus papers?

Manufacturing chlorine.

## Burning in chlorine

Chlorine reacts with metals. Magnesium burns in it. The solid product is magnesium chloride.

$Mg + Cl_2 \rightarrow MgCl_2$

Sodium bursts into flame in chlorine. Cubic crystals of sodium chloride are formed.

$2Na + Cl_2 \rightarrow 2NaCl$

Chlorine reacts with non-metals too. Phosphorus burns in it forming phosphorus chlorides.

$2P + 3Cl_2 \rightarrow 2PCl_3$

Candle wax is a hydrocarbon. It burns in chlorine. The flame is red and sooty. The soot is carbon. The other product is hydrogen chloride.

$C_{16}H_{34} + 17Cl_2 \rightarrow 16C + 34HCl$

## Chlorine and alkalis

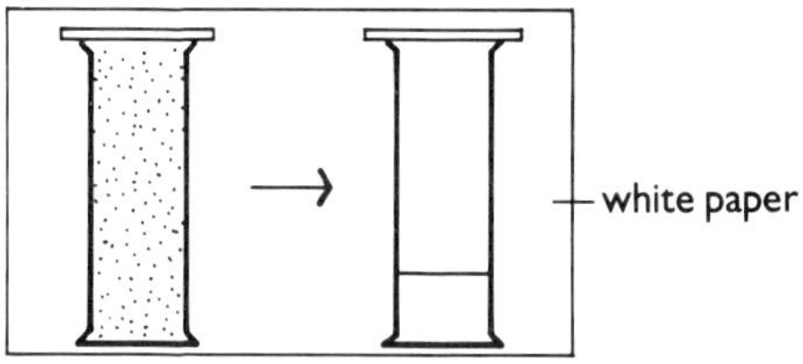


White paper makes it easy to see chlorine. Alkalis remove the gas. They must react with it. Remember that chlorine reacts with water. The solution is acid. It bleaches litmus paper white.

Chlorine and water give an acid which bleaches. It is hypochlorous acid, HClO. Its salts are called hypochlorites. Acid and salts both bleach.

$Cl_2 + H_2O \rightarrow HClO + HCl$

$HClO$ + coloured dye $\rightarrow$ $HCl$ + colourless substance

If water + chlorine $\rightarrow$ two acids $\longrightarrow$ $HClO + HCl$

then alkali + chlorine $\rightarrow$ two salts $\longrightarrow$ $NaClO + NaCl$

Sodium hydroxide and chlorine react. The solution is the household bleach we buy.

Calcium hydroxide and chlorine give 'bleaching powder'. Shaken with water it turns litmus blue. Acid makes the other end of the litmus paper red. Acid and bleaching powder bleach the middle. We get a red, white and blue strip.

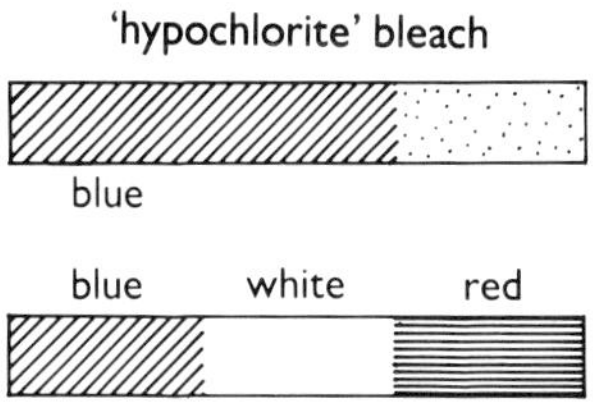


Chlorine belongs to a family. All the elements in it are called halogens. The word means 'salt former'. They are fluorine F, chlorine Cl, bromine Br, iodine I, astatine At. Their properties are very much alike. We know about chlorine. We shall test bromine and iodine.

# The halogen family

Fluorine and chlorine are pale green gases. Bromine is a brown liquid. Iodine is a shiny grey solid. Astatine is a solid. It is rare and radioactive.

### *Experiment 6.13 Properties of bromine and iodine

**a) Put one drop of bromine in a test tube. Stopper the tube. Let it stand. Add a little water. Shake the mixture in the tube. Add a blue litmus paper. Add 1 $cm^3$ of trichloromethane. Shake the tube.**

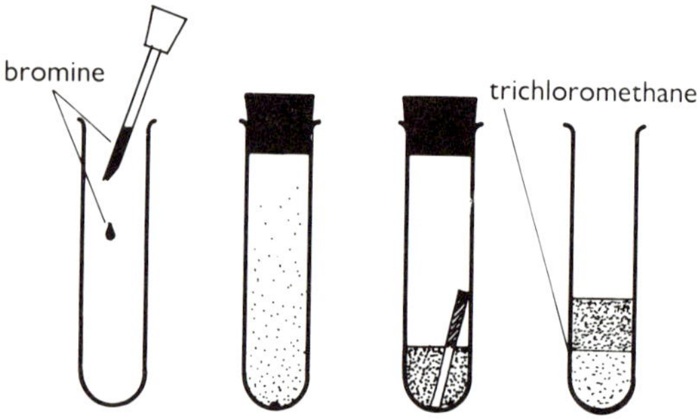


What happens to the drop of liquid bromine?
Does bromine dissolve in water and affect litmus?
What happens to the layer of trichloromethane?

**b) Put two or three iodine crystals in a test tube. Gently heat them. Let the tube cool. Add water. Stopper the tube and shake it. Add a blue litmus paper. Add a crystal of potassium iodide. Shake again. Shake the mixture with 1 $cm^3$ of trichloromethane.**

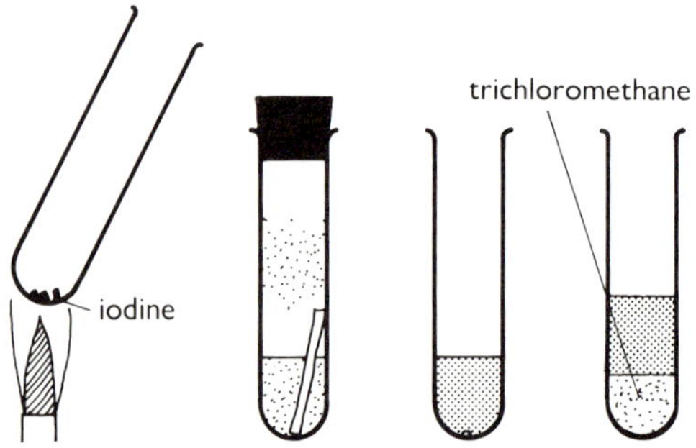


What happens when iodine is heated?
Does it dissolve in water?
What change does the potassium iodide make?
What happens to the layer of trichloromethane?

We know that chlorine dissolves slightly in water. The pale green solution bleaches litmus. Bromine turns into vapour. It also dissolves a little in water. The brown solution bleaches litmus slowly. Trichloromethane is more dense than water. It falls to the bottom. It becomes brown.

Iodine turns to vapour when heated. It sublimes. Iodine dissolves very little in water. The solution is very pale brown. It has little effect on litmus. Potassium iodide makes it dissolve much more. It dissolves in the trichloromethane layer. This solution is violet in colour.

### *Experiment 6.14 Halogens and metals

**Pass chlorine over heated iron as shown. Put two drops of bromine in a test tube. Put iron wool halfway down the tube. Heat just below the iron. Do it again. Use iodine crystals in place of bromine.**

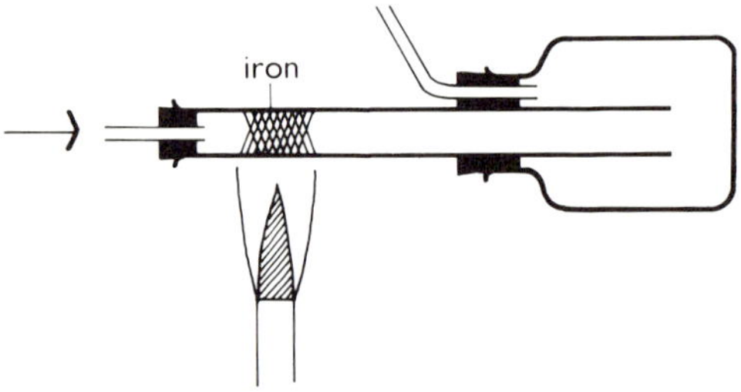


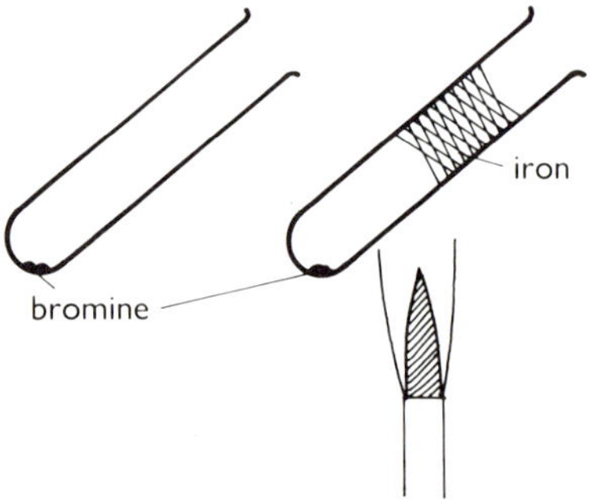


Do the three halogens react with iron? Put them in order of how well they react.

All halogens react with metals. Chlorine is the most vigorous of the three. Iodine is least active. Chlorides, bromides and iodides are formed. They are all salts.

## Experiment 6.15 Chlorides, bromides and iodides

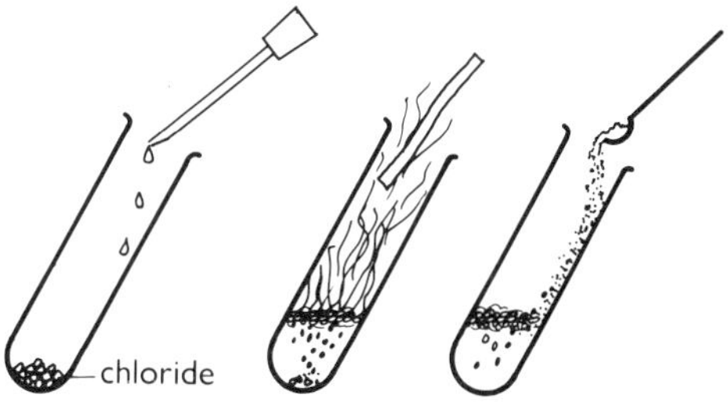


***a) Put sodium chloride crystals in a test tube. Add drops of concentrated sulphuric acid. Hold a wet litmus paper in the gas. Add a pinch of manganese(IV) oxide. Test the gas with litmus paper again. Add concentrated sulphuric acid to a bromide and an iodide. Test the gases with wet litmus paper.**

All three give misty gases. Name them.
What else appeared in the bromide tube?
What other product forms in the iodide tube?
What effect does the manganese(IV) oxide have?

A chloride gives misty hydrogen chloride. Bromide and iodide give misty gases. They must be hydrogen bromide and hydrogen iodide. Manganese(IV) oxide oxidizes hydrogen chloride. Chlorine is formed.

Brown bromine forms in the bromide tube. Grey iodine forms in the iodide tube. The misty gases have been oxidized. The sulphuric acid does this.

**b) Use solutions of chloride, bromide and iodide in water. Use them for these two tests.**

**1. Add drops of silver nitrate solution. Add a little dilute nitric acid. Add aqueous ammonia.**

**2. Add chlorine water to each solution. Put in 1 $cm^3$ of trichloromethane. Shake each tube gently.**

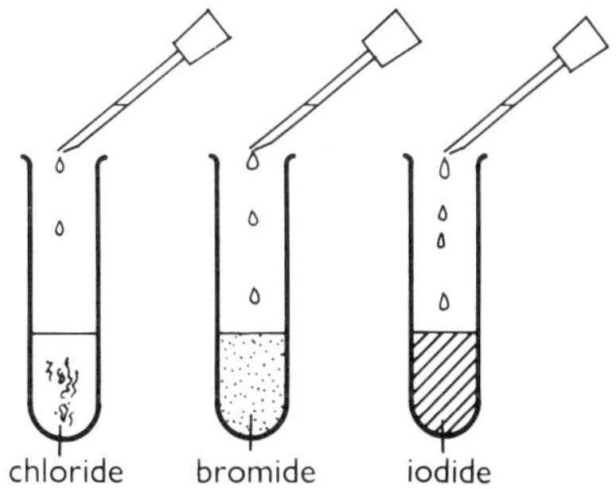


What colour is each ppt in 1?
What effect does aqueous ammonia have on each ppt?
What effect does chlorine have on the three solutions?

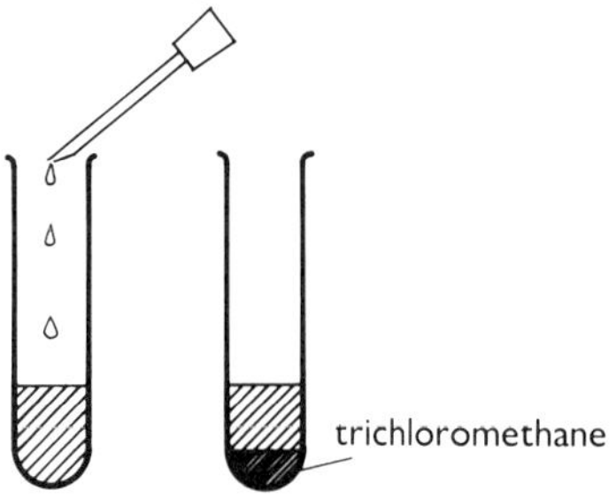


All three give ppts. Silver chloride is white. Silver bromide is cream coloured. Silver iodide is pale yellow. Ammonia dissolves silver chloride. It nearly dissolves silver bromide. Silver iodide remains unchanged.

Chlorine is the most active. It displaces bromine and iodine. Both solutions are brown. Trichloromethane shows us which is which. Bromine makes it brown. Iodine makes it violet.

We have crystals of chloride, bromide or iodide. These tests will tell us which.

# *Happy families?*

We have tested chlorine, bromine and iodine. We cannot test fluorine or astatine. The halogens are very much alike. So are their compounds. They react in the same kind of way. In our tests chlorine was the most active.

Bromine comes next. Iodine is least active. This is why chlorine reacts with bromides. Chlorine pushes out the less active bromine. It also displaces iodine. Both solutions become brown. We used trichloromethane to tell us which was which. It dissolves bromine. The solution is brown. It dissolves iodine. The solution is violet.

The compounds of the halogens are alike. A summary shows this.

| Reaction with | Chloride | Bromide | Iodide |
|---|---|---|---|
| 1. concentrated sulphuric acid | misty hydrogen chloride forms | misty hydrogen bromide + bromine | misty hydrogen iodide + iodine |
| 2. chlorine water<br><br>add trichloromethane | no reaction<br><br>no change | brown solution of bromine<br>brown solution in this liquid | brown solution of iodine<br>violet solution in this liquid |
| 3. silver nitrate solution | white ppt unchanged by acid<br>dissolves in ammonia | cream ppt unchanged by acid<br>nearly dissolves in ammonia | pale yellow ppt unchanged by nitric acid or ammonia |

All three tests can be used to test for chloride, bromide or iodide. All three give similar results. They differ enough to say which compound we started with.

Every element belongs to a family. Lithium, sodium and potassium do. They are called the alkali metals. As in all families their properties are alike. Potassium is the most active. Lithium is least active.

Look at their relative atomic masses or mass numbers.

Li = 7, Na = 23, K = 39

Can you see a connection?

## Summary

To make chlorine we use concentrated hydrochloric acid. The change is oxidation. Manganese(IV) oxide can oxidize the acid. Chlorine dissolves in water.

Chlorine reacts with metals and non-metals. The compounds formed are called chlorides. Sodium and magnesium both burn in chlorine. The equations are

$$2Na(s) + Cl_2(g) \rightarrow 2NaCl(s)$$
$$Mg(s) + Cl_2(g) \rightarrow MgCl_2(s)$$

Other metals heated in chlorine react.

Phosphorus is a non-metal which burns in chlorine. Candle wax is a hydrocarbon. It is a compound of hydrogen and carbon. A candle burns in chlorine. It has a smoky flame because soot is formed. Soot is carbon. Hydrogen chloride is also formed.

Chlorine reacts with alkalis. In water it gives two acids. With alkali it forms two salts. Both solutions bleach.

$$Cl_2 + 2NaOH \rightarrow H_2O + NaCl + NaClO(aq)$$

NaClO is sodium hypochlorite or sodium chlorate(I).

It bleaches by oxidizing the coloured dye.

$$NaClO + dye \rightarrow NaCl + \text{colourless substance}$$

Slaked lime is calcium hydroxide, an alkali. Chlorine reacts with it. The result is bleaching powder.

Chlorine is a member of the halogen family. The others are fluorine, bromine, iodine and astatine. They have similar properties. Chlorine is more active than bromine. Bromine is more active than iodine. Chlorine reacts with bromides and iodides.

It displaces bromine and iodine. They appear as brown solutions. Trichloromethane dissolves both. Bromine gives a brown solution, iodine a violet one.

Chlorides, bromides and iodides are alike. All three give a misty gas with concentrated sulphuric acid. The gases are hydrogen chloride, hydrogen bromide and hydrogen iodide. The last two are oxidized by the acid. Bromine and iodine are formed as well.

All three, in solution, give a ppt with silver ions. The ppts do not dissolve in nitric acid. The chloride ppt dissolves in ammonia. The bromide ppt nearly dissolves. The iodide ppt is not soluble.

Every element belongs to a family. The members of the family are alike. Their properties are similar. Some members react more vigorously than others.

## Questions

1. Fill in the blanks.

   Chlorine can be made from concentrated ______ acid. This is an example of an ______ reaction. Manganese(IV) oxide provides the ______. Chlorine is ______ in colour. Sodium ______ in chlorine. This gives white crystals of ______ ______. Some metals react if ______ in chlorine gas.

   A non-metal which burns in chlorine is ______. Hydrocarbons such as candle wax contain ______ and ______. They react with chlorine. The products are hydrogen ______ and soot. Soot is the element ______.

   Chlorine dissolves in water. The solution turns litmus ______. It then ______ it white. The first change shows that the solution is ______.

   $Cl_2 + H_2O \rightarrow HCl +$ ______. The second acid does the ______. It is hypochlorous ______ or chloric(I) acid.

   $HClO + dye \rightarrow HCl +$ ______ ______.

2. A salt A consists of white cubic crystals. Concentrated sulphuric acid is added to A. The gas B is formed. It is misty in moist air. It turns litmus red. Mixed with ammonia it gives white smoke. This settles as crystals of substance C. Manganese(IV) oxide is added to the sulphuric acid and salt mixture. A green gas D is formed. It will bleach a moist litmus paper.
   Name the salt A and the gases B and D.
   What is the white smoke C?
   Why does D bleach litmus paper?
   How would you make a sample of household bleach from gas D?

# Chemistry and disease

Disease means a lack of health. We become ill because our bodies are not working properly. There are three main reasons why this can happen.

1. The body may be short of a substance it cannot do without.
2. The body may have been invaded by tiny living creatures. These are called micro-organisms.
3. A part of the body may not be working properly.

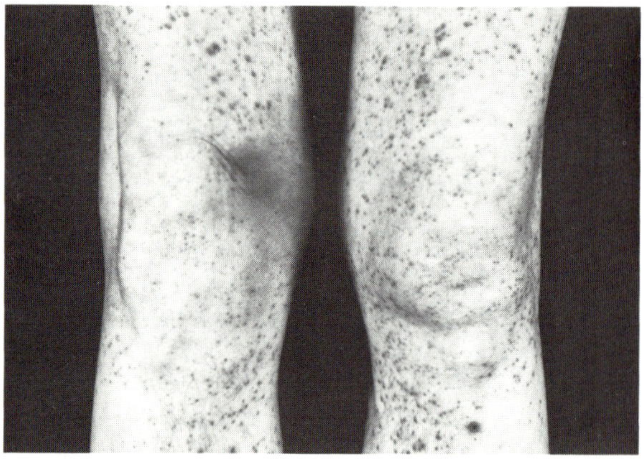

The scabs on these legs were caused by scurvy, a deficiency disease.

## A missing substance

A disease caused by a missing substance is called a **deficiency disease**. Scurvy is an example. It causes bleeding gums. It starts internal bleeding. It can cause death. It was once a very common disease.

In the days of sailing ships voyages were long. The sailors often suffered from scurvy. So did people living in poor city areas. The cure was simple. People had only to eat fresh fruit or vegetables.

Vitamin tablets help prevent deficiency diseases.

Sailors out of touch with land could not get them. Poor people in cities could not afford them. Lime juice was first carried by British ships. Fruit juice prevented the disease. This is why British sailors are still called 'limeys'.

Chemical methods proved that fruit contains a necessary substance. So do fresh vegetables. It is called vitamin C. It is the substance ascorbic acid. The pure substance can be manufactured. We buy it as vitamin C tablets. They are not as much fun to eat as oranges and currants. They do prevent scurvy.

Only Third World people are likely to have scurvy now. Other deficiency diseases have been dealt with. Chemists make the substances which prevent them.

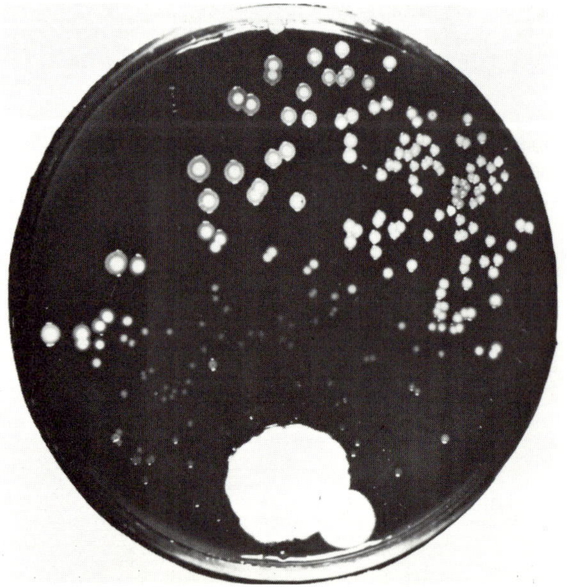

Penicillin is a mould. It can be grown on a petri dish.

## Micro-organisms

Bacteria and viruses are the common ones. They get into the body. They live and multiply there. Some bacteria are helpful. Over 100 years ago it was proved that others cause disease. They can be

Spraying crops with a pesticide.

Some villages rely on one water supply. It is disastrous if this water becomes infected.

passed on from person to person. The body has defences against them. Chemical compounds can destroy them.

From early times man has used such substances. He got them from plants. For example, Indians in Peru suffered from malaria. They chewed the bark of the cinchona tree. It prevented and cured the disease.

The bark was proved to contain the substance quinine. Quinine was manufactured. It took the place of the bark. Medicines of this kind are called **antibiotics**.

Some parts of our bodies absorb harmless dyes. So do micro-organisms. The dye may kill them. Science has found out how dyes do this. New ones are then designed. They destroy particular micro-organisms.

Some are destroyed by substances produced by living materials. A mould called penicillium gives a group of these substances. They are called penicillin. They destroy many bacteria. The diseases the bacteria caused, such as diphtheria, have almost disappeared.

## Other ways of controlling disease

Bacteria get into the body in many ways. One way is through wounds. These may come from injury or from surgery. We can use substances to destroy bacteria around wounds. They are called **antiseptics**. They reduce the risk of infection. The first was 'carbolic acid', used over 100 years ago.

Many diseases are handed on by animals and insects. Malaria is one example. The micro-organisms are carried by mosquitoes. A mosquito bite puts them into the blood. The human being gets malaria.

The insects can be killed by substances like DDT. So can their larvae. The places where they live are sprayed. Destroying them saves lives. It makes the land fit for farming. DDT is a **pesticide**.

Pesticides have two drawbacks. a) they may harm the birds which feed on the insects. b) insects build up resistance to a pesticide. It may become harmless in time. Pesticides may also kill useful insects.

Harmful micro-organisms may infect water supplies. Chlorine destroys them. Providing a pure water supply reduces disease. This is one way of helping poorer countries in the Third World.

# How do elements combine?

Chlorine is a green gas. Sodium is a metal. They are both elements. Like all elements they contain atoms. Sodium burns in chlorine. Their atoms combine.

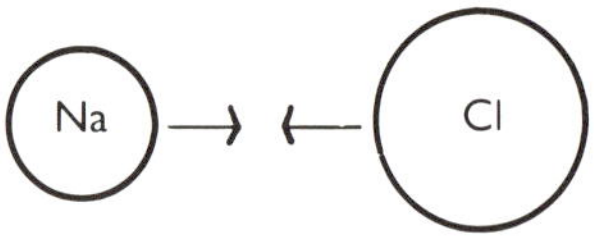


To do this the atoms must meet. They end up as white salt crystals. How do they combine? Check again on what you know about atoms.

Every atom has a **nucleus**. It is very small compared with the atom. It contains protons and neutrons. Protons give it a positive charge. Neutrons have no charge. Both have the mass of a hydrogen atom.

nucleus = protons + neutrons

An atom contains electrons. They are equal in number to its protons. They have a negative charge. They are in groups called shells. These surround the nucleus. You need to know more about the shells.

electrons in shells

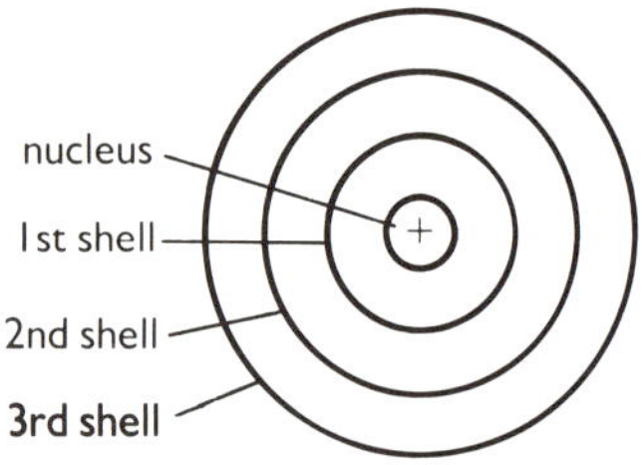


The first shell is the one nearest to the nucleus. It can hold at most only two electrons.

The second shell is further from the nucleus. It can hold up to eight electrons. It is then full. The third shell is full when it contains eighteen.

Apply these ideas to the first twenty elements.

**Hydrogen** Atomic Number 1. Mass Number 1.
Its atom has one proton in the nucleus.
It has one electron in the first shell.

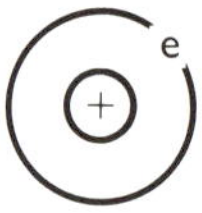


**Helium** Atomic number 2. Its nucleus has two protons.
Mass Number 4. The nucleus has two neutrons.
It has two protons so it will have two electrons as well.
They are both in the first shell. This shell is then full.

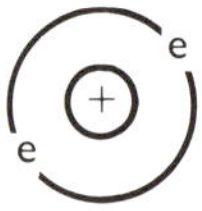


**Lithium** Atomic number 3. Mass Number 7.
Its atom contains three electrons. Two of these fill the first shell. The third will be in the second shell. This arrangement of electrons is called the electron structure.
It is written 2.1.

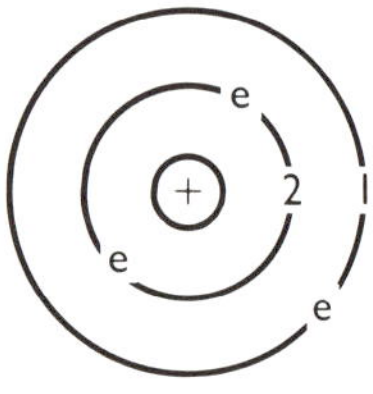


The table opposite shows twenty elements. Only the *electron* structure of each is worked out. Can you see why the *nucleus* is less important?

*When sodium, soft and shiny metal,*
*Meets chlorine, green and poisonous gas,*
*The two combine and crystals settle.*
*So now we have some salt to pass!*

| Element | Atomic Number | Number of electrons in each shell 1st | 2nd | 3rd | 4th | 5th |
|---|---|---|---|---|---|---|
| Hydrogen | 1 | 1 | | | | |
| Helium | 2 | 2 | (shell full) | | | |
| Lithium | 3 | 2 | 1 | | | |
| Beryllium | 4 | 2 | 2 | | | |
| Boron | 5 | 2 | 3 | | | |
| Carbon | 6 | 2 | 4 | | | |
| Nitrogen | 7 | 2 | 5 | | | |
| Oxygen | 8 | 2 | 6 | | | |
| Fluorine | 9 | 2 | 7 | | | |
| Neon | 10 | 2 | 8 | (shell full) | | |
| Sodium | 11 | 2 | 8 | 1 | | |
| Magnesium | 12 | 2 | 8 | 2 | | |
| Aluminium | 13 | 2 | 8 | 3 | | |
| Silicon | 14 | 2 | 8 | 4 | | |
| Phosphorus | 15 | 2 | 8 | 5 | | |
| Sulphur | 16 | 2 | 8 | 6 | | |
| Chlorine | 17 | 2 | 8 | 7 | | |
| Argon | 18 | 2 | 8 | 8 | (part shell full) | |
| Potassium | 19 | 2 | 8 | 8 | 1 | |
| Calcium | 20 | 2 | 8 | 8 | 2 | |

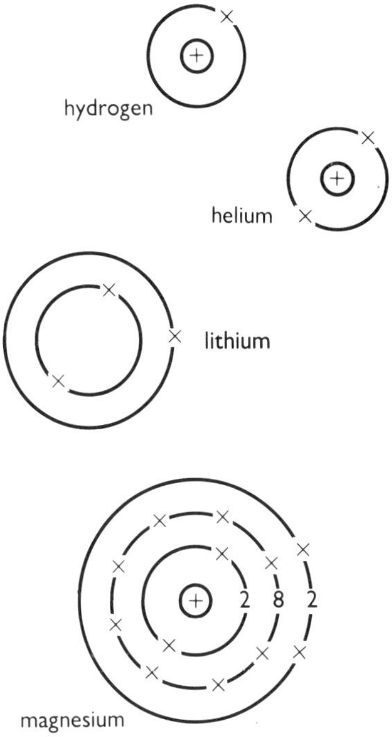


Atoms of sodium and chlorine combine. To do so they must meet. The shells surround the nucleus. So the shells meet first. The nucleus is less important. The shells must control combination.

Use the table to find answers to these questions.

1. Which two elements have full outside shells?
2. Which other element has eight electrons in its outside shell?
3. The list has three alkali metals. Which are they?
4. Check their outside shells. How many electrons in each?
5. Which is the outside shell of chlorine, 1st, 2nd or 3rd?
6. How many electrons does this outside shell contain?
7. What other element has the same number in its outside shell?
8. Is this element a halogen?

The first shell is filled by two electrons. So helium has a full outside shell. The second shell is full when it has eight electrons. Neon has a full outside shell. Both are noble gases. So is argon. Its structure is 2.8.8.

| | |
|---|---|
| He | 2 |
| Ne | 2.8 |
| Ar | 2.8.8 |

The alkali metals are lithium, sodium and potassium. Their atoms each have an outside shell with one electron. Chlorine has the electron structure 2.8.7. Its outside shell has seven electrons. So does the fluorine atom, 2.7. Both are halogens.

| | |
|---|---|
| Li | 2.1 |
| Na | 2.8.1 |
| K | 2.8.8.1 |

# The ionic bond

All atoms of noble gases have either

a) a full outside shell

or b) an outside shell of eight electrons.

All other atoms tend towards this. When they combine they reach the structure of a noble gas atom.

The electron structure of a sodium atom is 2.8.1. The nearest noble gas is neon, structure 2.8. To reach this, the sodium atom loses one electron. It now has only ten electrons. Their charge is 10−. The atom still has 11 protons. Their charge is 11+. It has one more positive than negative charge. It has become a sodium ion, $Na^+$, structure 2.8.

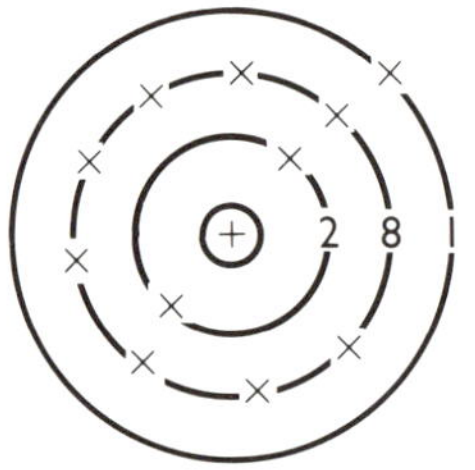


A chlorine atom has the electron structure 2.8.7. The nearest noble gas is argon, 2.8.8. A chlorine atom therefore gains one electron. Now it has eighteen electrons and a charge of 18−. It still has seventeen protons with a charge of 17+. It has one more negative charge than positive. It has become a chlorine ion, $Cl^-$ (2.8.8.).

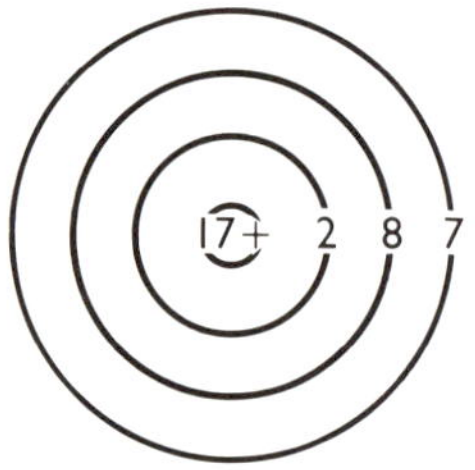


Can you see how a reaction works?
Put a small piece of sodium in chlorine gas.

| | |
|---|---|
| A sodium atom loses an electron (e). It becomes $Na^+$. | $Na \rightarrow Na^+ + e$ |
| A chlorine atom gains this electron forming $Cl^-$. | $Cl + e \rightarrow Cl^-$ |
| These two ions have opposite charges. | |
| They attract each other. They join up as $Na^+.Cl^-$. | $Na^+.Cl^-$ |

Another sodium atom loses an electron: $Na^+$ ion. Which of the ions already formed will attract it? Will the arrangement become

$Na^+.Cl^-.Na^+$ or $Na^+.Na^+.Cl^-$?

Forming this $Na^+$ provides an electron. This turns another chlorine atom into a $Cl^-$ ion. Which arrangement is it most likely to form?

If 23 g of sodium burns, L atoms of it lose L electrons. L atoms of the chlorine gain electrons. L ions form. Each ion is attracted to one of opposite charge. They join up in all directions. The result is 58.5 g of salt. It will be in the form of cubic crystals.

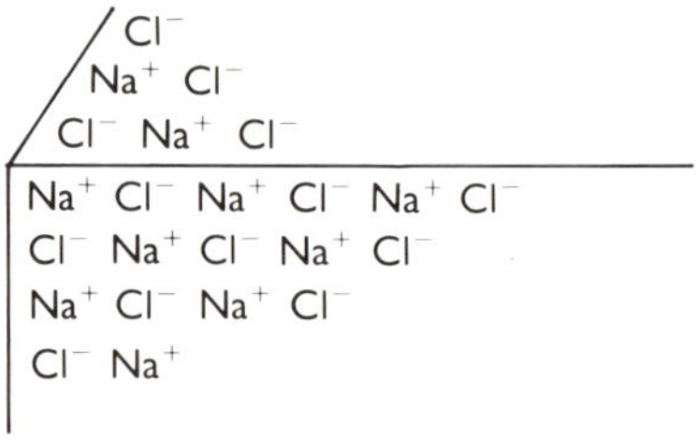

Now you can see why electron structure is important. The most important part is the outside shell. The outside shell is what other atoms first bump into. It decides whether the atom gains or loses electrons. It also decides how many electrons it gains or loses.

Look again at the table on page 63. Make a list of the metals in it. Check the number of electrons in their outside shells. Is the number small or large?

Will all metal atoms lose electrons or gain them?
Will they form positive or negative ions?
Will metal ions be attracted to the cathode or anode?

List the non-metals in the table. Check their outside shells. Do they contain small or large numbers of electrons? Non-metal atoms gain electrons. They form negative ions. Hydrogen is the only non-metal with a small number.

Attraction between ions is called the **ionic bond**. Compounds formed in this way are **ionic compounds**. This bonding explains why
a) One atom of sodium reacts with one atom of chlorine,
b) one atom of magnesium reacts with two Cl atoms.

Copy this into your book. Fill in the blanks.

Magnesium burns in chlorine forming magnesium ______. The electron structure of magnesium is 2.8 ______. The nearest noble gas is neon, structure 2.______. A magnesium atom will therefore lose ______ electrons. It loses these from its outside ______. It now has ______ electrons and ______ protons. It has ______ more positive than negative charges. It has become the ion Mg—.

Chlorine has the electron structure 2.8.______. A chlorine atom gains ______ electron. It becomes the negative ion Cl—. A magnesium atom loses 2 electrons. They turn ______ Cl atoms into Cl— ions. One magnesium atom combines with ______ chlorine atoms.

## Summary

Atoms have electrons in one or more shells. The outside shell is the most important. When atoms collide their outside shells meet. Atoms lose or gain electrons. They reach the same electron structure as the nearest noble gas. This gives ions.

Metals lose electrons. They form positive ions. Non-metals gain electrons. They form negative ions. Ions of opposite charge attract each other. This holds them together in huge numbers. The attraction is called the ionic bond. Compounds made of ions are ionic compounds. They are crystalline solids.

**Answers**
chloride
2.8.2
2.8
two electrons
outside shell
ten electrons
twelve protons
$Mg^{2+}$
2.8.7
gains one
$Cl^-$
two Cl atoms
$Cl^-$
two

# *Why do elements combine?*

We have seen how elements can combine. They do so by the transfer of electrons. One atom loses them. Another atom gains them. Both become ions.

The ions have opposite charges. They attract each other. Huge numbers join up. This is ionic bonding. The result is a solid crystal lattice.

This is **how** it happens. **Why** do atoms do this?

The chief reason is simple. Everything tends to lose energy. Energy is what is needed to do work. In Science, **work is done when a force moves through a distance**.

Take a simple example.

My case is on the floor. I need it on the table. The earth pulls it downwards. This pull is the weight of the case. To lift it, I must use a force bigger than its weight. This force moves through a distance. In lifting the case I have done some work.

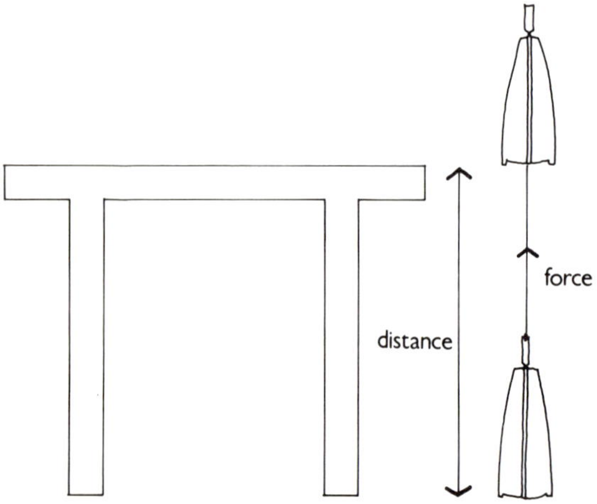


The same work can be done in many other ways. George falls asleep in Science lessons. Tie a rope to him. Pass the rope over pulleys. Tie the other end to my case. Let George fall asleep. Put a mattress behind him. Give him a gentle push.

He falls off his stool. This pulls the rope. It lifts the case to the table top. George has done work. So he must have used energy. What energy?

He had energy because of his position on the stool. It is called **potential energy**. He lost it when he fell to the floor. It was used to do work. On the floor he has no potential energy. He cannot do work. Now my case has potential energy.

**Heat** is another form of energy. We can use it to boil water. The steam given off will drive an engine. The engine makes a wheel go round. The wheel has energy of movement. This is called **kinetic energy**. We can use it to lift the case.

I can put an explosive under my case. The explosive is a chemical compound. Setting it off will lift my case. It may be whole or it may be in pieces. Energy stored in compounds is **chemical energy**.

No energy is ever lost. It is just turned into a different form. One kind of energy can be turned into any other kind. Chemical energy of an explosive is turned into

kinetic energy (it makes things move),
heat energy (from the reaction),
sound energy (the bang),
light energy.

All things tend to a lower energy level. Substances do. They give up energy when their atoms react. This appears mainly as heat.

Noble gases have no simple reactions. Their atoms must already be at a low energy level. They are like George on the floor. They cannot fall further.

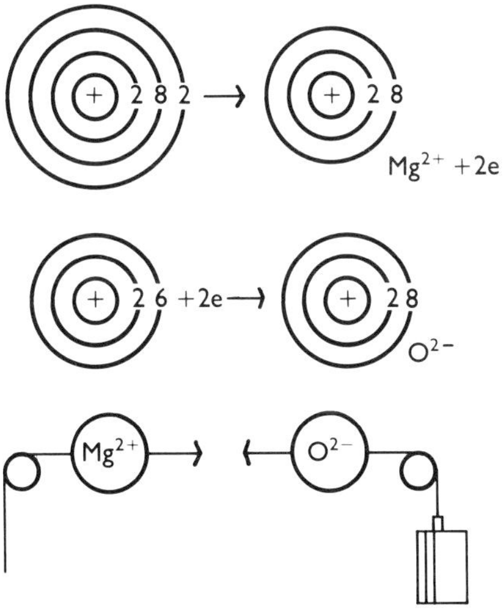

Burning petrol in a car engine gives the car energy to move.

A rocket turns chemical energy into kinetic energy.

This explains why other atoms lose or gain electrons. They become like noble gas atoms. They reach a lower energy level. The 'lost' energy appears as heat.

Burn magnesium in oxygen. The electron structure of magnesium is 2.8.2. The nearest noble gas is neon, 2.8. A magnesium atom loses 2 electrons. It gives up energy. It becomes a magnesium ion, $Mg^{2+}$.

Oxygen has electron structure 2.6. Again the nearest noble gas is neon, 2.8. An oxygen atom therefore gains 2 electrons. It gains those given by the magnesium atom. It becomes the ion $O^{2-}$. By becoming like a neon atom it too gives up energy.

The two ions have potential energy. They attract each other. In moving together they can do work. Can you imagine them lifting my case? In fact the energy of all three changes appears as heat.

Atoms turning into ions give heat. Ions joining up to form a crystal lattice give heat. This is why magnesium burns with a white hot flame. Other substances react with oxygen. Fuels burn. They give energy. It appears as heat. We can turn heat energy into other useful forms.

Petrol burns in motor engines. Gas and heat form in the cylinder. Gas molecules have kinetic energy. They hit the piston. It goes down. Its up and down movement rotates an axle. This turns the car wheels.

chemical energy of petrol → heat → kinetic energy of moving car

# Another kind of bond

Atoms combine only if they meet. An atom in Bath cannot combine with an atom in Aberdeen. When they meet their outside shells meet first. Both shells contain electrons. In ionic bonding these are transferred from one atom to the other. Ions form.

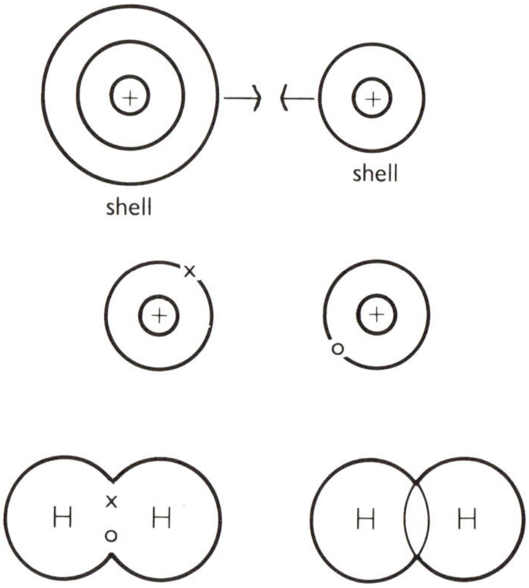


Atoms can combine by a second method. They can share electrons. Their outside shells overlap. By sharing electrons each reaches noble gas structure. The need to share holds the atoms together. Take hydrogen as an example.

Two hydrogen atoms move towards each other. Their outside shells overlap. Each contains one electron. So each shell has a share of two electrons. Each atom has noble gas structure, as long as they stay together.

The atoms are held together by a shared pair of electrons. Each atom provides one of the pair. The shared pair is called a **covalent bond**. Substances held together by covalent bonds are **covalent compounds**.

All electrons are exactly alike. In drawings, one electron is shown as x. The other is shown as o. This shows which atom each comes from.

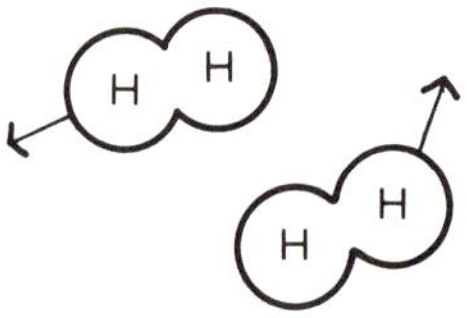


## The properties of covalent compounds

What properties does the theory suggest? It explains why hydrogen has diatomic molecules, $H_2$. The two H atoms are exactly alike. They will share the two electrons equally. So neither atom has an electrical charge. Hydrogen molecules do not attract each other. They can move freely. Molecules move freely in gases and liquids. Covalent compounds are usually gases or liquids. Large covalent molecules give solids.

Do you understand covalent bonding?
If not, this may help.
Grace keeps a rabbit. Its name is Electron x. It lives in a pen. The pen is called Shell G. Willie has a rabbit too. Its name is Electron o. It lives in a pen. This is called Shell W.

Grace and Willie would both like two rabbits. Each pen can hold two. Willie and Grace decide to share rabbits. They let the pens overlap. The rabbits occupy both shells. Each shell has a share of two rabbits, if they stay joined.

Try this example. Fill in the blanks. The drawings will help you.

The electron structure of chlorine is ______ ______ ______. The outside shell of its atom contains ______ electrons. To be like argon, 2.8.8, it needs ______ electron.

A hydrogen atom has ______ electron. With a chlorine atom it can make one ______ pair. The H atom has two electrons like the noble gas ______. The chlorine now has an outside shell of ______. The atoms are held together by a ______ pair. The formula of hydrogen chloride is ______. Like many covalent compounds it is a ______. The shared pair of electrons is a covalent bond.

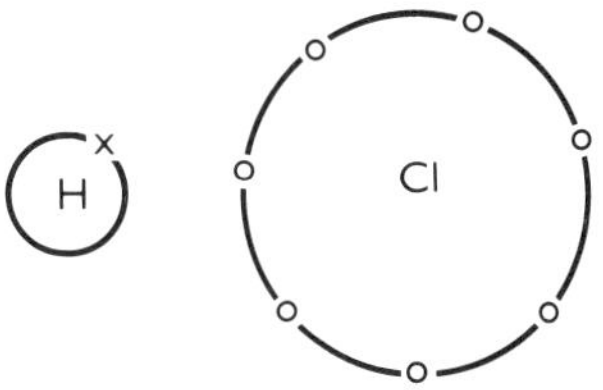


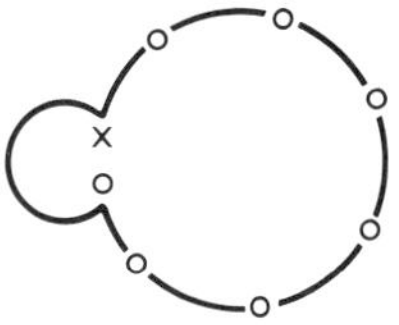

$H^+ - Cl^-$

A covalent bond is shown by a short line. It stands for a pair of electrons. Each atom provides one.

A hydrogen molecule contains two atoms. They are held together by a shared pair. They share them equally.

An HCl molecule contains two different atoms. They do not share the electron pair equally. A chlorine atom attracts electrons. The electron pair is more with chlorine. The Cl atom has a slight negative charge. The hydrogen atom will have a positive charge. $H^+ - Cl^-$

Grace likes rabbits more than Willie does. She attracts them. The rabbits are more often in Shell G. It has a bigger share of them than Shell W.

## Summary

Atoms can combine by sharing electrons. By doing this they reach noble gas structure. They have fallen to a lower energy level. Each shared pair is called a covalent bond. Each atom provides one electron of the pair. A line represents the bond.

Substances with this bonding are covalent compounds. In some the atoms share the pair equally. Neither atom carries a charge. They do not attract other molecules. They move freely. They are gases or liquids. If they have large molecules they may be solids. Ionic bonding gives crystalline solids.

Covalent bonding explains why some elements are diatomic. Atoms share electron pairs. Some atoms attract electrons. They may have a greater share. They will have a slight negative charge.

## Questions

1. Write down the electron structure of an oxygen atom. Use it to show that oxygen molecules are diatomic. Work out the formula of hydrogen oxide.
2. What is a covalent bond? Compare covalent with ionic bonding. Which compounds are more likely to be solids?

# *Ionic and covalent compounds*

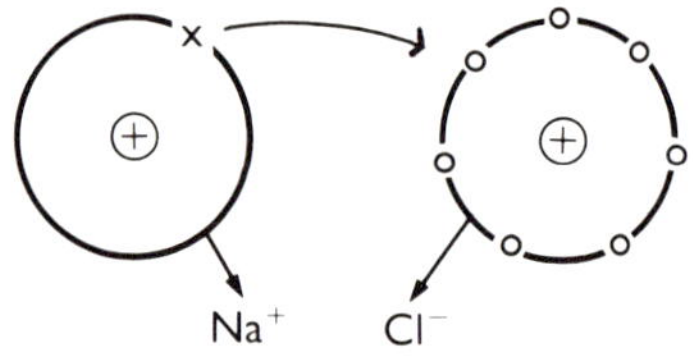


We have shown two ways in which atoms combine. One method is by the transfer of electrons. Loss and gain of electrons turns the atoms into ions. These collect in crystal lattices. Ionic compounds are solid.

In the second method atoms share electrons. Each shared pair is a covalent bond. The bond holds the atoms together. Molecules are formed. They are able to move freely. Covalent compounds are liquids or gases. Only those with large molecules are solids.

Sodium chloride is the typical ionic compound. Candle wax is a solid covalent compound. We shall compare their simple properties.

### Experiment 7.1 Ionic and covalent properties

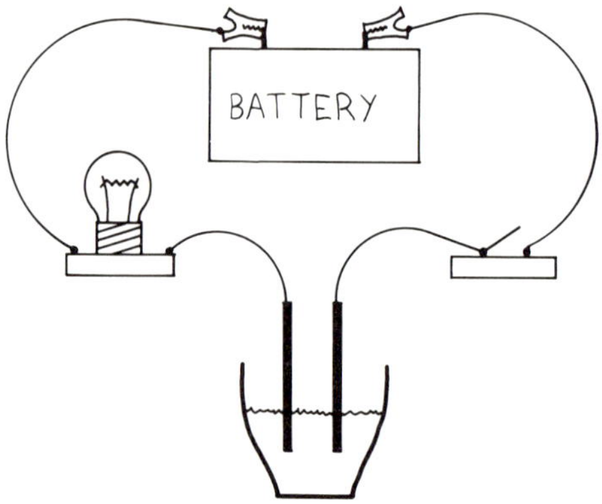


**Set up the apparatus shown. Switch on the current. Touch the carbon rods together.**

**a) Take a lump of solid wax. Press a carbon rod against one side of it. Press the other rod to the opposite side. Test a lump of salt in the same way.**

***b) Put wax into a crucible. Heat it gently on a pipeclay triangle. Hold the carbon rods in the molten wax. Switch on. Bring the rods close together.**

**Gently heat salt in a crucible. Then heat it more strongly. If it melts, dip the rods in the liquid. Switch on the current. Watch the two carbon rods.**

**c) Put wax and salt in separate beakers. Add water and stir. Use the carbon rods to find out if either liquid is a conductor.**

> You have seen some of these tests before.
> Is solid wax or solid salt a conductor?
> Which has the higher melting point, wax or salt?
> Is molten wax a conductor or an insulator?
> Does the bulb light up when the rods are in molten salt?
> Does wax dissolve in water?
> Does salt solution conduct a current?

When the rods touch the bulb lights up. A current flows. With wax between the rods the bulb does not light up. Solid wax is a non-conductor. So is solid salt.

Wax melts with gentle heating. Its melting point is low. Its molecules are easy to separate. They do not carry a current.

Salt is difficult to melt. It needs very strong heating. Melting breaks down the crystal lattice. The $Na^+$ and $Cl^-$ ions have to be pulled apart. This needs a great deal of energy. Its melting point is high, over 800 °C.

The ions move freely in the liquid. $Na^+$ ions move to the cathode. Electrolysis can happen. Sodium forms at the cathode. $Cl^-$ ions move to the anode. Chlorine gas forms there.

Salt dissolves in water. The $Na^+$ and $Cl^-$ ions separate. They can move toward cathode and anode. The solution conducts a current. Electrolysis can happen. The current consists of moving ions.

Wax does not dissolve in water. We can try other covalent compounds which do.

*Two atoms as a general rule*
*Join up to form a molecule.*
*What keeps them linked together there*
*Is a shared electron pair.*
*For this covalent bond the sign*
*Is the two symbols joined by line (C – H).*

## Experiment 7.2 Solutions of covalent compounds

**Use the apparatus of Experiment 7.1. Put ethanol (meths) in a beaker. Dip the carbon rods into it. Switch on. Take the temperature of the ethanol. Pour an equal volume of water into the beaker. Take the temperature again.**

**Take the temperature of some water. Dissolve hydrogen chloride in it. Take the temperature again. Find out if this solution is a conductor.**

Is ethanol a conductor?
Does it dissolve completely in water?
Does the temperature change?
Is the solution able to conduct a current?
Does hydrogen chloride solution conduct?
Are new substances formed at the cathode and anode?

Ethanol is not a conductor. It dissolves completely in water. The solution is not a conductor either. Hydrogen chloride dissolves in water. The solution conducts. It is dilute hydrochloric acid The temperature rises slightly. Perhaps a reaction is taking place.

Ionic compounds are solids. They have high melting points. The molten liquid conducts. So does the solution in water.
Covalent compounds are gases or liquids. Those with large molecules may be solids. They have low melting points. Some dissolve in water. Some of the solutions conduct. This means that some of them form ions in solution.

# Acid, alkali and pH

Did you work out a formula for water on page 69?

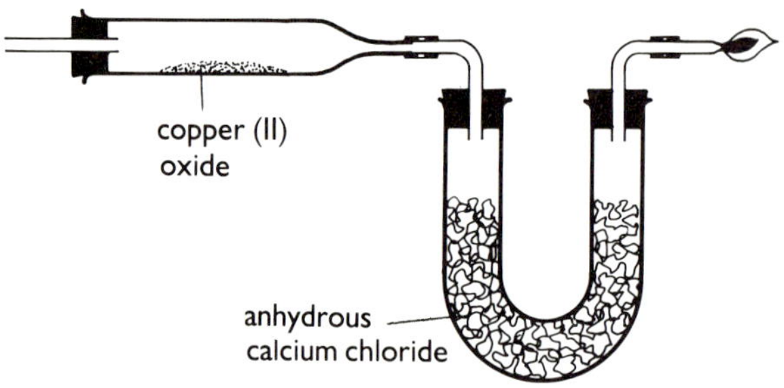


We did this by experiment in Book 1. We heated copper(II) oxide in hydrogen. Copper oxide was reduced to copper. Water was formed. We know the mass of oxygen in this water. It came from copper oxide. We can measure the mass of this water. From it we can work out the mass of hydrogen in it.

loss in mass of oxide = 2.00 g
total mass of water = 2.25 g
mass of hydrogen = 0.25 g

2.00 g of oxygen combine with 0.25 g of hydrogen.
16 g of oxygen will combine with 2 g of hydrogen.
O = 16. One mole of oxygen atoms is 16 grams.
H = 1. Two grams of hydrogen contain 2 moles of H atoms.
L atoms of oxygen combine with 2L atoms of hydrogen.
The formula of water is $H_2O$.

Theory shows this too. The electron structure of oxygen is 2.6. Its atom will gain two electrons. A hydrogen atom provides only one. Each oxygen atom needs two hydrogen atoms. The formula is $H_2O$. Water is a liquid. It is a poor conductor. These are covalent properties. Water is a covalent compound.

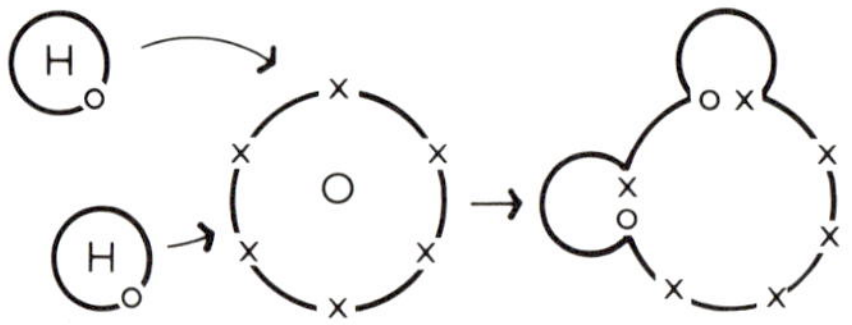

Oxygen attracts electrons. The O in $H_2O$ has a greater share of each electron pair. It is negatively charged. Hydrogen chloride is covalent. It dissolves in water. HCl and $H_2O$ molecules will meet. The O atom of $H_2O$ attracts the H atom of HCl. The Cl keeps the electron pair.

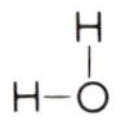

This makes it a $Cl^-$ ion. The H atom becomes an $H^+$ ion. All acids form $H^+$ ions in water in this way.

$$HCl \text{ in water} \rightarrow H^+(aq) + Cl^-(aq)$$

Acid properties in water are caused by hydrogen ions.

Sodium hydroxide is an alkali. It is a solid. It contains $Na^+$ and $OH^-$ ions. These ions separate when the solid dissolves. Alkalis put $OH^-$ ions into water. Alkaline properties are caused by hydroxyl ions in water.

$Na^+$ $OH^-$ $Na^+$ $OH^-$ $Na^+$
$OH^-$ $Na^+$ $OH^-$ $Na^+$ $OH^-$
$Na^+$ $OH^-$ $Na^+$ $OH^-$ $Na^+$

An indicator is a coloured substance. It is affected by acid or alkali. Many indicators come from plants. Litmus is one of these. Hydrogen ions make it red. Hydroxyl ions make it blue. The colour shows acid or alkali to be there. It does not say how much.

Concentration (how much) is important. HCl = 36.5. A molar solution of hydrogen chloride has 36.5 g of HCl in 1000 $cm^3$ of solution.

A molar solution of hydrogen chloride contains L molecules. Each of them turns into ions. Every one gives a hydrogen ion. The solution is very strongly acid.

Vinegar contains ethanoic or acetic acid. A molar solution will contain L molecules. Only about two in every hundred of them turn into ions. The solution has far fewer hydrogen ions. As an acid it is very much weaker.

The concentration of hydrogen ions is measured by pH.

pH numbers run from 0 to 14. Acids have pH from 0 to 6. pH 7 is neutral. Alkali solutions have pH from 8 to 14. Universal Indicator has a range of colours. They show pH.

| pH 0 1 2 3 4 | 5 | 6 | 7 | 8 | 9 | 10 11 12 13 14 |
|---|---|---|---|---|---|---|
| red | orange | yellow | green | blue | dark blue | violet |

→ acid getting weaker → neutral → alkali getting stronger →

*When water and an acid mix*
*The pH range is 0 to 6.*
*If to alkali we change*
*8 to 14 is the range.*

## Experiment 7.3 To test the pH of solutions

**a) Use 0.1 M solutions of hydrochloric acid and acetic acid. Put 10 $cm^3$ of the acid into a small beaker. Stir it with a glass rod. Take a Universal Indicator paper. Touch it with the wet rod. Record the pH.**

**Add two drops of M sodium hydroxide solution. Stir with the rod. Touch the paper. Write down the pH. Add two more drops. Stir. Find the pH of the liquid. Go on doing this. Draw a graph of pH against drops.**

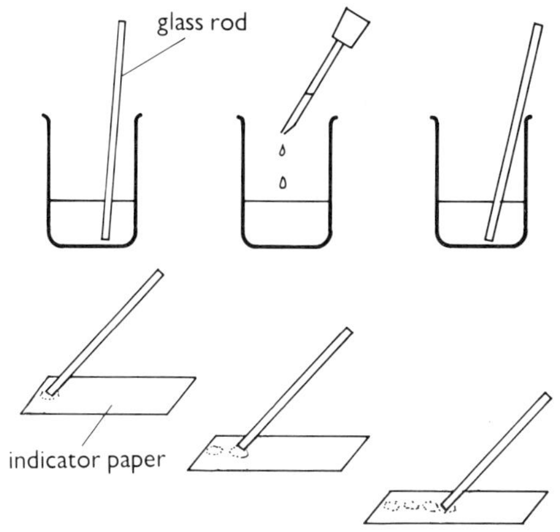


**b) Take solutions of as many substances as possible. Use drops of Universal Indicator to test their pH. Salt, lime water, aqueous ammonia, carbon dioxide, magnesium oxide in water, 'bicarbonate of soda', copper(II) sulphate, ammonium chloride, detergent can all be used.**

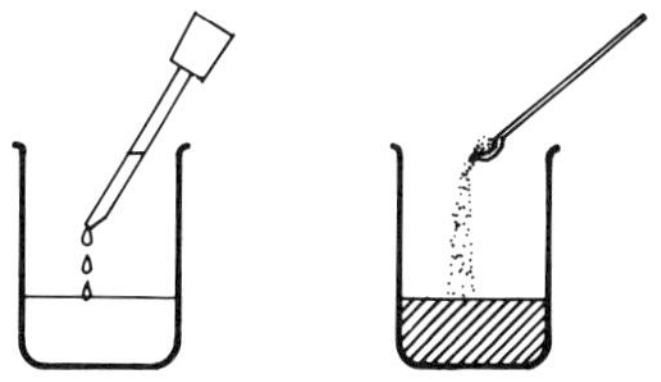

**c) Put 10 $cm^3$ of M hydrochloric acid into a small beaker. Add two drops of Universal Indicator. Drop in a small pinch of sodium hydrogencarbonate. Stir with a glass rod. Add another pinch. Stir. Repeat this. After each addition note the final pH.**

What does the graph show?
Is each solution in b) acid, alkaline or neutral?
Is it strongly acid or alkaline?
What is 'bicarbonate of soda' used for?

The graphs show neutralization of acid by alkali. At neutral there is a large change of pH.

Some salt solutions are not neutral.

# Energy from chemical change

We have found out *how* elements combine. We also know the main reason *why* they do this. By combining they reach a lower energy level. The compound formed has less energy than the elements. They have fallen down the energy ladder.

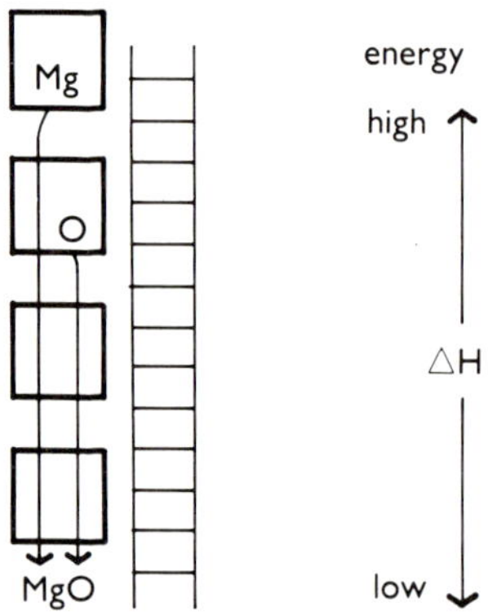


The energy they lose appears mainly as heat. Other reactions happen for the same reasons. The products have less energy than the reactants. This means that nearly all reactions give heat. If they do, they are exothermic reactions.

We use heat from exothermic reactions. It warms the rooms we live in. We use it to get hot food and hot water. In power stations it is turned into electrical energy. Measuring this heat is important.

How do we measure heat? We can only measure it by its effects. Heat makes things get hotter.

We put heat into water. Its temperature rises. The unit of energy or heat is the joule. To make 1 gram of water rise 1 °C in temperature we need 4.2 joules. One joule, J, is a small amount, A better unit is the kilojoule, kJ. It is 1000 joules.

We shall now try to measure the heat from a reaction.

### Experiment 8.1 To measure the heat from burning

**a) Fill a spirit lamp with ethanol. Cover the wick with a cap. Measure the mass of the lamp. With a measuring cylinder put 250 $cm^3$ of water into a metal can. 250 $cm^3$ of water has a mass of 250 grams.**

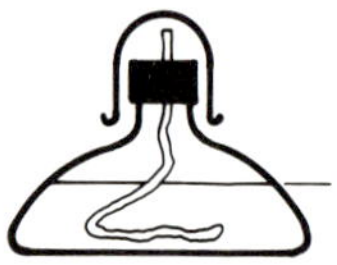


**Stir the water. Take its temperature. Support the can in a stand. Put the lamp under it. Remove the cap. Light the wick. Let the flame heat the can.**

**Stir the water steadily. Let its temperature rise about 15 °C. Remove the lamp. Quickly put the cap over the wick. Measure the new mass of the lamp. Go on stirring the water. Note its highest temperature. Work out how much heat has entered the water.**

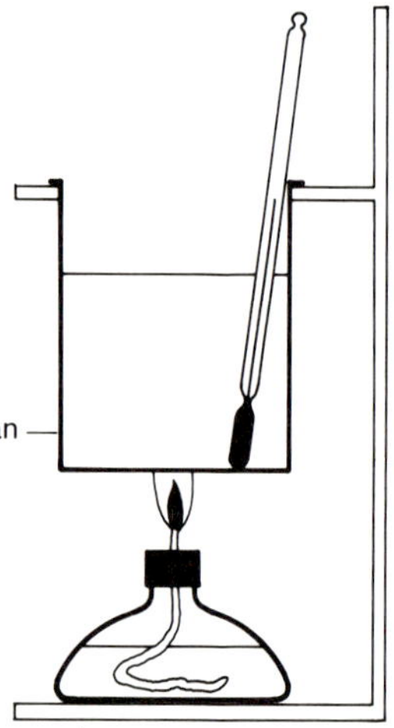


Ethanol burns in air. The reaction gives heat.
Does all this heat go into the water?
Where else could some of it finish up?
Does the result you worked out include this heat?
Is this result the exact heat given by burning?
How much ethanol did you burn?

In my result the temperature of the water rose 16 °C. The mass of the lamp got less. It fell by 0.8 g.

To raise the temperature of 1 g of water 1 °C needs 4.2 J. 250 g of water need 250 times as much heat as 1 g. The temperature of the water went up by 16 °C. This would need 16 times as much heat as for 1 °.

$250 \times 4.2$ J

$250 \times 4.2 \times 16$ J $= 16800$ J $= 16.8$ kJ

This is the heat which went into the water. The metal can also become hotter. It took in heat. The air around the flame gets hotter. None of this heat is in the water. So none of it is measured.

That means our result is only a rough one. We can make it more accurate. We can cut down heat losses. This means that more of the heat gets into the water. We can measure the heat used by the metal can.

We need to compare the heat given by different fuels. How much of each fuel shall we use? 1 g? 1 kg? 1 mole?

Burning is a chemical change. Molecules of fuel react. We ought to use the same number of molecules of each fuel. A mole of particles of each contains the same number. This number is L. It is Avogadro's number.

The mass of the lamp gets less. The loss is the mass of ethanol which burnt. It was 0.8 g. The formula of ethanol is $C_2H_6O$. H = 1, C = 12, O = 16. One mole of it has a mass of 46 grams.

$C_2 \quad H_6 \quad O$
$24 + 6 + 16 = 46$

0.8 g of ethanol burning gives 16.8 kJ.

46 g of ethanol burning gives $\dfrac{16.8 \times 46}{0.8} = 966$ kJ

This is the heat of combustion of one mole

Burning is combustion. This heat quantity is called the **heat of combustion of ethanol**. We did not measure all the heat. An accurate value is much higher than this.

Ethanol belongs to a family of compounds. Measure the heat of combustion of some others. Methanol is $CH_4O$. Propanol is $C_3H_8O$. Butanol is $C_4H_{10}O$.

***b) Use the apparatus shown in the photograph. The spirit lamp burns inside the apparatus. The pump draws air through. The flame burns in this air. The hot air passes through the spiral tube. It gives up all its heat to the water. Determine the heat which the apparatus uses.**

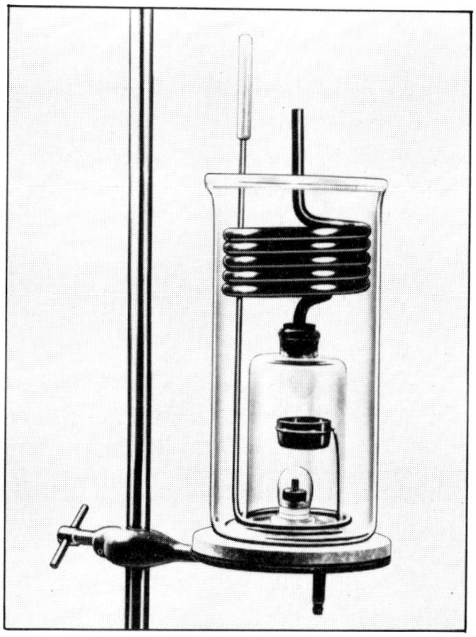

# Energy from other reactions

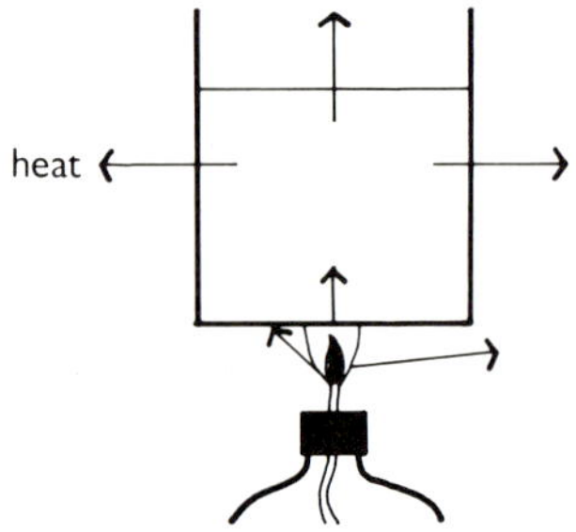


The burning fuel gives heat. Some of it goes into the water. Some is used in heating other things, such as the can. We measure only the heat which ends up in the water. Our result was not accurate. We must try to measure *all* the heat from a reaction.

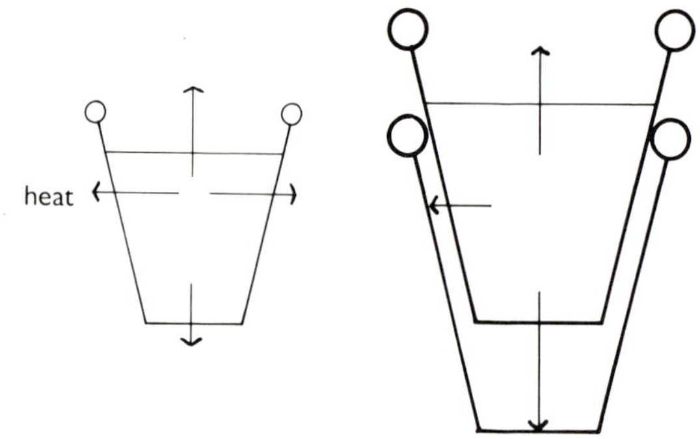


| | |
|---|---|
| The can | We can find out how much heat it takes in. Or we can use a different vessel. A thin plastic cup uses almost no heat. |
| Thermometer | This gets hotter. The heat it uses is very small. It hardly affects the result. |
| The air | Some heat from the flame warms the air. The water in the can becomes warm. Warm water cools. It does so by losing heat to the air. We can reduce both losses. Do the reaction inside the cup. Stand the cup in another one. |

Acid neutralizes alkali. This reaction gives heat. We shall try to measure this heat accurately. We shall use molar solutions of the alkali and acid.

### Experiment 8.2 To measure the heat of neutralization

Measure acid and alkali with measuring cylinders. Put 50 $cm^3$ of M hydrochloric acid in a plastic cup. Stand this cup in an empty one. Put 50 $cm^3$ of M sodium hydroxide solution in another plastic cup.

Take the temperature of each solution. Use thermometers marked in tenths of a degree. Stir the acid. Pour in the alkali. Record the temperature of the mixture.

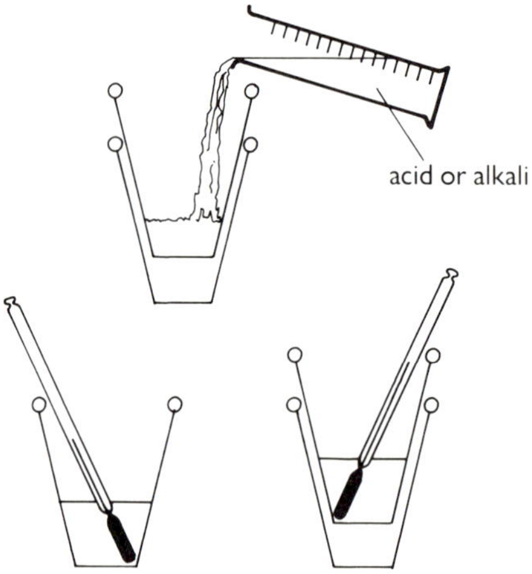


Is the reaction exothermic?
What is the rise in temperature of the acid?
How much does the alkali temperature rise?
Work out how much energy the reaction gives.

Acid and alkali react as soon as they mix. The reaction is exothermic. The heat is produced *inside the liquid.* It reaches its highest temperature at once.

The plastic cup gets warmer too. It uses very little of the heat. There is an air space between the cups. Very little heat is lost to the outside air. Nearly all the heat stays in the water and is measured.

We can take 1 $cm^3$ of each liquid as one gram. One gram of each needs the same heat as 1 g of water.

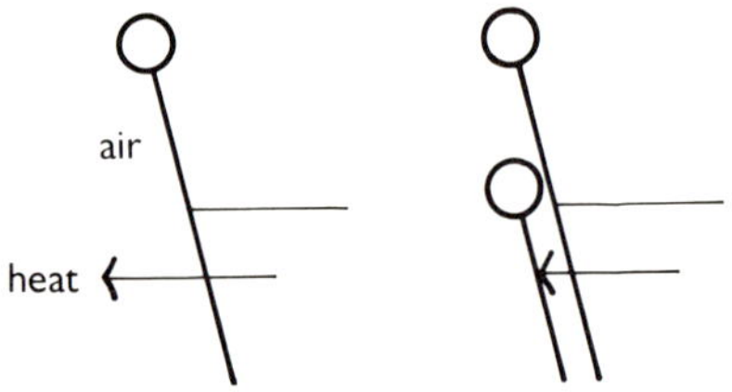

## Working out the result

In one experiment acid and alkali were at 16 °C. The mixture reached a temperature of 22.8 °C. The rise in temperature of both liquids was 6.8 °C. Altogether 100 g of water rose in temperature 6.8 °C.

1 g of water rising 1 °C in temperature needs 4.2 J.
100 g rising 1 °C in temperature needs 100 × 4.2 J.
100 g rising 6.8 °C in temperature needs 420 × 6.8 J.
To avoid large numbers we write this as 2.86 kJ.

420 joules
2860 joules
2.86 kilojoules

Neutralizing 50 $cm^3$ of M acid gives 2.86 kJ of energy.
Neutralizing 1000 $cm^3$ would give twenty times as much.
1000 $cm^3$ of M solution contains one mole of acid.
Neutralizing one mole of acid gives 57.2 kJ of heat.

57.2 kJ

From this reaction *we gain* 57.2 kJ of heat energy.
The *substances which react give up*, or lose it.
So heat from an exothermic reaction is given a minus sign.
When moles of a substance react, we use the symbol $\Delta H$.

−57.2 kJ

$\Delta H$ is delta H

$$HCl + NaOH \rightarrow NaCl + H_2O \qquad \Delta H = -57.2\ kJ$$

This equation shows the result. It does not show how it happens. The acid is in solution as ions $H^+$ and $Cl^-$. Sodium hydroxide is a solid ionic compound. Its solution contains the ions $Na^+$ and $OH^-$.

$H^+$ and $OH^-$ ions combine. They form molecules of water. This is because water is a covalent compound.

$Na^+$ and $Cl^-$ ions remain in the solution. If the water evaporates, crystals of salt will form. Neutralization of acid by alkali is summed up by

$$H^+(aq) + OH^-(aq) \rightarrow H_2O(l) \quad \Delta H = -57.2\ kJ$$

$H^+ + Cl^-$ acid
$OH^- + Na^+$ alkali
↓ ↓
$H_2O$
$Na^+ + Cl^-$
↙
salt solution
↓
$Na^+\ Cl^-\ Na^+\ Cl^-$
$Cl^-\ Na^+\ Cl^-\ Na^+$
crystal

## Experiment 8.3 Other acids and alkalis

**Use other acids in place of hydrochloric acid. Put 50 $cm^3$ of M acid solution into a plastic cup. Stand it in an empty one. Use ethanoic (acetic) acid, nitric acid and sulphuric acid.**

**Add to each 50 $cm^3$ of M sodium hydroxide solution. Take the temperatures of acid, alkali and mixture. Work out $\Delta H$ for each mole of acid neutralized.**

Are the results for all four acids the same?

# *Displacement reactions*

Do you remember the Activity Series? It shows the metals in order of how active they are. The most active is at the top. The bottom metal is the least active. The Series also includes hydrogen.

Each metal is more active than those below it. It can push these metals out of their compounds.

In Book 1 we put zinc into copper(II) sulphate solution. Copper formed on the surface of the zinc. Zinc displaces copper. It is more active. It will appear above copper in the Activity Series.

We shall find out if this reaction gives heat. If so, we shall measure it. Will the result be accurate? Only if we avoid heat losses.

potassium
sodium
calcium
magnesium
aluminium
zinc
iron
lead
hydrogen
copper
silver
gold

Activity Series

**Experiment 8.4 Heat from a displacement reaction**

**Measure 25 cm$^3$ of 0.5 M copper(II) sulphate solution. Put it into a plastic cup. Stand this in another cup. Measure out about 1.5 g of zinc powder.**

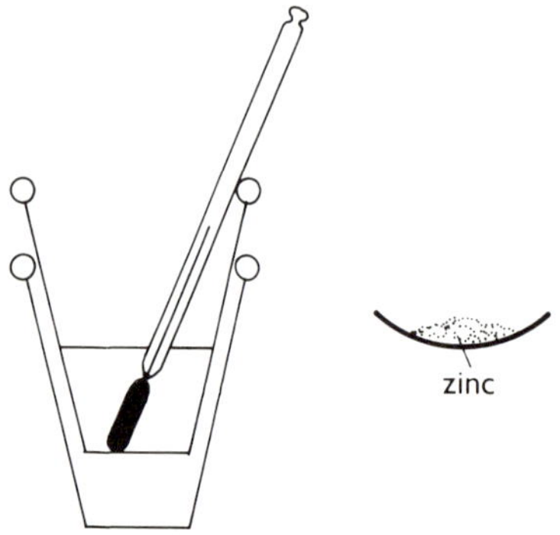


**Work in pairs. Start a stop clock. Stir the liquid steadily. Take its temperature every half minute. When it is constant, record it.**

**At the next half minute exactly, pour in the zinc. Keep stirring. Take the temperature each half minute for four or five minutes.**

Record the results as a table.
Use them to plot a graph.
Is the reaction exothermic?

Reaction takes a little time to complete. It is exothermic.
The graph shows how temperature changes.
AB shows the rapid rise caused by the reaction.
BC shows the hot solution cooling.
The dotted line CD shows how this would go on.
E shows what the temperature would have been
*if* reaction had taken place instantly
*and* no heat had been lost from the solution.

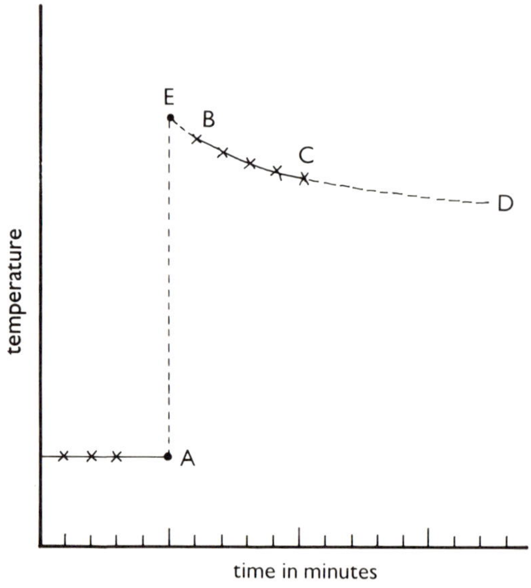

To raise the temperature of 1 g of water 1 °C needs 4.2 joules.
25 $cm^3$ of solution needs the same heat as 25 g of water.

The solution starts at temperature A, say 16 °C.
It would have risen to temperature E, say 40 °C.

25 g of water rising 24 °C takes in 25 × 24 × 4.2 joules. — 2520 joules = 2.52 kJ

We need to know the heat given by one mole.
25 $cm^3$ of 0.5 M solution gives 2.52 kJ.
1000 $cm^3$ of solution would give 40 times as much. — 40 × 2.52 = 100.8 kJ

The solution is 0.5 M. 1000 $cm^3$ contains 0.5 mole.
One mole gives twice as much heat as 0.5 mole. — 2 × 100.8 = 202 kJ

This energy is given up by the reactants. They are losing energy. This energy is given a minus sign. — $\Delta H = -202$ kJ

The equation is

$$Zn(s) + Cu^{2+}(aq) + SO_4^{2-}(aq) \rightarrow Zn^{2+}(aq) + SO_4^{2-}(aq) + Cu(s)$$

zinc — copper sulphate solution

The sulphate ions do not change. They are there all the time.
So the change is

$$Zn(s) + Cu^{2+}(aq) \rightarrow Zn^{2+}(aq) + Cu(s)$$

Zinc is better at turning into ions than copper is.
This is what being more active means.

## Experiment 8.5 Other displacements

**Repeat Experiment 8.4. Use aluminium, iron and lead powders with copper(II) sulphate solution.**

Compare the heats of displacement. Can they be used to place the metals in the Activity Series?

## Things to do

1. Measure heats of reaction for metals and dilute acid. Use 25 $cm^3$ of M hydrochloric acid. Drop in 1 g of metal. Place the metals in order.
2. Find out if there are energy changes when a substance dissolves. Put 25 $cm^3$ of water in a cup. Stir in 1 g of substance. Record any change in temperature. Work out the change for one mole of dissolved substance. Are any changes endothermic?

## Summary

In chemical changes new substances form. They usually have less energy than the reactants. The energy difference is set free. It appears in most cases as heat. Light, sound and electrical energy can appear.

Most reactions give out heat. They are exothermic. A few take in heat. They are endothermic. The energy change is shown as $\Delta H$. It is − for exothermic and + for endothermic reactions.

We use heat of combustion to compare the heating value of fuels. Heat of displacement can be used to place metals in the Activity Series.

# Chemical energy → electrical energy

In Experiment 8.4 copper sulphate solution and zinc react. Zinc sulphate solution and copper are formed.

$$Zn(s) + Cu^{2+}(aq) + SO_4^{2-}(aq) \rightarrow Zn^{2+}(aq) + SO_4^{2-}(aq) + Cu(s)$$

The sulphate ions take no part. The real change is

$$Zn(s) + Cu^{2+}(aq) \rightarrow Zn^{2+}(aq) + Cu(s) \quad \Delta H = -202\ kJ$$

The reaction is exothermic. Chemical energy is being turned into heat. It can be turned into electrical energy instead. The device for doing this is a cell.

The Daniell cell makes use of this reaction. It is named after its inventor. A copper can holds copper(II) sulphate solution. A porous pot stands in it. It holds a zinc rod in zinc sulphate solution. We can make and test this cell.

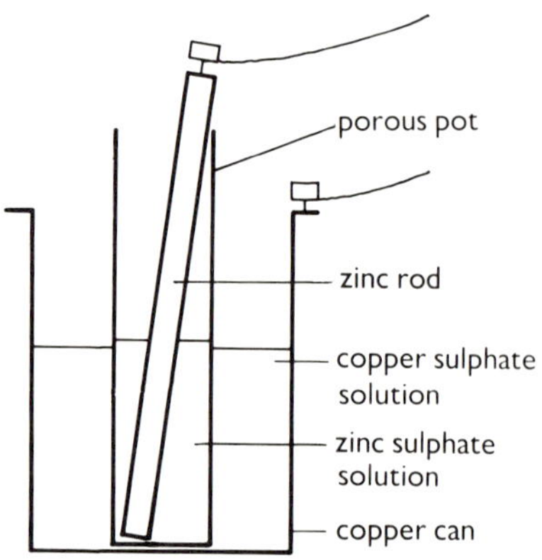


### Experiment 8.6 Testing simple cells

**Put two 100 $cm^3$ beakers side by side. Half fill one with copper (II) sulphate solution. Support in it a strip of copper foil. This makes a half cell.**

**Make a second half cell in the other beaker. Use zinc foil in zinc sulphate solution. Wet a strip of filter paper with dilute sulphuric acid. Put one end of it in each solution.**

**Connect each metal to one terminal of a voltmeter. Use wires joined to crocodile clips. If no reading shows, reverse the connections. Note which metal is joined to the + terminal. Record the highest voltage shown by the cell.**

**Set up other half cells. Hold the clean metal in a solution of its sulphate. Connect each in turn to a copper half cell. Use filter paper dipped in dilute acid. Record the voltage for each full cell. Use magnesium, iron and lead as suitable metals.**

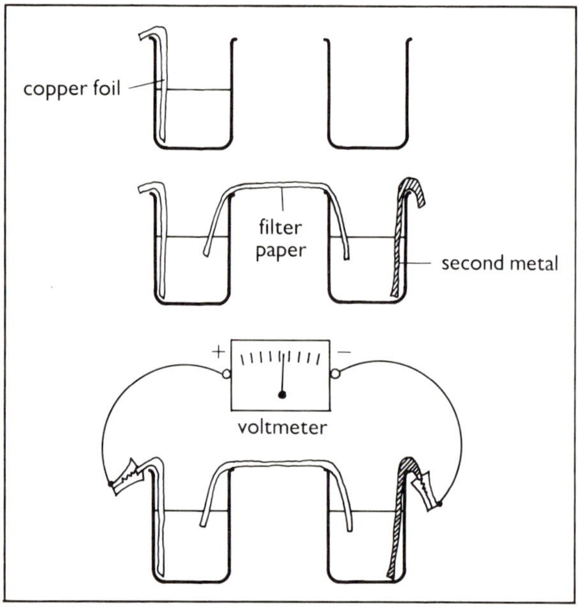


Two half cells joined in this way make a complete cell.
Which metal is the positive pole of each cell?
Which metal gives the highest voltage?
List the metals in order of voltage size.
Does the voltage shown by each cell change?

$Cu^{2+}$ is pronounced C U two plus. The 2 explains why we call its compounds copper(II) compounds.

*They put Daniel in the den of lions*
*The lions gave him L.*
*So Daniell used the den of ions*
*To make the first electric cell.*

These cells provide electric current. How do they work? They are easy to set up. What disadvantages do they have?

Take the Daniell cell. Zinc atoms form ions, $Zn^{2+}$. Each atom loses two electrons. *These electrons remain on the zinc.* They make it the *negative pole* of the cell. The zinc ions pass into solution.

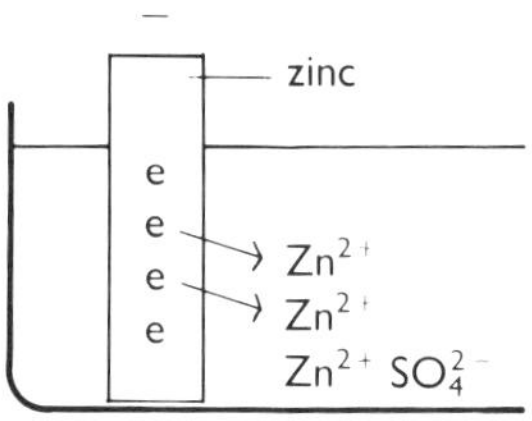


Copper atoms ionize less easily than zinc atoms. In fact, copper ions leave the solution. They join the copper plate. It becomes the positive pole.

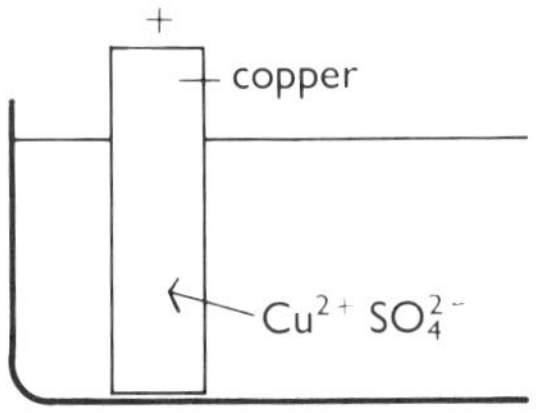


A voltmeter is a conductor. It connects copper and zinc. Electrons flow through it from zinc to copper. This flow of electrons is the current. More zinc ionizes to replace them. The zinc slowly dissolves.

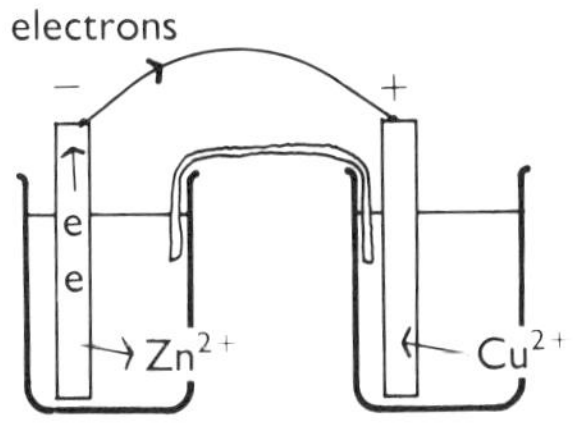


The reaction which provides energy is in two parts. One half cell gives electrons

$$Zn(s) \rightarrow Zn^{2+}(aq) + 2e$$

The other half cell uses them

$$Cu^{2+}(aq) + 2e \rightarrow Cu(s)$$

Copper is deposited on the copper plate.

Solutions in the two half cells must be connected. In the Daniell cell the pot is porous. In the experiments we used filter paper wet with acid.

Magnesium is more active than zinc. More of its atoms ionize. It will have a *bigger negative charge* than zinc. Its half cell gives a bigger voltage. Voltages fit in with Activity Series position.

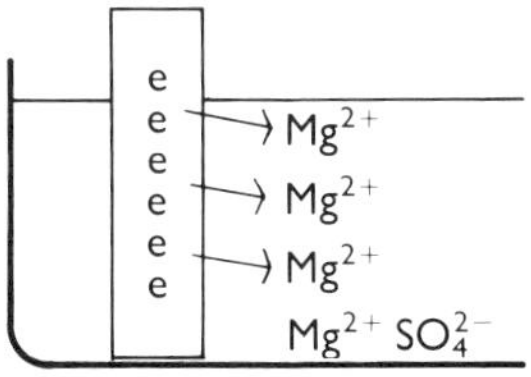


These cells have three disadvantages.
The solutions in them make them awkward to use.
They fail when a substance in them is used up.
The voltage drops quickly because hydrogen may form.

## The dry cell

This is what we call a 'battery'. It avoids some difficulties. Solutions are replaced by a wet paste. The battery's negative pole is a zinc pot. The zinc ionizes giving electrons. It is slowly used up. Zinc ions pass into the wet paste. The pot is slowly used up. It reacts even when the cell is not in use. Paste leaks out through the holes.

The positive pole is the carbon rod. Electrons flow to it. Manganese(IV) oxide oxidizes any hydrogen to water. The cell fails when it is completely used up.

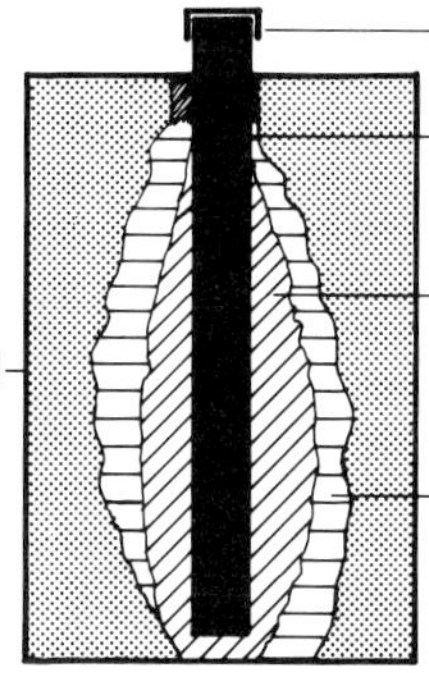

# Cells – primary and secondary

A cell makes ions and electrons move. The force which moves them is called the e.m.f. of the cell. E.m.f. stands for electromotive force. It is measured in volts, V. In a solid, current is a flow of electrons. In a solution it is a flow of ions.

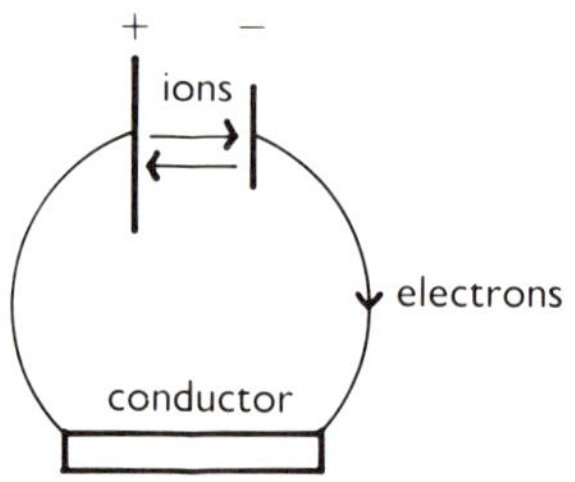


A battery is a set of cells joined in series. This means the negative pole of one cell is joined to the positive pole of the next. The e.m.f. of a dry cell is 1.5 volts. A battery of four cells has an e.m.f. of 6 V.

In the cell substances react. When they are used the cell is dead. We cannot reverse these chemical changes. This kind of cell is a primary cell. In some cells we can reverse the changes. These are called secondary cells. We shall make and test one.

Repeat the electrolysis of dilute sulphuric acid, Experiment 4.1. What gases are formed? Do they react with platinum electrodes? Will they react with lead?

*Judge: What are the prisoners' names?*
*Constable: Anne Ode and Cath Ode, your Honour.*
*Judge: Have they been charged?*
*Constable: Yes, your Honour, with assault and battery.*
*Judge: Put them in a dry cell.*

### Experiment 8.7 To make a lead cell

**Clean two strips of lead foil. Support them in 4 M sulphuric acid. Connect them to a six-volt power pack. Note which strip is the positive anode.**

**Switch on. Let the current run for five minutes. Disconnect the pack. Connect a bulb across the electrodes. Use the power pack again. Run the current for ten minutes. Test with the bulb again.**

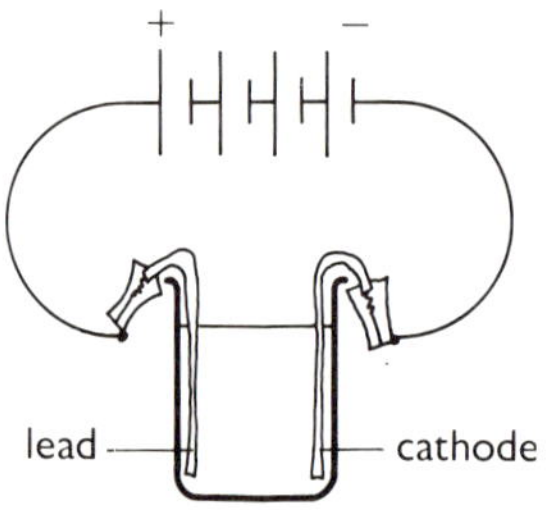


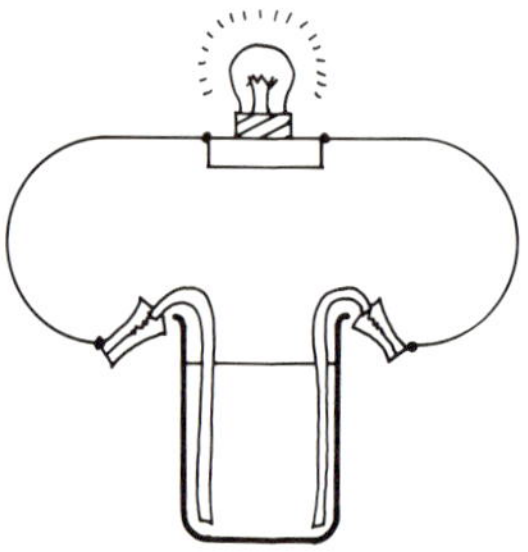

Which lead electrode changes and in what way?
The bulb lights up then dims. What does this show?
Does the bulb light up for longer the second time?

At the anode oxygen is set free. It reacts with the lead. Brown lead(IV) oxide forms.

$$Pb(s) + O_2(g) \rightarrow PbO_2(s)$$

At the cathode hydrogen forms. It does not react with lead.

The bulb shows that current flows. We have made a cell. It is the lead-acid accumulator. Its e.m.f. is 2.05 V. The bulb dims. The cell fails as the brown oxide is used up. Passing a current reverses this. The cell is charged again.

## The lead–acid accumulator

Its negative pole, or electrode, is spongy lead. It provides electrons

$Pb(s) \rightarrow Pb^{2+}(aq) + 2e$

Its positive pole is brown lead(IV) oxide (lead 4). It uses electrons

$Pb^{4+}(s) + 2e \rightarrow Pb^{2+}(s)$

As current flows these changes continue. $Pb^{2+}$ ions at both poles form white lead(II) sulphate. This uses sulphuric acid. The acid in the cell becomes weaker. The cell runs down. It fails to give current.

The changes are easy to reverse. A current is passed through in the opposite direction. The cell is 'charged'. At the cathode, hydrogen forms. It reduces lead(II) sulphate. The cathode becomes lead metal again. At the anode oxygen forms. The anode becomes lead(IV) oxide again. Both changes produce sulphuric acid. Acid concentration and voltage go back to normal.

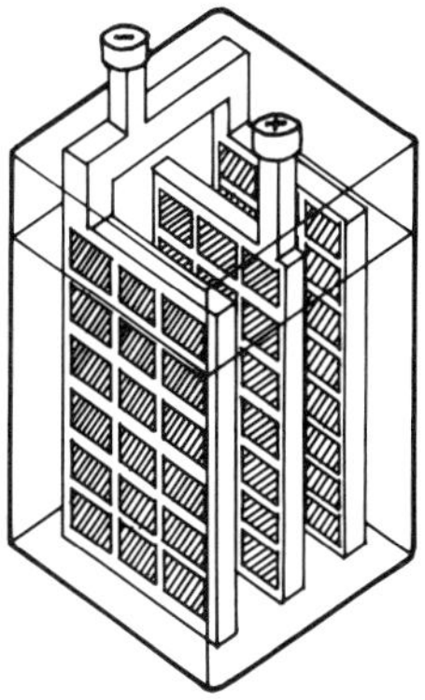

car battery

six cells in series = 12 volt battery

## Summary

Cells provide electrical energy, or current. It comes from chemical change. A cell has two poles or electrodes. They stand in solutions of ions.

The negative pole gives electrons. They come from a metal turning into ions.

$Zn(s) \rightarrow Zn^{2+}(aq) + 2e$

They flow through any conductor connecting the poles. This flow of electrons is the current. The positive pole uses the electrons for a chemical change. Current in the solution is a flow of ions.

Electrical pressure in the cell causes these flows. It is the e.m.f. of the cell, measured in volts. Chemical changes in some cells cannot be reversed. The cell is dead when the substances are used up. This kind of cell is a primary cell.

In secondary cells the changes can be reversed. The cells can be 'charged'. The lead accumulator has a negative pole made of lead. Its positive pole is lead(IV) oxide. The poles stand in sulphuric acid.

## Questions

1. Glucose is a sugar, $C_6H_{12}O_6$. It burns in oxygen.
   Relative atomic masses: C = 12, H = 1, O = 16.
   $C_6H_{12}O_6(s) + 6O_2(g) \rightarrow 6CO_2(g) + 6H_2O(g)$
   $\Delta H = -2800$ kJ.
   What does $\Delta H$ stand for?
   What does kJ mean?
   What does the minus sign in $-2800$ kJ mean?
   How many grams of glucose make one mole?
   How much heat is given by burning one mole of it?
   Glucose is a food. How does it give us energy?
   Plants make glucose from carbon dioxide and water. Is this reaction exothermic or endothermic?
   Where does the energy stored in glucose come from?
   In sunshine, pond weed gives bubbles of gas. Which gas is it? Write an equation for the reaction.
2. A metal can displace other metals from solutions of their salts. Describe an experiment to determine the heat of reaction. The results can be used to place the metals in the Activity Series. How?
3. You are given zinc and copper metals and solutions of their sulphates. Say how you would use them to make a cell.
   How would you measure its e.m.f.?
   What is a primary cell?
   How is it different from a secondary cell?
   What materials make up a lead–acid cell?
   How many make a 12 volt car battery?

# *Fuels and the oil industry*

A fuel is any substance which provides energy. We use energy in many ways. It heats and lights our buildings. It cooks our food. It drives our transport by land, sea and air. We need it to make new substances.

The earliest fuel was wood. Burning it gives heat. Coal was the next common source of energy. It occurs in layers called seams. Most of them are underground. Some may appear above ground as 'outcrops'.

Other seams are close to the surface. The earth above them is removed. The coal is taken out. The earth is put back as it was. This is opencast mining.

**Cutting coal underground.**

A mine is sunk down to deeper seams. Miners once hacked out the coal by hand. Now it is cut by machine. It is loaded on to trucks or conveyor belts. These take it to the bottom of the mine shaft. It is hauled up to the surface. Taking a seam out leaves a gap. So the roof has to be supported. The land may still sink.

Coal is useful in three ways. Firsty, it is burnt as fuel. Finely powdered coal is blown into a furnace. It burns like a gas. The heat is used to boil water. The steam drives generators. They produce electricity. Power stations are built near mines to save transport.

**Heating water using gas!**

The second use is to make coke. Coal is heated in special ovens. Then the white hot coke is pushed out. It is cooled with water. It is used as a smokeless fuel. Coke also reduces metal oxides to the metal.

The third use of coal is that making coke also produces a liquid and a gas. The liquid is a source of chemical compounds (Book 1).

**A gas works producing gas from coal.**

The gas was once the common gas fuel. Most towns had a gas works in which 'coal gas' was made.

Today, coal gas has been replaced by natural gas. This, like oil, is found underground. It is often below the sea bed. Huge amounts of both are found under the North Sea.

To extract the oil or gas a hole is drilled down into the sea bed. A diamond tipped drill is used. It is worked from a platform. Gas is brought ashore by pipe line. The oil found is crude oil, or petroleum. It must be refined. It is taken to a refinery. Overland it travels by pipe line. When it travels by sea huge ships called tankers are used.

A crude oil distillation unit.

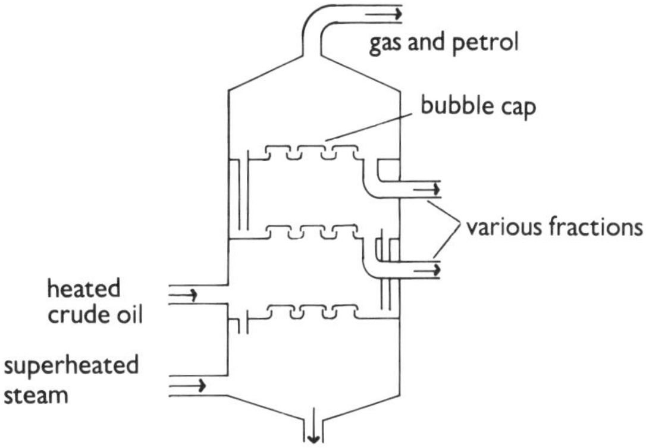

What a distillation unit looks like inside.

To refine crude oil a process called distillation is used. The oil is strongly heated and passes into a tall tower. Vapour rises, cools and turns to liquid. The liquid falls down the tower. It fills trays or shelves. These are fitted with bubble caps. They make the rising vapour pass through the falling liquid. The oil separates into fractions.

The fractions are drawn off at intervals down the tower. Each of them is a mixture. The first fraction is gasoline, or petrol. The substances in it boil below 65 °C. This means that they have small molecules.

The crude oil may not contain all the gasoline we need. Other fractions boil at higher temperatures. They have larger molecules. 'Cracking' breaks them down into smaller ones. More gasoline is formed. Smaller molecules can be built into bigger ones. The proportion of each fraction can be changed. These changes need a catalyst.

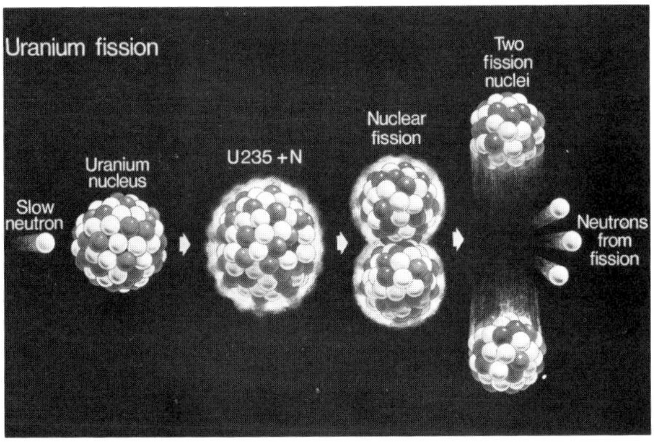

Nuclear fission of uranium.

Coal, oil and gas are 'fossil' fuels. They come from decayed vegetation (Book 1, The Coal Industry). We are using them very rapidly. The supply of natural gas and oil could dry up. There are large unused reserves of coal. There are also other problems.

Fuels have hazards. Accidents still occur in coal mines. Waste tips near the mines can collapse. Oil tankers may leak, sink or burn. Oil slicks are washed up on the shore. The oil kills plant and animal marine life. Burning fuel pollutes the air (Book 1, page 138).

Burning fuel uses oxygen. It puts carbon dioxide into the air instead. Green plants do the opposite. The two changes balance (Book 1, page 153). The balance is being lost. The amount of fuel burnt is increasing. We cut down and use more and more green trees and plants.

Carbon dioxide in air is increasing. It absorbs and traps heat. The average temperature of our air is rising. Our weather system may change as a result.

Some radioactive elements act as fuels. Uranium–235 does. If its atom is hit by a neutron the nucleus splits. Two new atoms are formed. Three neutrons are set free. They strike other uranium atoms. This change is called nuclear fission. It gives huge amounts of energy. This kind of change is used in nuclear power stations. The heat is used to make electricity (page 45).

# Carbon compounds

Carbon is an element. We studied it in Book 1. Two forms of carbon occur in nature. They are diamond and graphite.

Diamond is very hard. It is transparent, like glass. Graphite is soft and grey. Both are crystalline solids. Their crystal shapes are different. When they are pure, both contain only carbon atoms.

Then why are they so different? Because their carbon atoms are arranged differently. Different forms of the same element are called allotropes. They are part of the allotropy of carbon.

We also met some carbon compounds in Book 1. Foods contain carbon compounds. So do many minerals. Many more are present in crude oil. Carbon atoms can link to atoms of other elements. They can also link up to other carbon atoms by covalent bonds.

The atomic number of carbon is 6. A carbon atom contains six electrons. Two fill the first shell. The other four must be in the second shell. The electron structure of the carbon atom is 2.4.

The nearest noble gases are helium and neon. Their electron structures are 2 and 2.8. To be like helium a carbon atom must lose four electrons. This is impossible. To be like neon it must gain four electrons. It can do this by sharing.

A hydrogen atom has one electron. It can join in sharing one pair. A carbon atom needs four. It can form shared pairs with four hydrogen atoms. This compound is methane. Its formula is $CH_4$.

Covalent compounds with small molecules are usually gases. Natural gas is mainly methane. It also comes from crude oil. We shall make it.

These diamonds are one allotrope of carbon . . .

. . . this graphite is another.

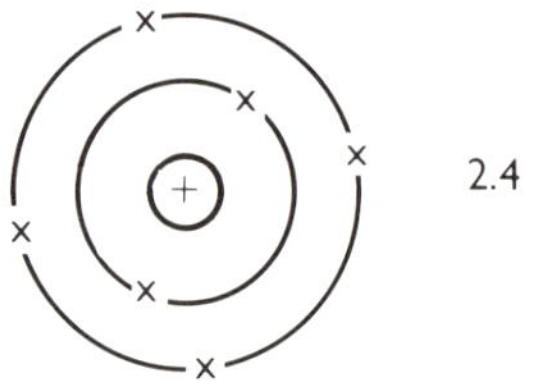


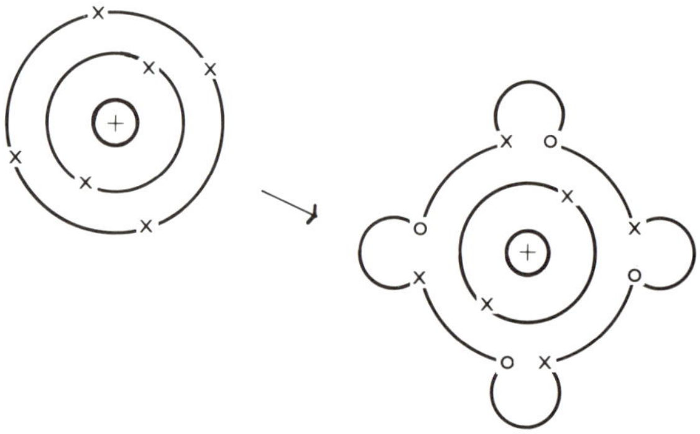

## Experiment 9.1 The properties of methane

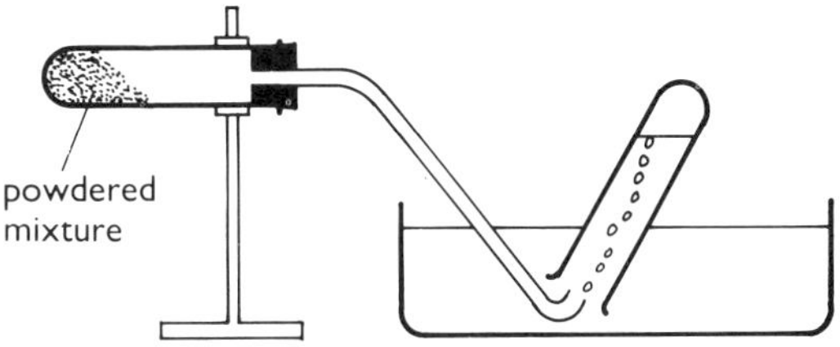


**Grind soda lime and anhydrous sodium ethanoate (acetate) to powder. Heat them separately in an oven at 200°C. Mix well equal parts of each.**

**Heat this mixture. Collect the gas in large test tubes. Stopper them. Use one for each test.**

**Test methane with a lighted splint. Hold a large test tube over the flame. Add lime water to this tube. Stopper it and shake the solution.**

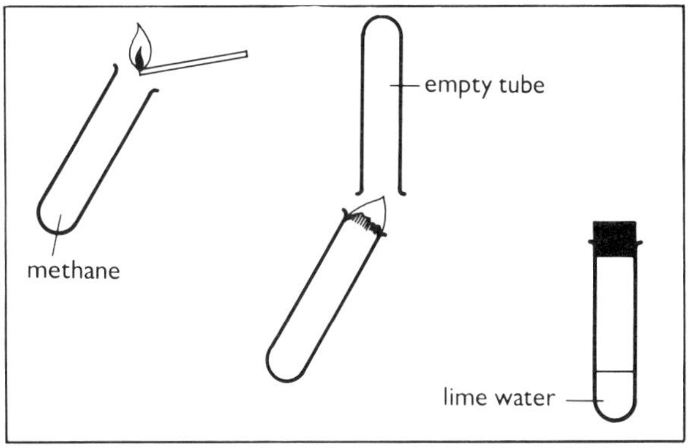


**Shake methane with water. Add a litmus paper. Put in drops of Universal Indicator. Shake methane with a) acidified manganate(VII) solution and b) a solution of bromine in water.**

Apart from burning, does methane react?

Methane burns at the mouth of the tube. The flame is like a bunsen flame with its air hole closed. Carbon dioxide and water form in the tube over the flame.

Methane does not react with water, acids or alkalis. It is not oxidized or reduced. The brown bromine colour fades. Methane reacts with bromine slowly.

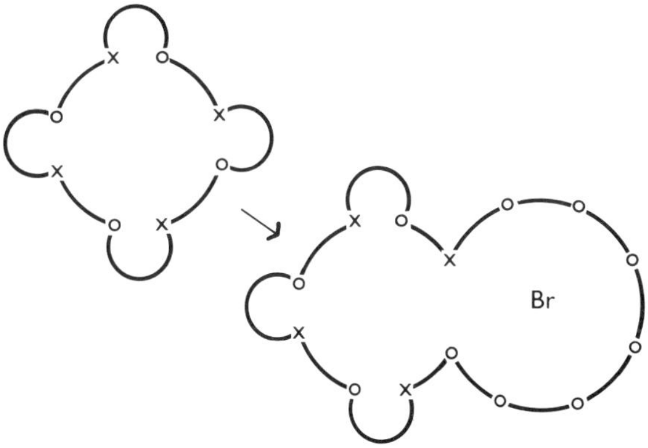


A carbon atom has four covalent bonds. In methane they are filled by hydrogen atoms. The molecule can change in only one way. A hydrogen atom can be taken away. Another atom can go in its place.

This kind of change is called **substitution**. It can happen to all four hydrogen atoms. A compound which can react only by substitution is **saturated**.

$CH_4 + Br_2 \rightarrow CH_3Br + HBr$

$CH_3Br$ is bromomethane.

Methane contains only carbon and hydrogen. It is a hydrocarbon. Hydrocarbons burn in air. The usual products are carbon dioxide and water.

Two carbon atoms can join by a covalent bond. Each provides one electron of the shared pair. Each now has five electrons in its outside shell. Both need three more. Each can link to three hydrogen atoms. This substance is a hydrocarbon too.

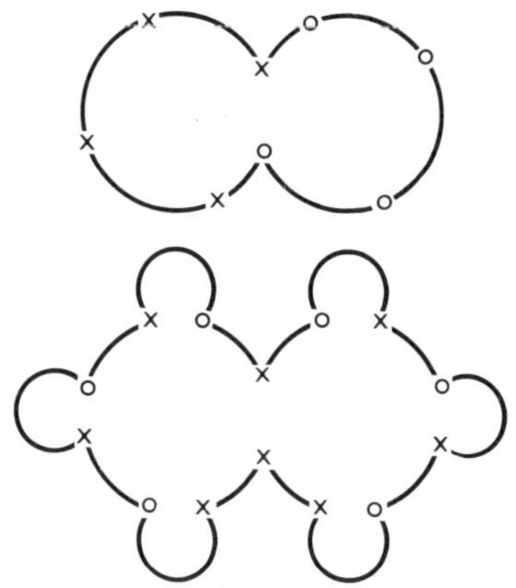

$CH_3.CH_3 = C_2H_6$

Like methane it is a gas. It has no smell or colour. It reacts only by substitution and by burning. It is saturated. It is called ethane, formula $C_2H_6$.

Methane and ethane are very much alike.

# Formula and family

Plants and animals are living 'organisms'. Many carbon compounds come from them. People once thought that they all did. They called the study of carbon compounds 'Organic Chemistry'. Over two million of them are known. Most of them are manufactured. This makes 'Carbon Chemistry' a better name.

Each compound has a formula. There are four ways of writing it. We can show how using methane and ethane.

| **Methane** | | **Ethane** |
|---|---|---|
| $CH_4$ | This is the molecular formula. Use it in equations. | $C_2H_6$ |
| 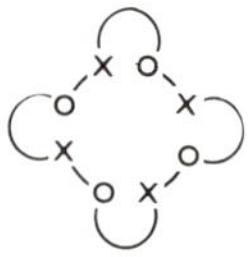 | These drawings show the shared pairs of electrons. | 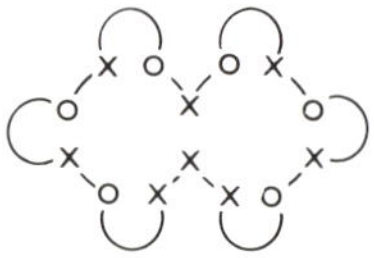 |
| H<br>I<br>H-C-H<br>I<br>H | A shared pair is a covalent bond. Each bond is shown as a short line. The result is a structural formula. It shows which atoms are bonded together. | H H<br>I I<br>H-C-C-H<br>I I<br>H H |
| $CH_4$ | A short form of this is often used. It shows which atoms are joined to each carbon atom. | $CH_3.CH_3$ |

We can think of each atom as a sphere. Hydrogen atoms are smaller than carbon atoms. They are roughly table tennis ball to tennis ball in size.

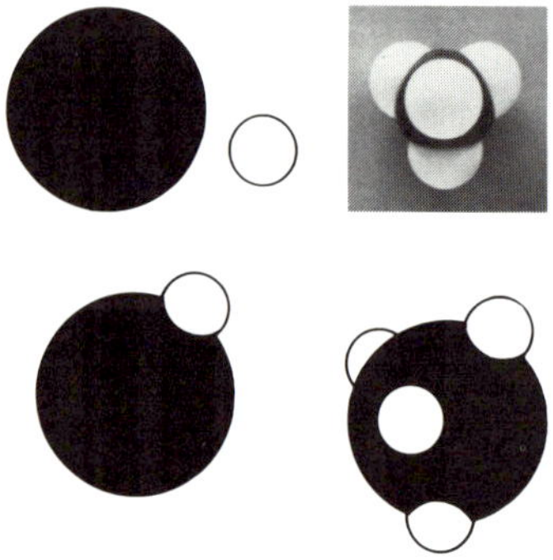

In methane four H atoms are evenly spaced round one C atom. Imagine four table tennis balls fixed to one tennis ball. Each table tennis ball is the same distance from the other three. Atomic models show this well. Remember that electron shells overlap.

In the drawings carbon atoms are black. Hydrogen atoms are white.

Three carbon atoms can join by covalent bonds. The middle one then has six electrons. It needs eight. It forms bonds with two hydrogen atoms.

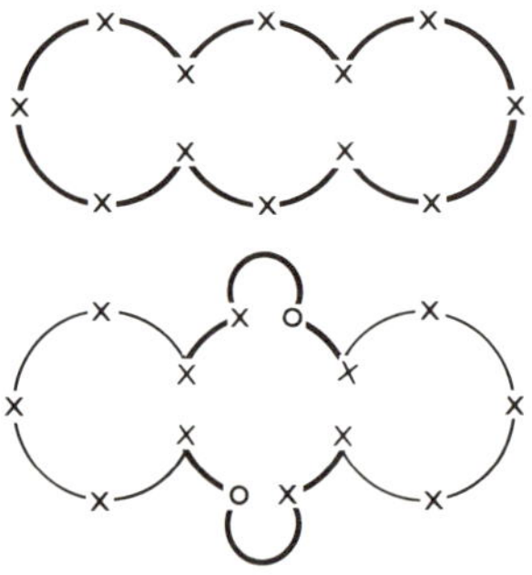

Each end carbon atom now has five electrons. Each carbon atom can form bonds with three hydrogen atoms. The molecular formula is $C_3H_8$. The structural formula is shown in both ways.

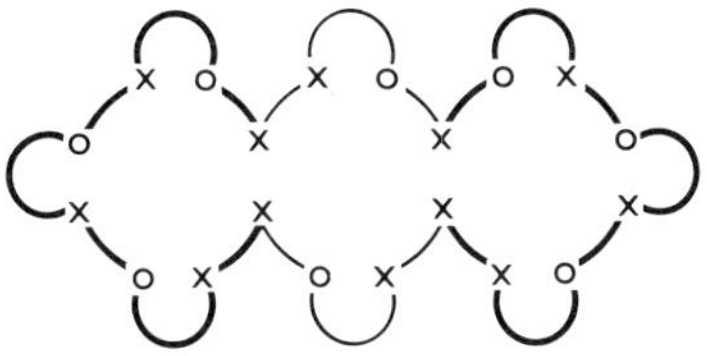

$C_3H_8$ is a hydrocarbon and a gas. It burns forming carbon dioxide and water. Apart from this it reacts by substitution only. It is very much like ethane and methane. It is called propane (pro-pane).

All three belong to the same family. This kind of family is called an 'homologous series'. This one is the alkanes. Their names are in two parts. The first part says how many carbon atoms. The second part is the family name. -ane stands for alkane.

meth- means one carbon atom
eth- means two
prop- means three
but- means four
pent- means five

Look at their formulae. The next one has four carbon atoms. How many H atoms in the molecule?

$CH_4$ $C_2H_6$ $C_3H_8$ $C_4H_?$

This is butane (bewt-ane). It has a chain of four carbon atoms. They are bonded to ten hydrogen atoms. Butane is a gas which burns and reacts by substitution. Its formula is $C_4H_{10}$. The next alkane is $C_5H_{12}$.

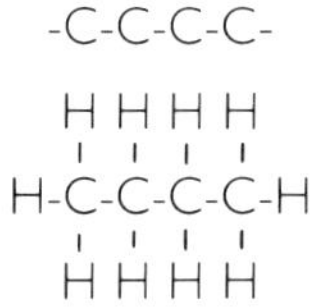


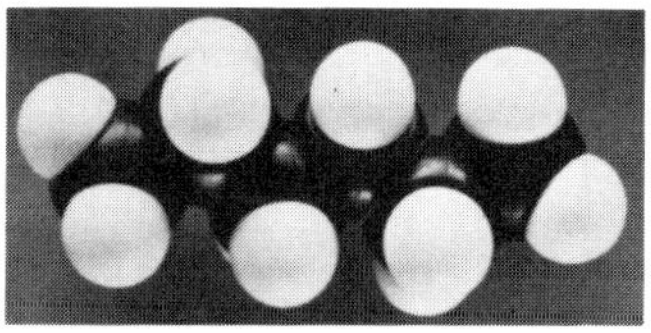

Four carbon atoms can be linked in a different way. We can put three in a chain. We can join the fourth to the middle one. Ten hydrogen atoms are needed. This means there are two compounds with molecular formula $C_4H_{10}$. Such different compounds are called isomers.

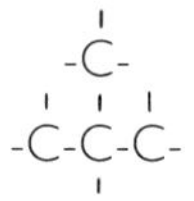


## Summary

A carbon atom can form four covalent bonds. They can be filled by four hydrogen atoms. This compound is called methane. Its formula is $CH_4$.

Methane is a gas hydrocarbon. It burns. It can react in only one other way. Its hydrogen atoms can be replaced by other atoms. This is substitution. Substances which react in this way are saturated.

A covalent bond can link two carbon atoms. Each can then link to three H atoms. The compound is ethane. Its formula is $C_2H_6$ or $CH_3.CH_3$. Methane and ethane belong to a family or homologous series. They are alkanes. The first part of the name shows how many carbon atoms. The ending is the family name, -ane.

A structural formula shows which atoms are joined. A short line stands for a covalent bond. Compounds can have the same molecular formula but different structural formulae. Such compounds are called isomers.

## Questions

1. Write down the formulae and names of the first four alkanes. Give the name and formula of the fifth.
2. What is meant by
   a) an homologous series,
   b) substitution reaction,
   c) hydrocarbon,
   d) isomers.

# Alcohols

For thousands of years people have made wine from grapes. Crushed grapes give a sweet juice. The skins carry a fungus like yeast. It helps to break down the sugar in the juice. A gas is formed. The mixture froths. The reaction is called fermentation.

Yeast will ferment sugar in the same way.

Picking grapes to make wine.

### *Experiment 9.2 New substances from fermentation

Dissolve 20 g of sugar in 80 $cm^3$ of water. Gently grind 10 g of yeast in 20 $cm^3$ of water. Pour both into a flask. Add crystals of potassium nitrate, ammonium phosphate(V) and magnesium sulphate.

Warm the liquid to about 25 °C. Plug the flask loosely with cotton wool. Put it in a warm place. When it froths, bubble the gas through lime water. When frothing stops, carefully pour off the liquid.

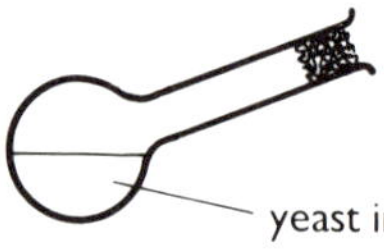


Distil the liquid as shown. Collect the distillate. Stop when the temperature rises above 80 °C. Smell the liquid. Pour a little of it on a watch glass. Touch it with the flame of a lighted splint.

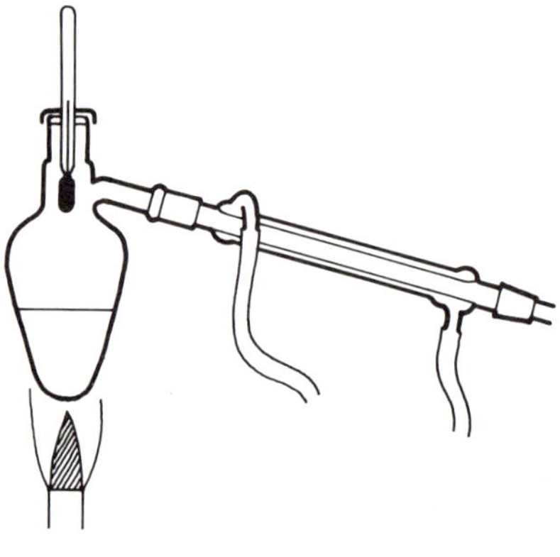

Put $\frac{1}{2}$ cm depth of it into each of four tubes.
*To 1 add a scrap of sodium. Test for hydrogen.
*To 2 add a pinch of phosphorus(V) chloride. Hold a damp litmus paper in the mouth of the tube.
Take potassium manganate(VII) solution. Add dilute sulphuric acid. Do the same to potassium dichromate(VI) solution. Add drops of each solution to test tubes 3 and 4. Warm the test tubes.

Fermentation gives carbon dioxide. A colourless liquid distils over.
What is its boiling point?
Did you recognize its smell?

The colourless liquid smells like 'meths'. It boils at 78 °C. It has always been called 'alcohol'. Experiments prove that its formula is $C_2H_6O$.

Wine, beer and other drinks are made by fermentation. They all contain this substance. This is why they are called alcoholic drinks. Yeast consists of living cells. They contain substances called enzymes. They are catalysts for the breakdown of sugar molecules.

What gases are formed in tests 1) and 2)?

$$C_{12}H_{22}O_{11} + H_2O \xrightarrow{\text{invertase}} C_6H_{12}O_6 + C_6H_{12}O_6$$

sucrose — glucose — fructose

$$C_6H_{12}O_6 \xrightarrow{\text{zymase}} 2C_2H_6O + 2CO_2$$

Sucrose is ordinary sugar. Glucose and fructose are sugars too. Invertase and zymase are two of the enzymes in yeast.

$C_2H_6O$ is a liquid. It has a low boiling point. We have shown that meths does not conduct a current. These are covalent properties. The atoms must be joined by covalent bonds. The structural formula of $C_2H_6O$ is

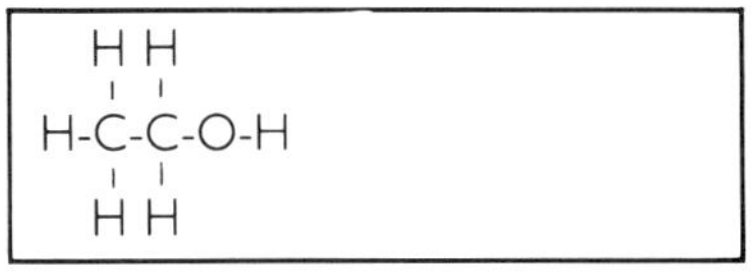

The $-O-H$ part is called a hydroxyl group. Apart from this the molecule is like ethane. Its name begins with ethan-. The ending-ol shows an $-O-H$. The correct name for 'alcohol' is ethanol.

$CH_3.CH_2OH$

this is ethanol

Ethane is not reactive. Ethanol is. The $-OH$ group is the only difference between them. It must be the active part of ethanol. It reacts with the metal sodium. Metals displace hydrogen from the $-OH$ group.

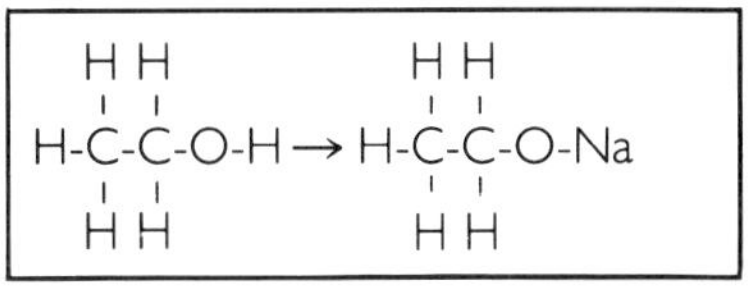

Ethanol reacts with phosphorus chlorides. A misty gas turns litmus red. It must be hydrogen chloride. The hydroxyl group is replaced by a chlorine atom.

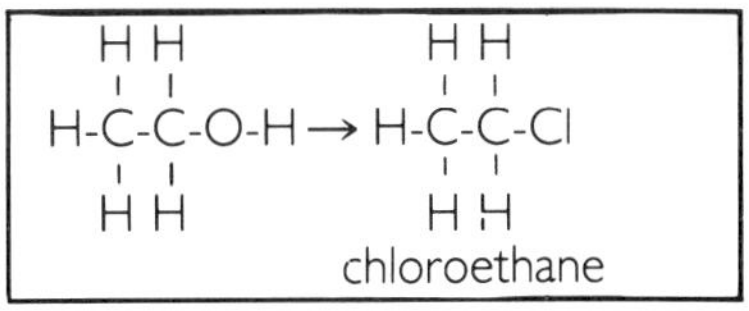


Ethanol reacts with purple potassium manganate(VII) solution. The products are colourless. Orange dichromate(VI) solution changes to green. What do these colour changes tell us? What has happened to the ethanol?

The colour changes show that oxygen is being given up. Ethanol is oxidized in two stages. The first stage forms ethanal. It is an aldehyde. Stage 2 forms an acid. It is ethanoic (acetic) acid.

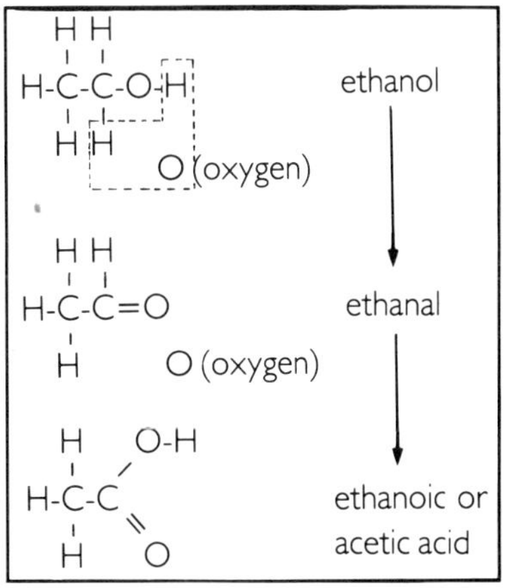


The aldehyde group is $-C{\overset{\diagup H}{\underset{\diagdown\!\diagdown O}{}}}$. The acid group is $-C{\overset{\diagup O-H}{\underset{\diagdown\!\diagdown O}{}}}$

Both contain a carbon atom linked to an oxygen atom. This needs two covalent bonds. Two bonds linking the same two atoms are called a double bond.

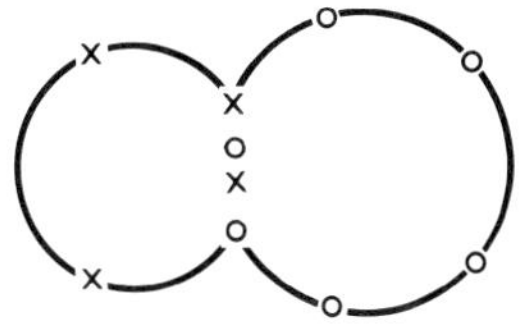

C = O

Like ethane, ethanol burns. The products are carbon dioxide and water. As meths, ethanol is a common fuel.

# Fermentation, food and drink

## Ethanol in everyday life

Wine comes mainly from grapes. At one time they were trampled on to get the juice. Now modern presses are used. The juice ferments for about a week. The wine is then run off into vats.

Here it becomes clear and matures. Then it is bottled. Dark-skinned grapes make the wine red in colour. White or yellow grapes give a white wine.

Sugar is added to some wines before bottling. This will ferment inside the bottle. Carbon dioxide builds up inside. The bottle will open with a 'pop'. The wine is 'bubbly'. Winning motor racing drivers spray it about quite a lot!

Beer is made from barley. The grain is made wet and warm. It sprouts. Some of its starch is turned into sugar. Heating it in a kiln kills the little plants. The result is malted barley.

This malt is crushed in hot water and filtered. The liquid is called wort. It is boiled in copper pots with sugar and roasted hops. After cooling yeast is added. It ferments for a few days.

The yeast grows and multiplies. Some of it is removed. It is sold as 'brewers' yeast. Substances are added to clear the beer. Beer is bottled or put into casks. It contains carbon dioxide. This is what makes the froth or 'head' when it is poured.

Whisky is made from malt too. The kiln is heated by burning peat. The smoke from it gives flavour to the fermented liquid. The fermented liquid has about 14% ethanol.

This liquid is distilled in copper pots. The distillate has a higher percentage of ethanol in it. If this is distilled the percentage becomes bigger still. The result is whisky. It may stand for years before it is bottled. This process is called maturing.

Liquids made by distillation are called spirits. Brandy is made by distilling wine. Molasses can be fermented. Distilling the liquid gives rum. All spirits have a high percentage of ethanol.

Pressing grapes to extract the juice.

Whisky is distilled in large copper pots.

*Grace has a favourite boy friend Mike*
*Who drank alcohol then crashed his bike.*
*He's lucky to be still alive:*
*If you drink you shouldn't drive.*

Alcoholic drinks contain ethanol. What does drinking it do to us?

Small amounts of alcohol make us more lively than usual. Our hearts beat faster. Alcohol sharpens our appetite for food. We worry less about what people think of us.

Larger amounts of alcohol slow us down. We react more slowly. Drivers are more likely to have accidents. They think they are still driving well. They risk other peoples' lives as well as their own.

Find out about breathalysers. The older model had crystals. Alcohol changed them from orange to green. Where have we met this change before? The new model shown has a meter. This shows the amount of alcohol breathed into it.

Constant drinking damages liver and kidneys. The habit is hard to break. Some people become alcoholics.

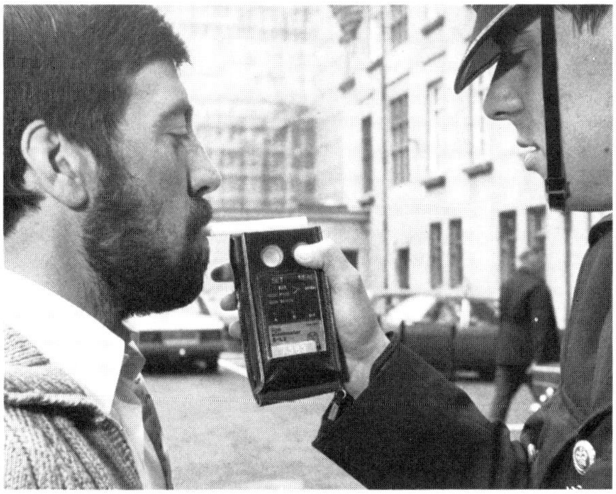

**The new breathalyser test.**

Bread is made using yeast. Flour and water are kneaded into dough. Yeast and sugar are mixed in. They ferment giving bubbles of carbon dioxide. This gas puffs up the dough, or 'raises' it.

The dough is shaped into loaves. They are baked in an oven. The carbon dioxide and ethanol escape. The high temperature kills the yeast. The bread is left full of holes. It is light and spongy in texture.

**Mixing dried yeast for breadmaking.**

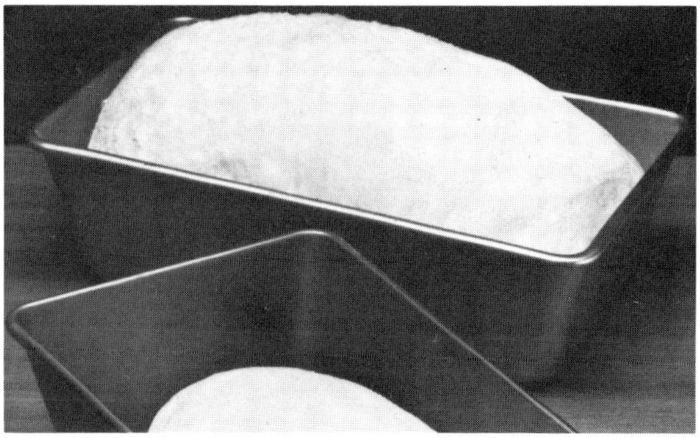

**Loaves are left in a warm place to let the dough rise.**

Vinegar is made from wine or beer. If wine or beer stand in air they become sour or sharp.
Ethanol reacts with oxygen. Ethanoic acid (acetic acid) is formed. Some bacteria speed up the change. Vinegar is a weak solution of the acid, $CH_3COOH$, in water.

## Ethanol in industry

Experiment 9.2 gave a liquid. At most the liquid contains about 96% alcohol. It is called rectified spirit. Removing water from it gives absolute alcohol. Both are used as solvents. They dissolve many substances from paint to perfume.

Methylated spirit is rectified spirit with methanol. A violet dye may be added to it. It is used as a fuel. Methylated spirit is cheaper because less tax is paid on it. The methanol makes the alcohol poisonous to drink.

# Alcohols and esters

There are many substances like ethanol. They belong to a homologous series. This series, or family, is the alcohols. Each has a hydroxyl group, $-OH$, in its molecule. Primary alcohols have a $-CH_2OH$ group.

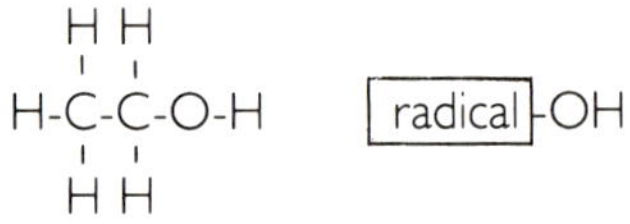


All primary alcohols contain these two groups. This is why they are alike. They all have the properties of the two groups. The $-OH$ group reacts with sodium. All alcohols react with it giving off hydrogen.

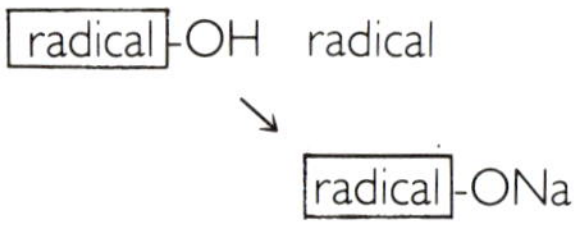


Each $-OH$ group is bonded to a group of atoms. These groups are called radicals. They are methyl $CH_3-$, ethyl $C_2H_5-$, propyl $C_3H_7-$, butyl $C_4H_9-$ and so on.

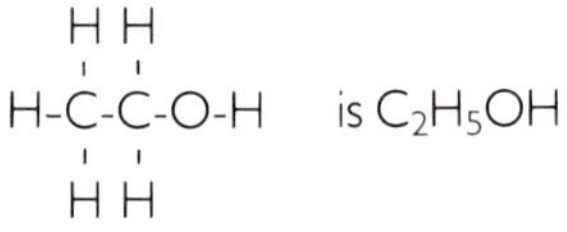

ethanol is ethyl alcohol

All alcohols react with acids.

### Experiment 9.3 Alcohol and acid

**Put 1 cm depth of ethanol in a test tube. Add about ten drops of pure ethanoic acid. Put in ten drops of concentrated sulphuric acid. TAKE CARE! Warm the mixture gently. Smell it with great care.**

**Let it cool. Pour it into sodium carbonate solution in a small beaker. Smell it again with care.**

Is the smell pleasant?
Do you recognize it?

The $-OH$ groups of acid and alcohol react. A molecule of water is formed. The sulphuric acid takes up this water. It also acts as a catalyst. The rest of the acid and alcohol molecules join to form an ester.

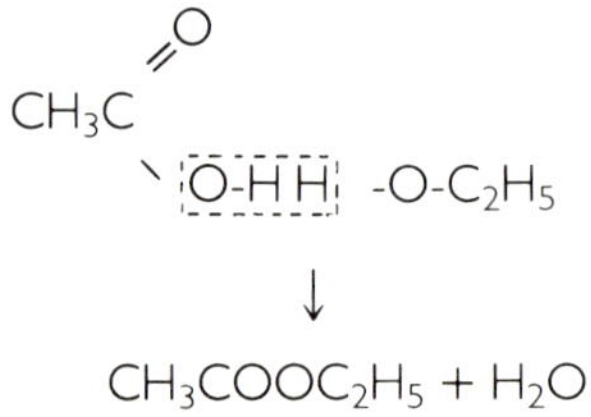


acid + alcohol → ester + water

Flowers and fruit produce esters. When we smell them we breathe in ester vapour. So esters have a 'fruity smell'. Most natural fats and oils are esters.

### The names of isomers

Naming radicals allows us to name isomers. Take the substance $C_4H_{10}$. The atoms can be bonded in two ways. One has a chain of four carbon atoms. It is butane. The chain is shown as a straight line. In the molecule the chain of carbon atoms is a zigzag.

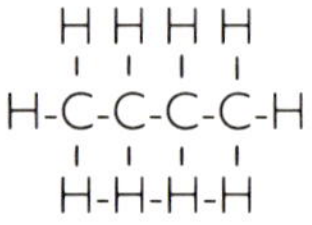

The other has a chain of three carbon atoms. The fourth is bonded to the middle one. The three chain molecule is propane. One H atom is replaced by $CH_3-$. $CH_3-$ is the methyl radical. The isomer formed is called methylpropane.

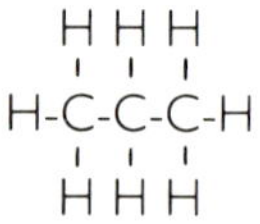
**propane**

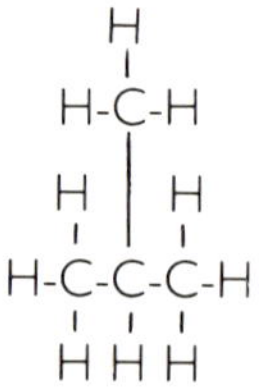
**methylpropane**

There are two alcohols with formula $C_3H_7OH$.
Their structural formulae are shown.
Both have three carbon atoms.
Both are like propane. Both names begin with propan-.
Each has an $-OH$ group. Each name must end in -ol.

Number the carbon atoms from right to left.
**A** has its $-OH$ group on carbon 1. It is propan-1-ol.
**B** has its $-OH$ group on carbon 2. It is propan-2-ol.
Propan-3-ol is the same formula as propan-1-ol.

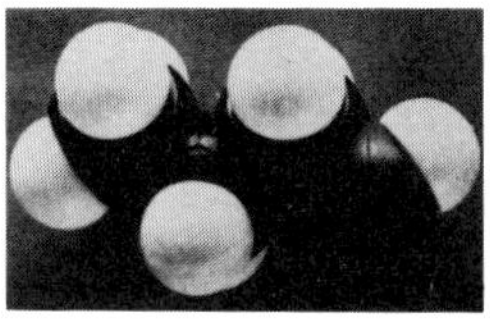

-C-C-C-

3 2 1

**A**

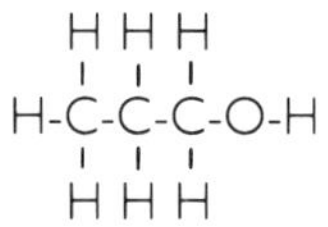

**B**

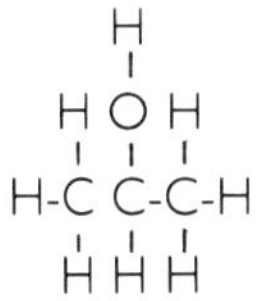

## Summary

Alcohol usually means ethanol, $C_2H_5OH$. It is formed when yeast ferments sugar. The enzymes in yeast act as catalysts. They cause the breakdown of sugar. The frothing during reaction is carbon dioxide bubbles.

This is how alcoholic drinks are made. Distilling these gives spirits. They have a high ethanol content.

Ethanol burns in air. It is a useful fuel. It is used in industry as a solvent. Ethanol is also used to make other important substances.

Rectified spirit is 95% ethanol and 5% water. Adding methanol, $CH_3OH$, makes it poisonous to drink. The mixture is called methylated spirit, or meths. A violet dye may be added as well. Pure ethanol is called absolute alcohol. It belongs to an homologous series called alcohols. They have hydroxyl, $-OH$ groups.

Sodium reacts with alcohols. It replaces the H atom of the $-OH$ group. Phosphorous chlorides replace the hydroxyl, $-OH$, group by a chlorine atom.

alcohol + acid → ester + water.

Concentrated sulphuric acid acts as a catalyst and absorbs water.

Alcohols with a $-CH_2OH$ group are primary alcohols. They can be oxidized.

$$-CH_2OH + O \rightarrow -CHO + H_2O$$

Substances with a $-CHO$ group are aldehydes.

Further oxidation gives acids. These acids all contain the group $-COOH$. $CH_3COOH$ is ethanoic acid or acetic acid. Vinegar is a weak solution of it.

## Questions

1. Fill in the blank spaces.
   Sugar is fermented by using ______. The frothing is caused by the gas ______ ______. The other substance formed is 'alcohol'. Its chemical name is ______. It belongs to a family, or homologous ______. Yeast contains substances called ______. They break down sugar by acting as ______. The reactive part of ethanol is the hydroxyl group ______. Metals such as ______ react with it. They replace the ______ of the $-OH$ group. Phosphorous chlorides replace the $-OH$ by a ______ atom. Alcohol and acid react to form ______ and ______.
2. Write one sentence for each word to explain what it means:
   alkane, structural formula, primary alcohol, ester, substitution reaction.

*Grace's science teacher taught her*
*Acid + base gives salt + water.*
*And one more change to interest her*
*Acid + alcohol gives us ester.*

# *Breaking down other molecules*

Sugar molecules are large. Fermentation breaks them down into smaller ones. One of the products is ethanol. We shall try to decompose ethanol.

sugar → ethanol → ?
$C_{12}H_{22}O_{11} \rightarrow C_2H_5OH \rightarrow$ ?

### Experiment 9.5 To decompose ethanol

**Put a 1 cm depth of ethanol into a test tube. Push rocksill in to soak up the liquid. Support the tube horizontally. Put a pile of porcelain bits in the middle of it. Broken evaporating dish will do.**

**Heat the porcelain fairly strongly. Collect the gas in large test tubes. Stopper them. Do the same tests on the gas as on methane, Experiment 9.1.**

What happens to a lighted splint in the gas?
Does the gas burn forming carbon dioxide?
Does it affect litmus or Universal Indicator?
Does the gas react with bromine?
Can potassium manganate(VII) solution oxidize the gas?

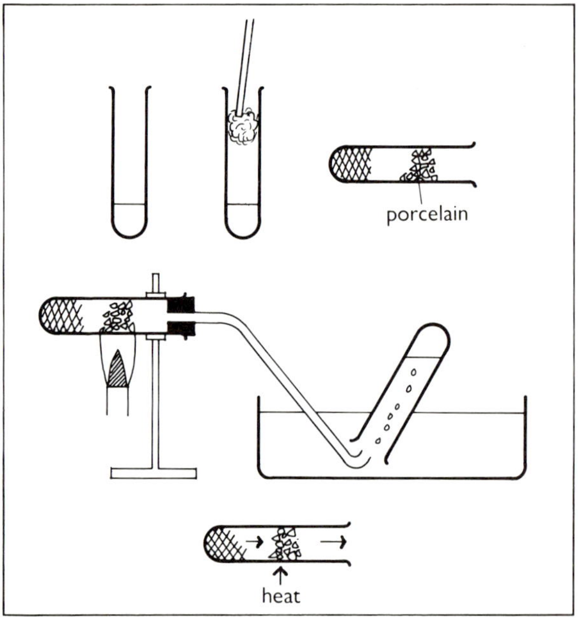


The broken porcelain acts as a catalyst. Heating it also heats the ethanol. So ethanol vapour passes over the catalyst. A colourless gas is collected. It burns with a yellow flame. The products are carbon dioxide and water. The gas is a hydrocarbon.

Its formula is $C_2H_4$. $C_2$ means that its name begins with eth-. It is ethene. Joining two carbon atoms leaves six covalent bonds. There are only four hydrogen atoms to fill them. Each carbon atom will have a spare bond. What happens to these bonds?

$C_2H_4$ 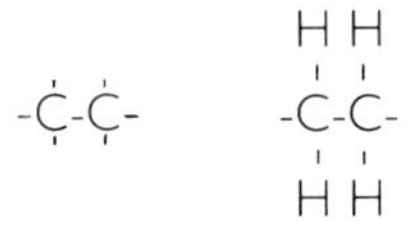

They also connect the two carbon atoms. They are joined by a double bond. A double bond makes the molecule reactive. Ethene has many reactions.

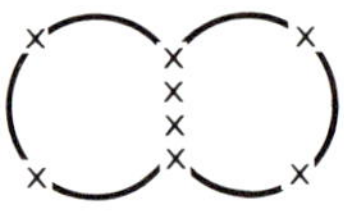

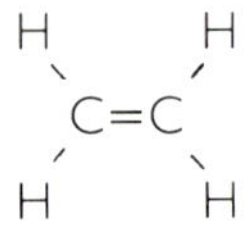

Ethene reacts with bromine. We know this because the brown colour of bromine disappears. A bromine atom adds to each carbon atom. The double bond changes to a single one. Two substances combine to form one. This is an addition reaction:

$$C_2H_4 + Br_2 \rightarrow C_2H_4Br_2$$

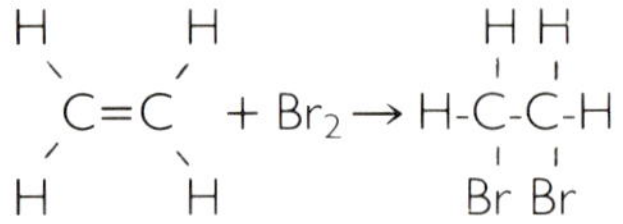

**In an addition reaction, two or more molecules react to form only one product.**

$C_2H_4Br_2$ is called dibromoethane. It could be made from ethane. Two H atoms of ethane are replaced by Br atoms. Two different compounds have this formula.

The one made from ethene has formula **A**. The other has both bromine atoms bonded to the same carbon. This is formula **B**. The two compounds are isomers. Their names must tell us which is which.

```
A    H H          B    H H
     | |               | |
   H-C-C-H           H-C-C-Br
     | |               | |
    Br Br              H Br
```

Number the two carbon atoms from the right. Use them to say where the bromine atoms are.

```
-C-C-
 2 1
```

**A** is 1,2-dibromoethane

**B** is 1,1-dibromoethane

Each molecule has a double bond.

In ethene, potassium manganate(VII) solution loses its purple colour. This shows it is losing oxygen. It is oxidizing ethene. The equation is shown.

```
H     H                                      H H
 \   /                                       | |
  C=C     + H2O + O →                      H-C-C-H
 /   \      potasssium                       | |
H     H     manganate (VII) solution        OH OH
```

This product has $-OH$ groups. It is an ______.
It has two carbon atoms. Its name begins ______. Can you name it?
The products $-OH$ groups are on separate carbon atoms.

Alkenes are very reactive. They react by addition. Work out the reactions of ethene with hydrogen, hydrogen chloride HCl, hydrogen bromine HBr, chlorine $Cl_2$. Name the product formed in each case.

Compare ethane, $C_2H_6$ with ethene, $C_2H_4$.
Ethane is an alkane. It is saturated. It reacts by substitution.
Ethene is an alkene. It is unsaturated. It reacts by addition.

Ethanol molecules can be broken down. One product is ethene. It belongs to an homologous series called the alkenes.

$$C_2H_5OH \rightarrow C_2H_4 + H_2O$$

We have decomposed sugar. Sugar comes from plants. We shall now try a mineral substance. It is medicinal paraffin. It comes from crude oil or petroleum.

## Experiment 9.6 Breaking down medicinal paraffin

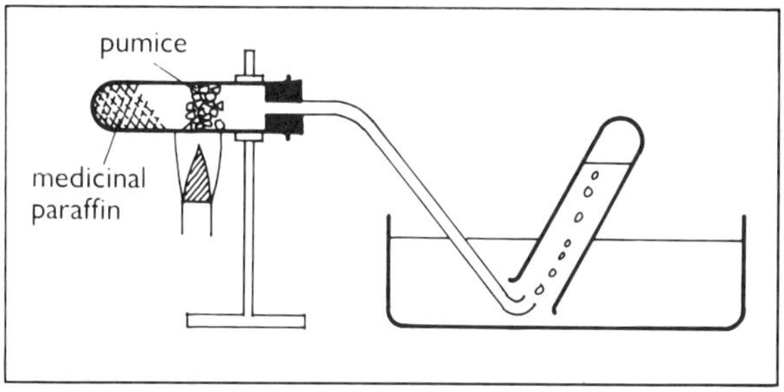


**Use the apparatus of the last experiment. Use the paraffin in place of ethanol. Use pumice in place of porcelain. Heat it strongly. Collect the gas.**

Is the gas likely to be a hydrocarbon?
What test will you use to find out?
Is the gas an alkane or an alkene?
What test will you use to find out?
What second test can be used to decide?
What suggests that the product has smaller molecules than the paraffin?

**Answer**

```
  H H
  | |
H-C-C-H is ethane-1,2-diol
  | |
 OH OH
```

# *Larger molecules to smaller molecules*

We can break down large molecules by other methods.

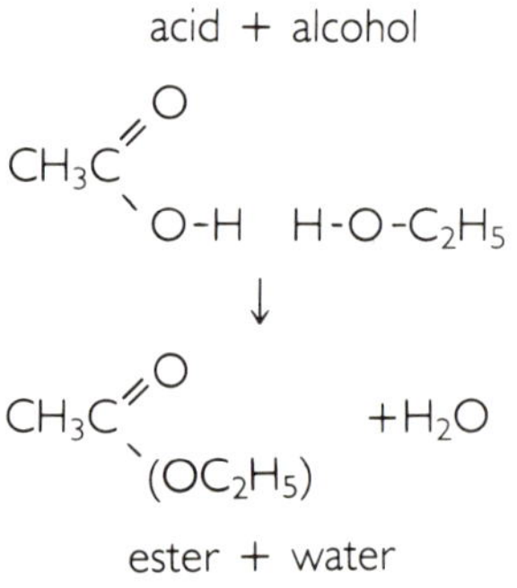


On page 92 we made an ester. We used the reaction

acid + alcohol → ester + water

The ester has a bigger molecule than the acid or the alcohol. This is a condensation reaction.

In a condensation reaction two or more molecules react. One product is a molecule larger than either. The other is a simple molecule such as $H_2O$.

This reaction can be reversed:

ester + water → acid + alcohol

The reaction is very slow. It can be made faster by using a catalyst. Acids and alkalis act as catalysts. The large ester molecule breaks down to smaller ones.

Most natural oils and fats are esters. Castor oil is.

### Experiment 9.7 The breakdown of esters

**a) Wear eyeshields. Put 2 cm$^3$ of castor oil in a 50 cm$^3$ beaker. Add with care 10 cm$^3$ of 5 M sodium hydroxide solution. Keep it away from clothes or skin. It is very caustic.**

**Stir the mixture and gently heat it. Let it boil very gently for about five minutes. Add an equal volume of distilled water. Stir in half a spoonful of salt. Filter. Wash the solid with distilled water.**

**Half fill one test tube with distilled water. Half fill another with hard tap water. Add a lump of the solid to each. Stopper and shake the two tubes.**

What happens to the castor oil?
How does the solid affect the two samples of water?
Do these results tell you what the solid is?

*** b) Put a 1 cm depth of castor oil into a test tube. Add twice the volume of concentrated sulphuric acid. TAKE CARE! Stir the mixture with a glass rod. Pour it into distilled water in a beaker. Stir it. Carefully pour the water away. Oil is left in the beaker. Wash it again with distilled water.**

**Take test tubes of hard water and distilled water. Add a little oil to each. Shake the tubes.**

How does the oil affect the two samples of water?
Are results for hard and soft water different?
Does this tell you what the oil is?

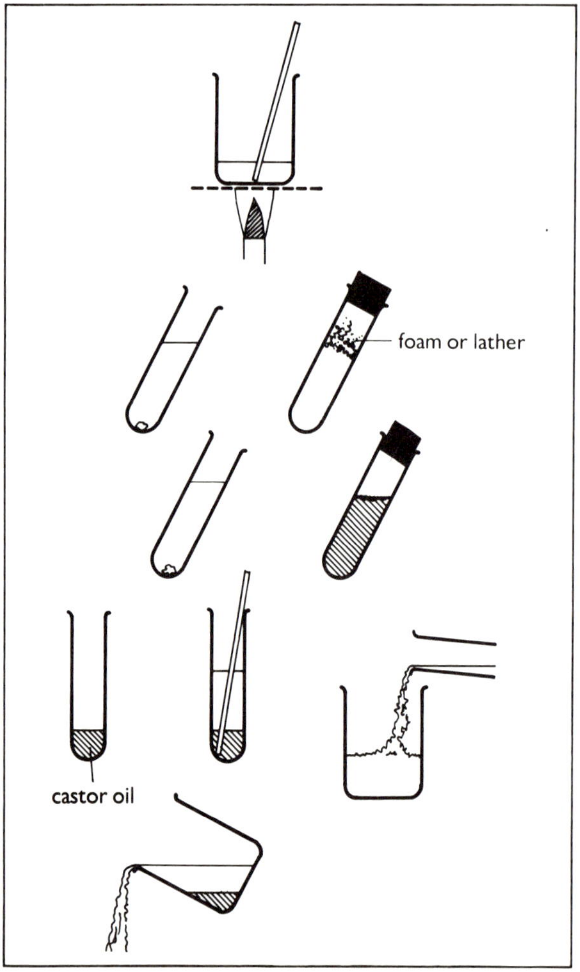

In Book 1, soap was added to water. It gave a lather. Distilled water needed very little soap. Lather formed at once. The water remained clear.

Most tap water is hard. It contains dissolved calcium compounds. These react with soap. The water becomes cloudy with scum. Lather forms when this change is complete. Much more soap is needed.

Detergents do not react with calcium compounds. Tap water and distilled water lather at once. They stay clear.

**Lather produced by soap in hard and soft water.**

The solid from castor oil behaves like soap.
The oil we made behaves like a detergent.
How does this happen?

oil + sodium hydroxide → soap
oil + sulphuric acid → detergent

We know that:

ester + water → acid + alcohol

Sodium hydroxide speeds up the change. It also reacts with the acid. Its sodium salt is formed. The alcohol formed is glycerol. The sodium salt has a long carbon atom chain. It is soap.

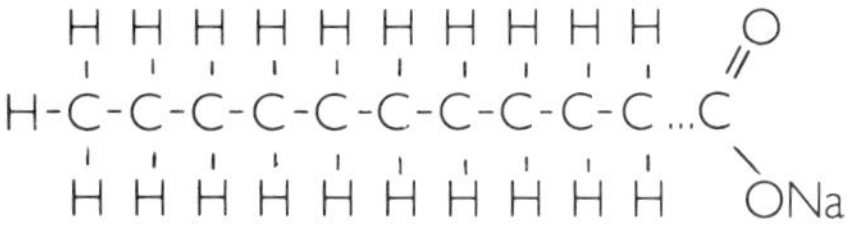

A detergent molecule has the same shape. The group at the end of the chain comes from sulphuric acid. It does not react with calcium compounds. It does not form scum. It can lather at once in hard water.

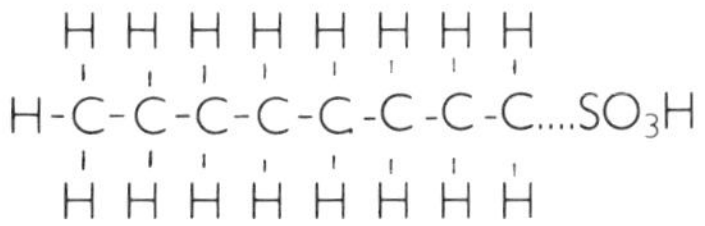

Our skins produce an oily substance. This collects dirt. Oily dirt rubs off on clothes. Oil and water do not mix. Water alone does not wash off oily dirt. Soap and detergent help oil and water to mix.

Their long carbon chains are attracted to oil. The other end of the molecule goes into the water. The boundary between oil and water is broken up. The two mix. Rinsing removes both and also the dirt.

Vegetable oils can be used to make food. Turning them into detergent is a waste so oils from petroleum are used instead.

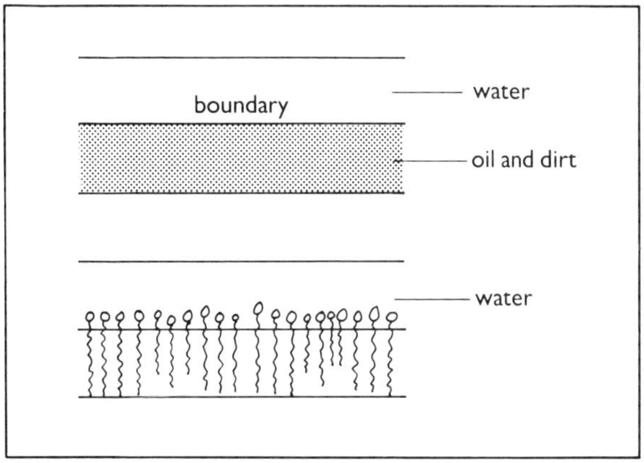

# Cosmetics

The word cosmetic comes from a Greek word. It means 'to make beautiful'. Anything we use to make us more attractive is a cosmetic. Cosmetics have been used through the ages. Do you remember malachite?

It is the green ore copper carbonate. It was used as eye-shadow in Egypt at least 6000 years ago.

### Do you wash?

Our skins produce a fatty substance called sebum. We also perspire. We wash these substances off. If we don't bacteria slowly decompose them. This gives rise to body odour. We don't think of soap as a cosmetic but shampoo is a cosmetic.

Our scalps produce sebum. Sebum collects dirt. Greasy dirt makes hair look dull and matted. Shampoo contains a good detergent to remove it. Colour and perfume make shampoo more attractive. Other extras are lemon juice, beer, egg – the list is endless. They don't help in washing hair but may have other useful effects.

Bath salts soften water. The crystals are sodium carbonate or sesquicarbonate. A coloured dye and perfume are usually added to the crystals. We use talcum powder to absorb water. It also makes our skin smooth or 'slippery'. It is mainly French chalk. Boric acid and fine chalk are also mixed in.

### Do you clean your teeth?

A sticky layer called plaque forms on teeth. It harbours bacteria. Bacteria decompose the sugars in food. Acids are formed. They attack the enamel layer of teeth. This causes tooth decay.

Cleaning prevents decay in three ways. First, it removes food from between teeth. No food sugars will form on them. Secondly, it rubs off the plaque. This reduces the bacteria which use the sugar. Thirdly, it washes off acid already formed. Decay is cut down to a minimum.

Using toothpaste helps both effects. It must be soft but not gritty. Grit may damage the enamel. Very fine chalk is usually used. It neutralizes any acid already formed. This also helps to avoid decay. Water and glycerol keep the paste soft and moist.

A little dental soap in the paste helps cleaning. A flavour such as peppermint helps the taste. Some pastes contain fluorides. They reduce decay quite a lot. People still argue about their usefulness.

## **Going out into the world?**

Setting lotion holds hair in place. So does hair lotion. Lotion contains a gum in solution. The solvent is mainly water. It contains some ethanol and glycerol. The ethanol is industrial meths.

Hair cream is mostly water and medicinal paraffin. A substance is added to make the oil and water mix. The mixture is an emulsion. Wax is dissolved in it.

Make-up includes lipstick, eye-shadow and mascara. It can make us more attractive. It may alter our appearance entirely. Make-up for stage and television often does this. We can 'put on a new face'.

Lipstick, eye-shadow and mascara provide colour. To do this well they must spread evenly and smoothly. They should also last and not easily rub off. All three contain an oil and a wax. This is to ensure even spread.

Lipstick contains beeswax in medicinal paraffin. It also has petroleum jelly. Colour and perfume are added. The melted mixture is poured into a mould. It cools and sets to a solid. This is a 'lipstick'.

Eye-shadow has a colour pigment. Mascara contains carbon black. Both are added to an oil and wax mixture. Thorough mixing is also important.

Finger and toe nails are often uneven. Nail varnish covers them with a smooth, hard layer. The varnish is a solution of shellac. This resin is dissolved in a mixture of liquids. A colour pigment is added. It is painted on the nail. The liquids evaporate quickly. This leaves a hard, coloured shellac layer. Meths and propanol are common solvents. They can be used to remove the shellac layer from the nail.

You can make these and other cosmetics. Two books will help. They are:

*Cosmetic Chemistry* by Anne Young (Mills and Boon)

*Cosmetic Science* by John Gostelow (Griffin and George).

# Building large molecules

We have broken down large molecules into smaller ones. The reverse can also happen. Small molecules can be built into larger ones. We already know two ways of doing this.

1. Ethene is unsaturated. It reacts by addition. Its molecules join to those of other substances. The result is one single bigger molecule.

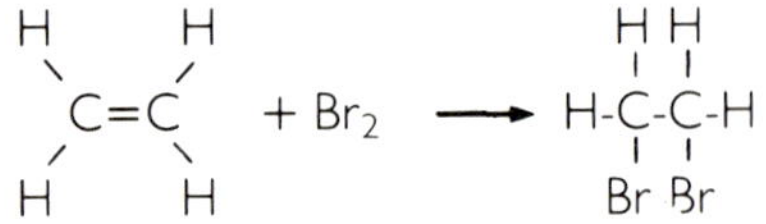


2. Alcohol and acid have active −OH groups. These react by losing a molecule of water. The rest of the two molecules join up. An ester is formed. Its molecule is bigger than those of acid or alcohol. This is a condensation reaction.

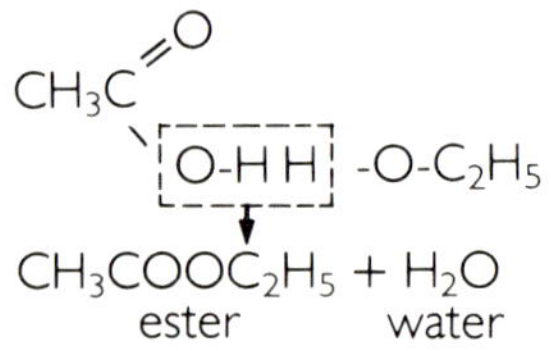


Neither molecule shown is really large. The methods are important. They can be used to make huge molecules.

## Polymers and plastics

Molecules of the same substance can react by method 1. Two ethene molecules link up. Their double bonds become single. Other $C_2H_4$ molecules join at the ends.

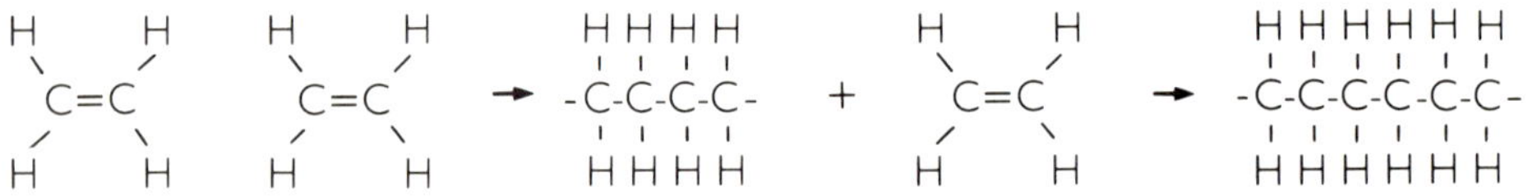

Thousands of molecules link up by addition. The result is a giant molecule. This must be a solid.

The prefix for one is mono–. The compound with single molecules is called a **monomer**. The prefix for many is poly–. The result of joining many single molecules is a **polymer**. The process is **polymerization**.

ethene — addition polymerization → polythene
(monomer) (polymer)

Ethene, $C_2H_4$, is the monomer. The polymer is poly–ethene. This has been shortened to polythene.

Molecules of different compounds can be used. They also react by addition. The result is a co-polymer. Many polymers are plastics (see page 108).

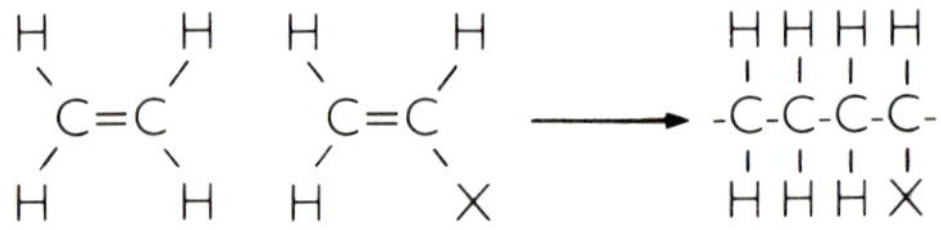

Look at these formulae.

vinyl chloride    styrene    acrylonitrile

The names given are the older ones.
Are these four substances saturated?
What part of each formula gives the answer?
Will they react by addition?
Which ones are likely to polymerize by addition?

These pipes are made from PVC.

All four molecules contain a double bond. It makes them unsaturated. All four react by addition. All four can act as monomers. This is why the older names are given. *Poly*vinyl chloride is known as PVC.

chloroethene

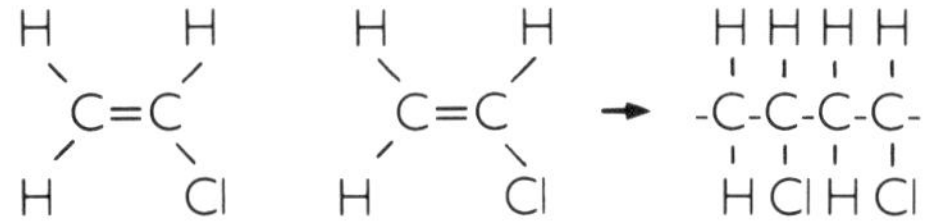

Polymerization of styrene gives polystyrene. It is a very strong solid. It is light in weight. It does not conduct heat or an electric current. These properties give it many uses. Find out what they are.

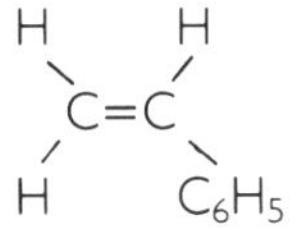

is phenylethene

The polymer from acrilonitrile gives man-made fibres. Their trade names are well known: Orlon, Acrilan etc. Look for them on the labels on your clothes.

propenenitrile

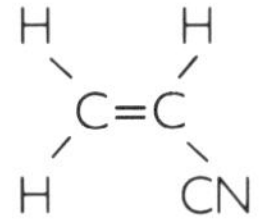

The fluoride monomer is tetrafluorethene. It gives a polymer called Teflon or Fluon. It is very hard. It has few reactions. It is used as a non-stick layer, for example in saucepans.

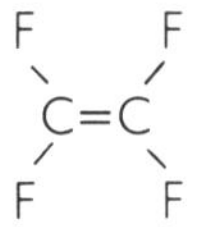

$CF_2{=}CF_2$

The polymers are named from the older names. The modern names are given with the formula. Perspex is a well known polymer.

## Experiment 9.8 Polymer to monomer and back

**Put perspex chips into a test tube to a depth of 3 cm. Fit the tube with stopper and delivery tube. Stand another tube in cold water. Put the delivery tube into it. Do the experiment in a fume cupboard.**

**Heat the perspex. Collect the liquid in the cooled tube. Stand the tube in hot water. Drop in a little di(dodecanoyl) peroxide. Let the mixture stand.**

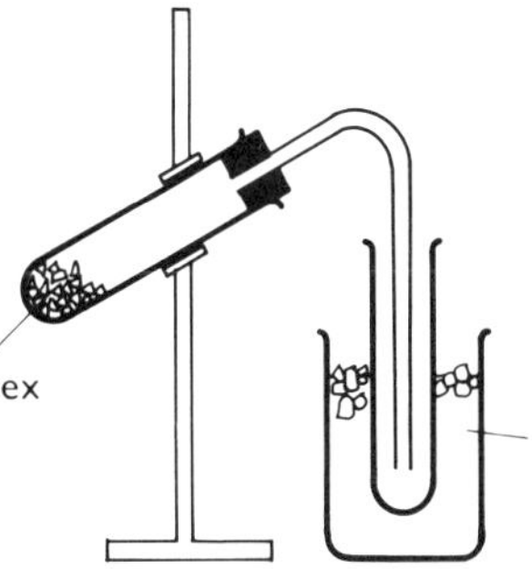


Which has the larger molecules, perspex or liquid?
What effect does the peroxide have on the liquid?

Perspex is an important polymer. It is a kind of super glass. It is used in making lenses. They are used in spectacles and optical instruments. The liquid has the smaller molecules. It is the monomer. The peroxide makes it polymerize to perspex again.

Polymers such as polythene are **plastics**. They can be moulded into almost any shape. They can be tailor-made for almost any purpose.

# The second method

Method 1 uses substances with double bonds. Method 2 uses compounds with active groups. To show how it works we shall make nylon. We need two different substances.

One is hexanedioyl dichloride. It is dissolved in tetrachloromethane. Call this solution A.

The other is hexane–1,6–diamine. It is dissolved in water. Call this solution B. A and B do not mix.

A dam wall made from plastic.

### Experiment 9.9 To make nylon

**Put 2 cm$^3$ of A into a 5 cm$^3$ beaker. Using a dropper add an equal volume of B. Add it carefully. It then forms a separate layer resting on solution A.**

**Gently put a pair of tweezers in the top layer. Pick up a bit of the boundary between A and B. Pull it slowly out of the liquid. Wind the thread round a glass rod. Slowly rotate the rod.**

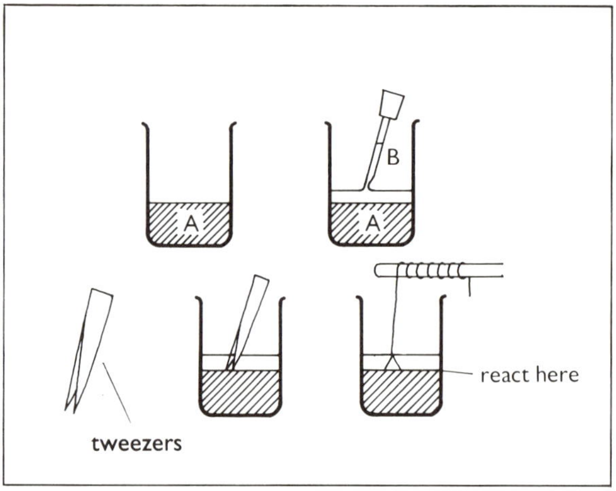


A and B react. Where does the reaction happen?
Describe the appearance of the thread formed.
It is a solid. Are its molecules likely to be large?

A and B do not mix. They can react only where they meet. The tweezers pick up one product of this reaction. It is a solid. This means it may have large molecules. It is like a thread of white cotton. It is nylon thread.

For easy reaction we used a dichloride. It is made from an acid. In the manufacture of nylon the acid itself is used. Its molecule has an acid group at each end. Both ends of the molecules will react.

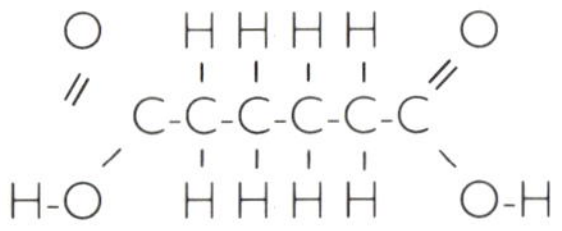


Diamine means that a molecule has two amine groups. This group is $-NH_2$. A nitrogen atom forms three covalent bonds. B has $-NH_2$ at each end of its molecule. Hexane means that a chain of six carbon atoms comes between them. Both ends react.

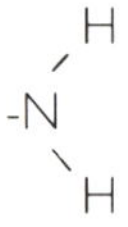


the amine group

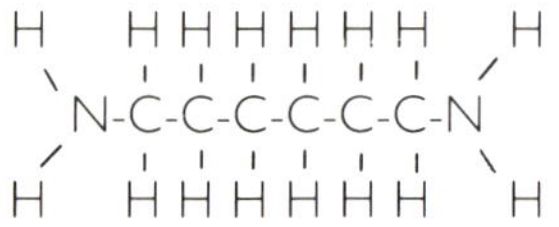


The acid and amine groups react. A molecule of water is formed. Free bonds are left at the ends of A and B. They join together. This is condensation.

This happens at both ends of B molecules. Both ends of A can react too. The product is a polymer.

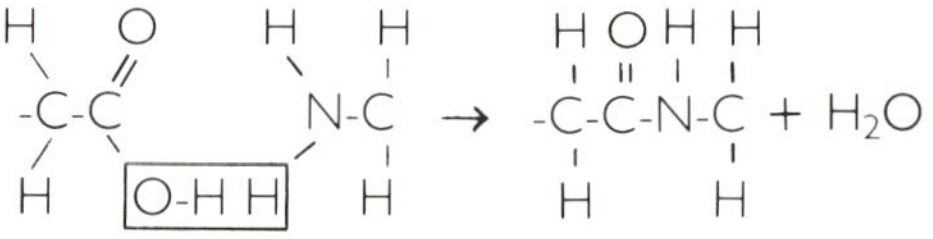

The new molecule is much larger. It still has an active group at each end. These groups react. The molecule becomes larger still. It still has an active group at each end. Two more units add on.

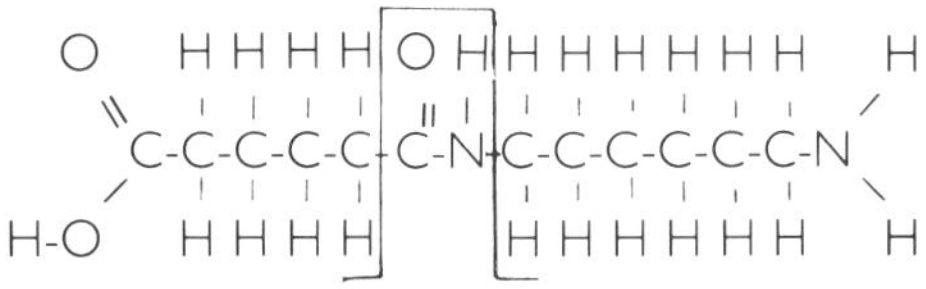

the join

Very long chain molecules form. Each reaction adds another unit to the chain. It may be 100 units long. Amine and acid molecules alternate. Each has a chain of six carbon atoms. The product is nylon. Nylon is very tough and strong. It melts at about 250 °C.

.... join-$(CH_2)_4$-join-$(CH_2)_6$-join-$(CH_2)_4$...

-A-join-B-join-A-

.... A-B-A-B-A-B-....

In this nylon each unit has six carbon atoms. It is called nylon 66. Other acids and amines can be used. The polymers formed will have slightly different properties. They will also be called nylons.

We used esters to explain condensation reactions. Suppose we use an alcohol with two −OH groups. Choose one with −OH groups separated by a carbon chain. Let it react with an acid at both ends.

Suppose we use an acid with two acid groups. Both ends of the molecule will be active. Both will react with the alcohol. Long chain molecules will form.

Terylene is an example of this kind of polymer.

**Polyester coming off the machine.**

One monomer is H-O-C(H)(H)-C(H)(H)-O-H Write it HO-□-OH

The other is $HOOC.C_6H_4.COOH$. Write it HOOC-□-COOH.
Condensation gives an ester. This has an active group at each end of its molecule. These react by condensation forming esters.

HOOC-□-CO [OH H] O-□-O [H HO] OC-□-CO [OH H] O-□ .....

HOOC-□-COO-□-OOC-□-COO-□-OOC- ....

**A spinneret is used in the manufacture of terylene.**

These polymers are called polyesters. The most well known example is terylene. It is very strong. Like nylon it is a man-made fibre. Look for it on the labels on clothes.

# *Natural polymers*

Many natural materials are polymers. For example, the sap from a rubber tree is a polymer. It is called latex. Acid turns it into solid rubber. The section on plastics will tell you more about it.

Starch is a polymer. Plants make it in their leaves. Potatoes and grain contain starch. Starch is part of our normal diet. It is insoluble. A soluble form can be made. We shall use it to test properties of starch.

### Experiment 9.10 The properties of starch

**Stir a pinch of soluble starch in a few $cm^3$ of water. Pour this into 100 $cm^3$ of boiling water. Put an iodine crystal into a test tube half full of water. Add a potassium iodide crystal. Shake the mixture. Use these solutions in the tests below.**

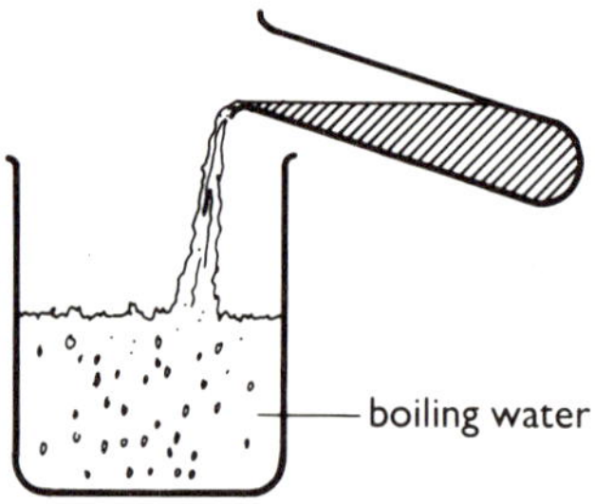


**a) Add a drop of iodine solution to some starch solution. Put starch solution in a test tube. Add an equal volume of Fehling's solution. Boil it.**

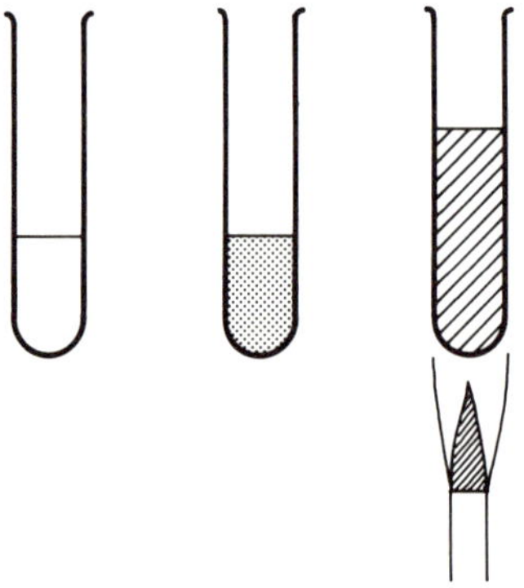

Which of these can be used as a test for starch?

Iodine and starch give a blue colour. It is used as a test for either of them. Starch does not affect Fehling's solution.

**b) Put 20 $cm^3$ of starch solution into a beaker. Add 3 $cm^3$ of dilute hydrochloric acid. Gently boil the solution. Remove a little of it every two minutes.**

**Divide each part removed into two. Test one half with iodine solution. Boil the other with Fehling's solution.**

**c) Fill a test tube one third full with starch solution. Dribble saliva into it. Shake the mixture. Take out a little every two minutes. Test each part as in b). Chew a small piece of bread for several minutes.**

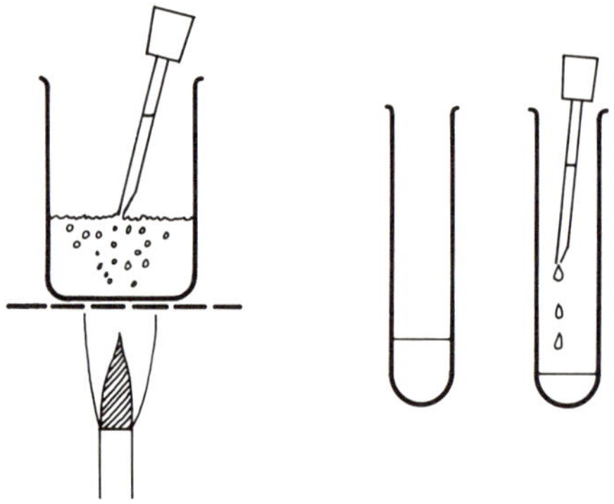

Is starch used up in the acid solution?
Does saliva cause the starch to disappear?
Does the taste of the bread change?

With each sample, iodine gives a paler blue than the sample before. Starch is being used up. Acid and saliva turn it into sugars. This is why the taste of bread becomes sweeter. Saliva contains an enzyme, ptyalin. It is a catalyst for the change starch → sugars. This change is part of digesting our food.

Some sugars react with Fehling's solution. The blue colour of copper(II) ions goes. An orange solid, copper(I) oxide, is formed.

$$-C_6H_{10}O_5-C_6H_{10}O_5-C_6H_{10}O_5-$$
$$+\,H_2O \qquad +\,H_2O \qquad +\,H_2O$$

ptyalin ↓ or acid

$C_6H_{12}O_6$ sugars

starch + water → sugar

## Things to do

Make a list of all plastic articles in your home. Find out the names of the polymers they contain. Check the labels on your clothes. What fibre does each of them contain? Do they contain wool or cotton?

## Summary

Large molecules can be broken down into smaller ones. Using a catalyst, ethanol decomposes. It gives a gas called ethene. This is a hydrocarbon, formula $C_2H_4$.

Ethene burns with a yellow flame. Its molecule has a double bond. It is unsaturated. It reacts by addition. In addition, two or more molecules react to give one product.

$$C_2H_4 + Br_2 \rightarrow C_2H_4Br_2$$

Ethene molecules react with each other. They form long chain molecules. The product is a solid polymer. It can be moulded into shape. It is called polythene. The process is polymerization. Many substances such as ethene polymerize. They are called monomers.

Large molecules are also made by condensation. Here the active groups of two molecules react. A small molecule such as $H_2O$ is formed. This allows the rest of the two molecules to link up. Monomer molecules have an active group at both ends. Both of these react. Long chain molecules of a polymer form.

Many natural substances are polymers. Starch has a giant molecule. It is made up of $C_6H_{10}O_5$ units. It gives a blue colour with iodine. It breaks down into sugars. Acid and saliva effect this change.

## Questions

1. Ethene is an unsaturated compound.
   a) What does 'unsaturated' mean?
   b) Draw a simple structural formula for ethene.
   c) Ethene reacts with hydrogen to form a saturated compound, ethane. What does 'saturated' mean?
   d) Write an equation for the last reaction.
   e) Draw a simple structural formula for ethane.
   f) Why are ethane and ethene called hydrocarbons?

2. Ethene is an unsaturated hydrocarbon.
   a) What does the term 'unsaturated' mean?
   b) What does the term 'hydrocarbon' mean?
   c) Bromine is added to ethene. What would you see?
   d) Ethene can be polymerized. What is a polymer?
   e) Name the polymer formed from ethene.
   f) Why is this reaction called 'addition' polymerization?

3.

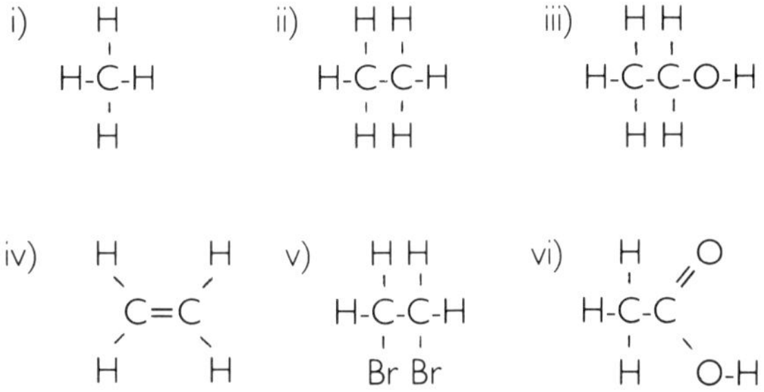

   a) Name the compounds from i) to vi).
   b) Three of them are hydrocarbons. Which ones?
   c) One of these hydrocarbons is unsaturated. Which?
   d) What everyday substance is made from substance iv)?
   e) Which two substances react to form an ester?
   f) Substances ii) and iv) both burn in air. Name the products formed by burning.
   g) Apart from burning the reactions of ii) and iv) are different. Explain why.
   h) Which of the six substances is made by fermentation? What part do enzymes take in fermentation?

# The plastics age

What time did you get out of bed?
What plastics did you use in the next hour?
Try to work out how many you use in a day.

A plastic is a substance which can be moulded into shape. Most plastics are polymers. They are manufactured in huge amounts. Many different monomers are used. There are many methods of manufacture.

Two types of reaction are used. Addition reactions use molecules with double bonds. They may be of one substance only. Two monomers may also be used together. In condensation two monomers are used. Each has active groups. These react. Both methods build long chain molecules. Polymers have giant molecules.

Their properties depend on three main factors: a) which monomers are used, b) the method used to make them react, c) cross linking between the chain molecules. So a plastic can be tailor-made. The factors can be chosen to give the properties needed.

Take polythene as an example. Solvent is fed into a reaction vessel. A catalyst is added. Ethene under pressure is passed in. The temperature used is about 75 °C. Ethene reacts to form the polymer.

It leaves the reaction vessel dissolved in the solvent. Any catalyst is removed. The solvent is evaporated. The solid plastic is formed. It is made into small pieces or granules. These can be heated.

Heating gives the chain molecules greater movement. The plastic softens. It can be shaped by a mould. On cooling the plastic hardens in this shape. It can also be made into thin film or sheet.

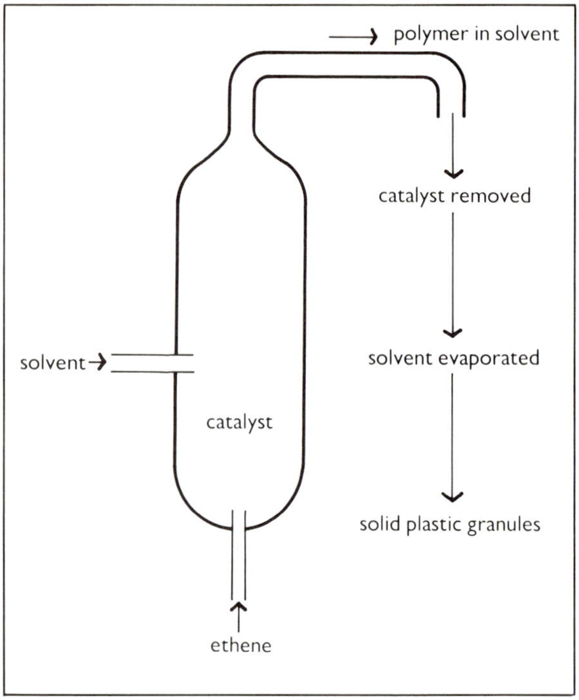


Polythene is a thermoplastic. Heat softens it. It can be moulded. It can be heated, softened and remoulded again. For some plastics this is not true. They are called thermosetting. Heat softens them. They can be moulded. The moulded substance will not soften on heating. The chains have become cross linked. They are held in rigid positions.

Plastics are moulded in many ways. One is called extrusion. Heated plastic is forced through a gap. Pipes and tubing are made in this way. So are rods, plastic sheet, tape and plastic coated wire.

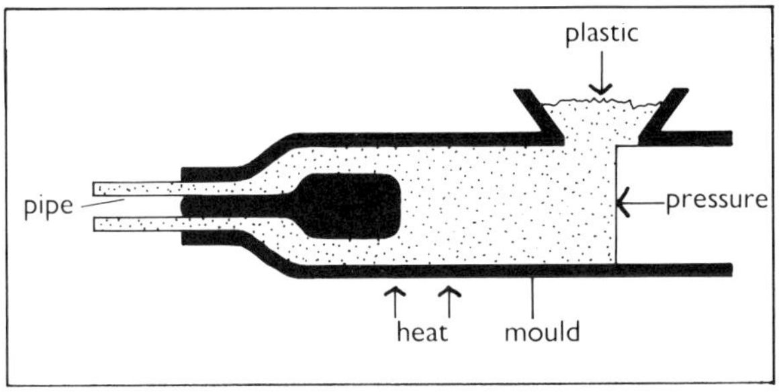


Blow moulding is used to make hollow objects.

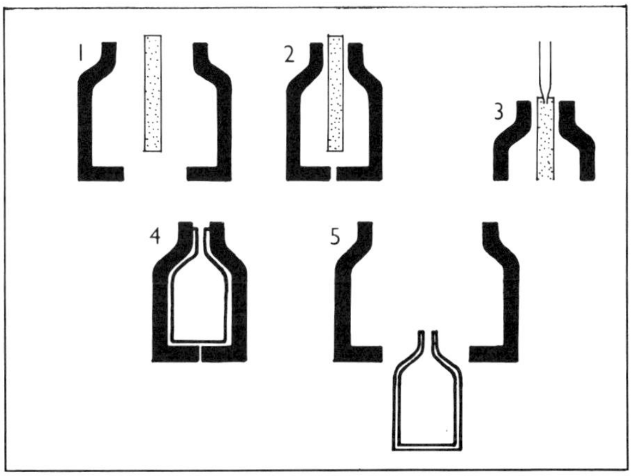


Heated plastic is fed into a mould. The mould closes. An air inlet is put into the plastic. Air is blown in. The plastic takes the shape of the mould. When the mould opens it drops out.

Rubber is a polymer made from latex. Some of this comes from rubber trees. Most of it is now man-made. Monomers such as butadiene are used. They are polymerized with monomers such as styrene. The polymer formed still contains double bonds.

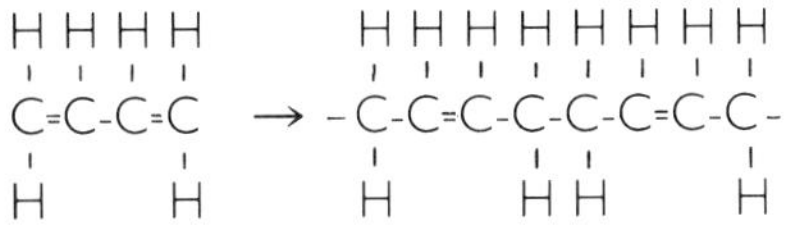

bewt-a-di-een

All rubbers are elastic. Forces applied to them change their shape. The forces do this by pulling the chain molecules apart. The molecules return to where they were when the forces are taken away. Cross linking between chains improves this effect.

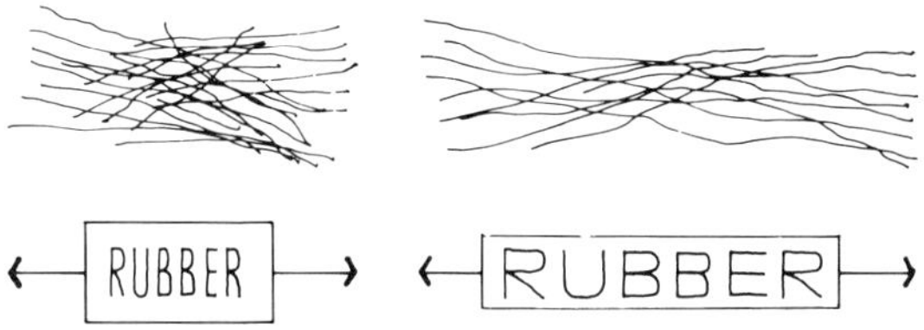


Sulphur atoms can link carbon atoms in different chains. Carbon atoms link directly as well. Both make the rubber more elastic. It improves strength and toughness. Cross linking makes it less plastic.

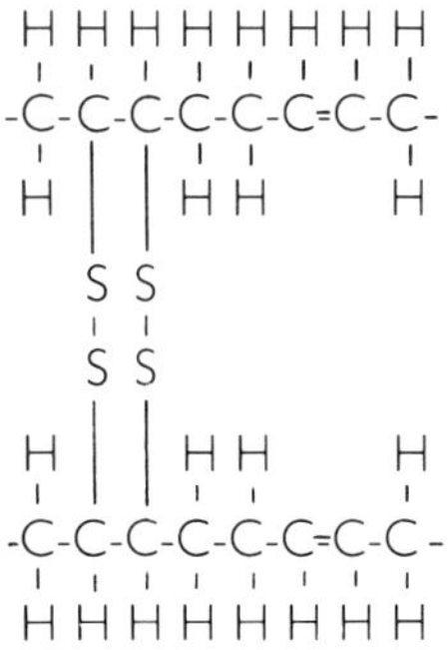

Rubber, sulphur and carbon black are mixed. The mixture is fed into a heated mould. It forms a hard, tough elastic shape. Tyres are made in this way. The process is called vulcanization. Foam rubber needs no mould. A substance is added to produce gas. The heated mixture forms a froth. It cools to a solid.

Plastics have thousands of uses. They are needed for contact lenses, tennis rackets, nylon rope, nylon stockings, pop records, T–shirts, roof insulation, floor carpets, tape decks, trousers and many more.

# Nitrogen

Write down all you know about the element nitrogen.

### Experiment 10.1 The properties of nitrogen

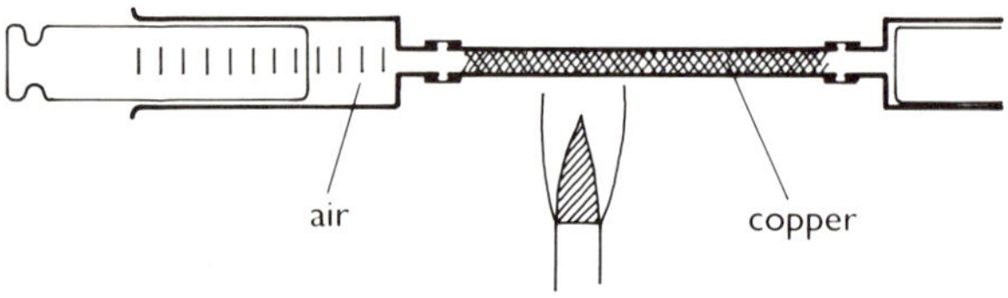


**Fill a tube with tiny pieces of copper wire. Connect a syringe at each end. Have one syringe full of air. Read off its volume. Heat a section of the copper. Push the air through it.**

**Heat the next section. Push the air back into the first syringe. Do this until the heated copper shows no change. Read off the volume of air remaining. Bubble it into test tubes.**

**Test the gas with a wet litmus paper, a lighted splint and burning magnesium. Invert a test tube of gas in dilute acid. Invert a second test tube of gas in sodium hydroxide solution.**

What gas remains in the syringe?
What percentage of air is this gas?
Is it a reactive element?

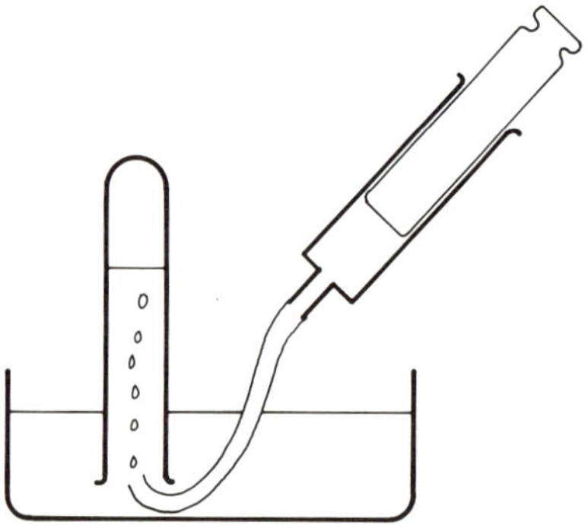

Air is mainly oxygen and nitrogen. Heated copper takes out the oxygen. About 78% of air is nitrogen. 0.03% is carbon dioxide. Carbon dioxide is in the nitrogen we tested. It is too small to matter.

Only magnesium reacts with nitrogen. It almost goes on burning. It combines to form a white solid. This is magnesium nitride. Nitrogen is not a reactive element.

The atomic number of nitrogen is 7.
Its relative atomic mass is 14. Its position is shown.

| **Element** | C | Nitrogen | O | F | Neon | Na | Mg | Al | Si |
|---|---|---|---|---|---|---|---|---|---|
| **Atomic Number** | 6 | 7 | 8 | 9 | 10 | 11 | 12 | 13 | 14 |

Answer these questions:
What is the symbol for nitrogen?
How many protons does a nitrogen atom contain?
How many neutrons are there in its nucleus?
How many electrons does a nitrogen atom have?
How many electrons fill the first shell?
How many does this leave for the second shell?
What is the electron structure of nitrogen?
What is the electron stucture of the nearest noble gas?

Atomic Number = number of protons in the atom.
Number of electrons = number of protons.
Number of neutrons = atomic mass − atomic number.

the N atom has 7 protons
7 electrons
$14 - 7 = 7$ neutrons

The electron structure of a nitrogen atom is 2.5.
For the nearest noble gas, neon, it is 2.8.
A nitrogen atom will gain three electrons.

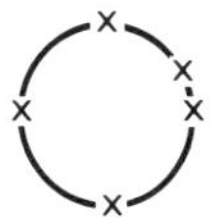

The structure of the magnesium atom is 2.8.2.
What is the formula of magnesium nitride? It is a solid. What type of bond is likely to be holding its atoms together?

A solid is likely to be ionic.
A magnesium atom provides two electrons. It becomes $Mg^{2+}$. Three magnesium atoms supply six electrons. They satisfy two nitrogen atoms. Each nitrogen atom becomes the ion $N^{3-}$.

$Mg\,(2.8.2) \rightarrow Mg^{2+} + 2e$
$N\,(2.5) + 3e \rightarrow N^{3-}$

The change from N to $N^{3-}$ needs a great deal of energy. Only very active metals can supply it. Calcium, sodium and magnesium burn in nitrogen.

$3Mg^{2+}.\ 2N^{3-}$

## Nitrogen and food

### Experiment 10.2 Heating foods with soda lime

**Heat a little powdered meat in a small test tube. Smell with care any gas given off. Hold a wet litmus paper in the mouth of the tube. Test any gas with a lighted splint.**

**Mix a little powdered meat with soda lime. Heat this in the same way. Use the same tests. Use other foods in place of meat. Milk, corn flakes, sugar, crisps, bread and fish may be used. They should be dry and powdered.**

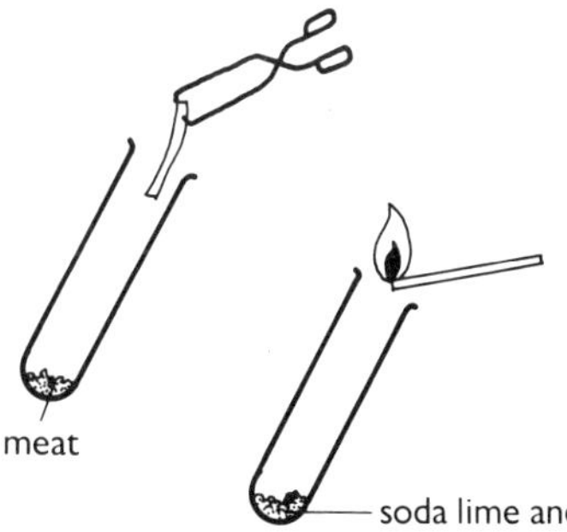


The smell suggests that a gas is given off.
Do you recognize it by its smell?
Is it given off by all foods or only some?
What happens to the litmus and the lighted splint?
Are other substances formed during the heating?

Foods contain carbon compounds. This is why heating makes then char. Condensation forms in the tube. This is probably water. Some foods give a gas on heating. It has a pungent smell. It turns litmus blue. It must be the gas ammonia. Ammonia has the same smell as smelling salts.

Not all foods give ammonia. Only those which contain protein do so. Soda lime makes the gas come off more quickly.

# *Ammonia*

We can buy ammonia as a concentrated solution in water. The solution is called aqueous ammonia.

**Experiment 10.3 To find out what elements ammonia contains**

**Put aqueous ammonia in the tube with a side neck. Add bits of pumice. Gently heat it to get ammonia. Pass the gas through quicklime to dry it.**

**At the same time heat the black copper oxide. Collect liquid in the cooled tube. Collect gas over water.**

**Test the boiling point of the liquid. Try other tests on it. Test the gas with litmus. Find out if magnesium burns in it.**

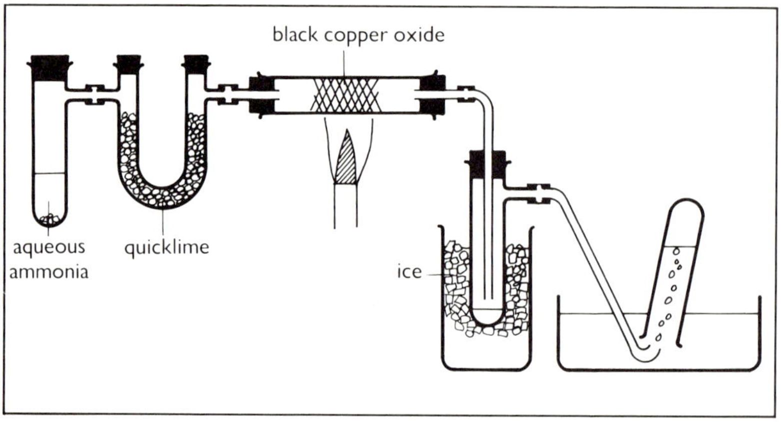


What happens to the heated copper(II) oxide?
What substance is the oxide giving up?
Does its boiling point show what the liquid is?
What other tests did you use on the liquid?
What is the gas collected in the test tubes?
Complete the word equation
ammonia + copper(II) oxide → ? + ? + ?

The gas puts out a lighted splint. Magnesium nearly burns in it. Litmus is not changed. The gas is nitrogen.

The boiling point of the liquid is 100 °C. It could be water. It turns white anhydrous copper sulphate blue.

The copper oxide is reduced to copper. It gives up oxygen.

Where does the water come from? The ammonia is dried. Water must be a product of the reaction. Its oxygen comes from the copper(II) oxide. Its hydrogen must come from ammonia. The reaction is

| | | | | | | | | |
|---|---|---|---|---|---|---|---|---|
| ammonia | + | copper oxide | → | nitrogen | + | water | + | copper |
| ? | + | $CuO$ | → | $N_2$ | + | $H_2O$ | + | $Cu$ |

Ammonia is a compound of nitrogen and hydrogen. You know their electron structures. Use them to work out a formula for ammonia.

The electron structure of nitrogen is 2.5. Its atom therefore needs three electrons to reach 2.8. It can get them by sharing with other atoms. Three shared pairs make three covalent bonds. The formula of the gas ammonia must be $NH_3$.

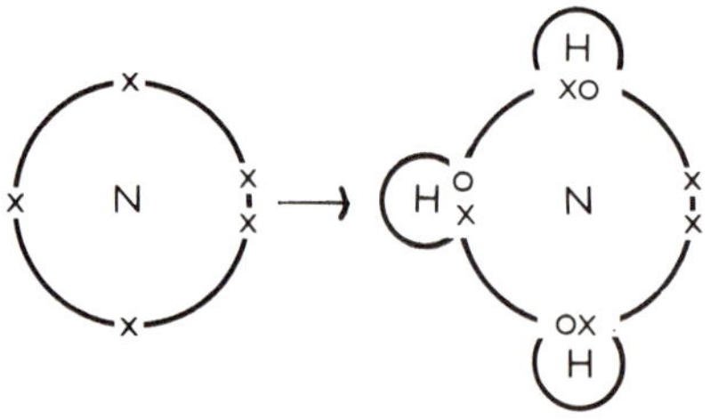

## *Experiment 10.4 To make and test ammonia

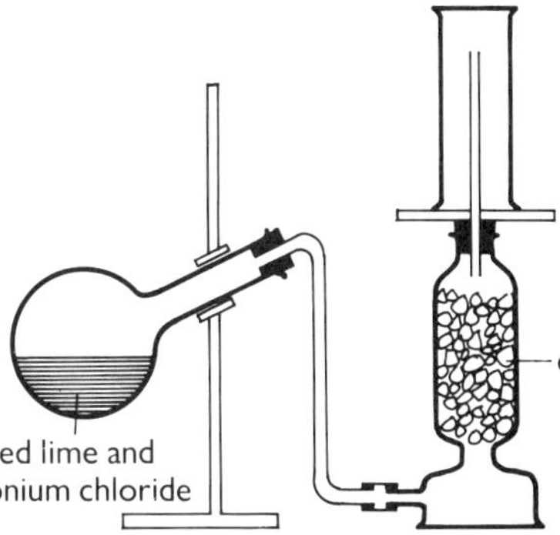


Mix equal amounts of slaked lime and ammonium chloride. Heat the mixture in a round bottomed flask. Dry the gas with quicklime in a tower. Fill four gas jars with the gas. Use a damp litmus to find out when each jar is full.

Invert a jar of gas in water. Remove the cover. Test the water with an indicator.

Invert a gas jar in dilute acid. Remove the cover.

Make a gas jar of hydrogen chloride. Invert it over a gas jar of ammonia. Remove the covers.

Hold a lighted splint over a gas jar of ammonia. Remove the cover from the jar. The ammonia rises.

Does water rise into the gas jar of ammonia?
Does the dilute acid rise into the jar?
How well does the gas dissolve in each case?
What do ammonia and hydrogen chloride form when mixed?

Fit a round bottomed flask as shown. Close the clip on the rubber tubing. Take out the stopper. Fill the flask with ammonia. Dip the end of the glass tube in water. Stopper the flask with it. Colour water with Universal Indicator. Put the rubber tube into the water. Open the clip.

What do you see?
Why does it happen?

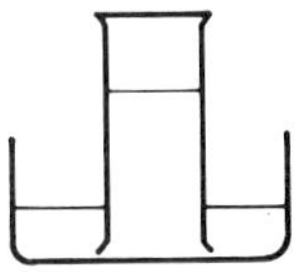

Water rises into the gas jar. So does dilute acid. Ammonia must be dissolving in each liquid. Water rushes into the flask. A fountain is formed. Water rushing in shows that the ammonia has gone. It can only have dissolved in water on the tube. Ammonia must be very soluble in water. Alkali forms.

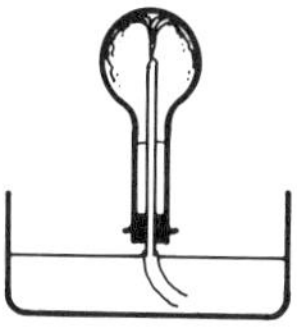

Ammonia and hydrogen chloride give white smoke. This settles on the jar as crystals like salt. Ammonia puts out a lighted splint. A pale yellow flame lingers above the splint. Ammonia nearly burns in air.

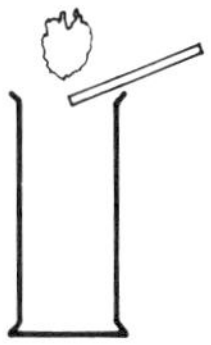

# *Ammonium compounds*

Here is the ammonia molecule again. Its atoms are joined by covalent bonds. Each bond is a shared pair of electrons. Both atoms supply one electron of the pair.

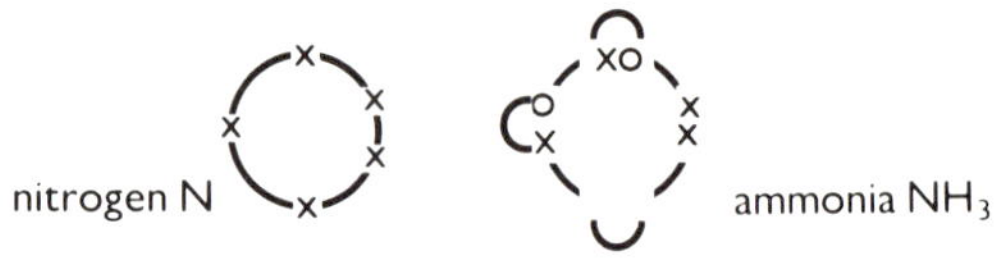


An ammonia molecule has an unused pair of electrons. This spare pair can be used for bonding. For example, a hydrogen ion, $H^+$, has no electrons. It can bond to ammonia using the spare pair. The result is $NH_4^+$. It behaves like the sodium ion, $Na^+$. It is therefore called the ammonium ion.

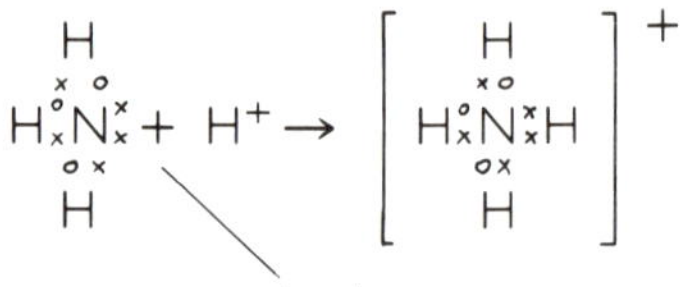


The bond is still a shared pair of electrons. Both electrons are supplied by one of the atoms. This explains why aqueous ammonia is an alkali. An ammonia molecule takes an $H^+$ ion from water. This leaves a hydroxyl ion, $OH^-$. Ammonia puts $OH^-$ ions into water.

$$NH_3 + H_2O \rightarrow NH_4^+ + OH^-$$

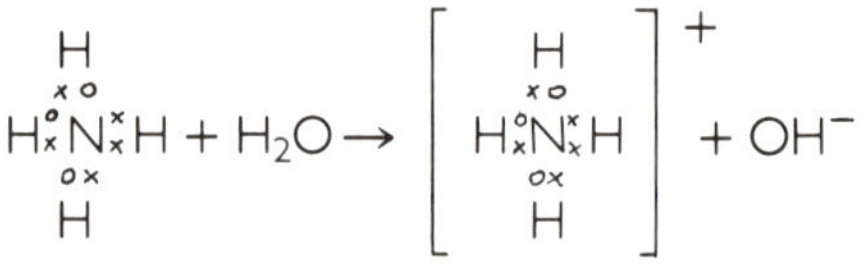

Ammonia and hydrogen chloride react. White crystals form. An ammonia molecule takes an $H^+$ from HCl. Together they form $NH_4^+$. This leaves a $Cl^-$ ion. The ions attract each other. They form a crystal lattice, as in sodium chloride. The white crystals are a salt. It is called ammonium chloride.

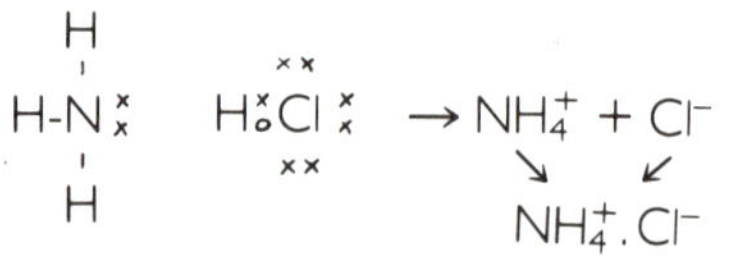

This bonding shows how ammonia reacts with acids. Nitric acid contains $H^+$ and $NO_3^+$ ions in solution. $NH_3$ reacts with $H^+$. The solution now contains $NH_4^+$ and $NO_3^-$ ions. When it evaporates crystals form. They are the salt ammonium nitrate.

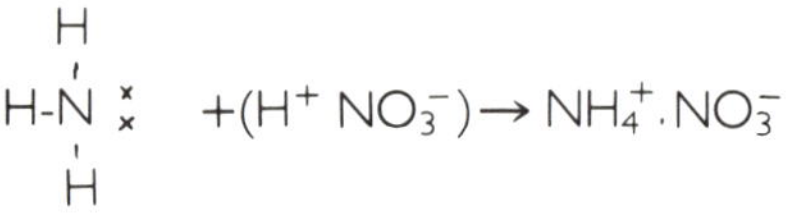

### Experiment 10.5 Heating ammonium salts

**Heat a few ammonium chloride crystals in a dry test tube.**

**Put some crystals in a second test tube. Stick a wet litmus paper just above them. Put in some rocksill fibre. Put a second litmus paper just above it. Heat the crystals. Watch the litmus.**

What happens to the heated crystals?
What changes in the litmus papers did you see?
Can you work out what these changes mean?

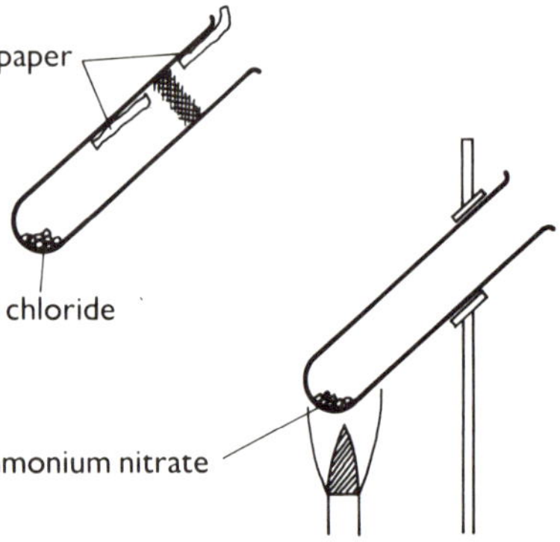


***Put a small pinch of ammonium nitrate crystals in a dry test tube. Hold it in a clamp. Put safety screens around it. Heat it gently.**

What happens?
What may one of the products be?

Heat does not melt ammonium chloride. No liquid forms. The crystals slowly disappear. They form again on the sides of the tube.

Both litmus papers turn blue. Ammonia must be formed by heating. The bottom litmus then turns red. This means that hydrogen chloride must be formed. Heat must make the crystals decompose. Ammonia and hydrogen chloride are formed. Ammonia molecules move the faster.

They reach the litmus first. The fibre helps separate the gases.

$$NH_4^+.Cl^- \underset{\text{cooling}}{\overset{\text{heating}}{\rightleftharpoons}} NH_3 + HCl$$

The reaction is reversible.

Ammonium nitrate decomposes. It explodes gently. It may blow smoke rings. One product looks like steam. The other is a gas. It is called dinitrogen oxide. It was once used as an anaesthetic called laughing gas. Its formula is $N_2O$.

$$NH_4NO_3 \text{ or } (NH_4^+.NO_3^-) \rightarrow N_2O + 2H_2O$$

Packing bags of fertilizer.

## The uses of ammonia and its compounds

Ammonia has many uses. It is a grease remover. It also softens v/ater. It is used in the manufacture of many other substances. Washing soda and nitric acid are two of these. One of the monomers needed to make nylon is another.

Ammonium salts are made by passing ammonia into acid solutions. The solutions are then evaporated to give crystals.

Ammonium chloride is used in dry cells. It is used as a flux. It cleans metal surfaces before soldering.

Ammonium nitrate is used as an explosive. It can be used alone or mixed with other substances. It is an important fertilizer. Mixed with chalk ammonium nitrate is called nitrochalk. Chalk makes acid soils neutral. Chalk is also there to reduce the risk of explosion.

Ammonium sulphate is a famous fertilizer. It is called 'sulphate of ammonia'. Ammonia and its salts put nitrogen into the soil. Large amounts of them are used. Read the section on fertilizers.

All these uses need large amounts of ammonia. A cheap method of making it on the large scale is needed. It is made from nitrogen and hydrogen.

Sulphate of ammonia silo.

# *The manufacture of ammonia*

About 8 million tonnes of ammonia are manufactured in Britain every year. Nitrogen and hydrogen are used. These gases react very slowly. The reaction is reversible. It also gives out heat.

$N_2(g) + 3H_2(g) \rightleftharpoons 2NH_3(g)$

$\Delta H$ for this reaction is minus

What methods can we use to speed up a reaction? Heating is one method. Another is to use a catalyst. We can combine both methods. The gases are passed through hot iron. This acts as the catalyst.

Look at the equation. Four molecules of the mixed gases react. They give only two molecules of product. Pressure affects this kind of change. High pressure makes the gas volume smaller. More ammonia is formed.

Nitrogen is made from liquid air (Book 1). Hydrogen is made from oil or natural gas. The two are mixed. The mixture is compressed to 250 times air pressure. It is passed through hot iron at 500 °C. The catalyst is in a strong steel cylinder.

The gases react. The mixture leaves the cylinder. It contains about 12% ammonia. Under pressure ammonia turns to liquid as its cools. This separates ammonia from unused gases. They are used again. Ammonia is stored under pressure in its liquid form. The method is called the Haber Process.

**Summary**

78% of air is nitrogen. Its molecule is diatomic. It is written $N_2$. Nitrogen is not reactive. It puts out a lighted splint. It does not burn. Nitrogen does not react with acid, alkali or lime water.

Its electron structure is 2.5. When it reacts a nitrogen atom needs to gain three electrons. Active metals burn in it. The ion $N^{3-}$ is formed.

$3Mg + N_2 \rightarrow 3Mg^{2+}.2N^{3-}$

($Mg_3N_2$) magnesium nitride

Protein foods heated with soda lime give the gas ammonia. It is also made by heating slaked lime with ammonium chloride. Ammonia turns moist litmus blue. It can be recognized by this and by its smell.

Ammonia has the formula $NH_3$. The atoms are joined by covalent bonds. $NH_3$ has a 'spare pair' of electrons. With them it bonds to a hydrogen ion. The result is an ammonium ion, $NH_4^+$.

$$\begin{matrix} & H & \\ H\text{-}N & & \overset{\times}{\times} + H^+ \rightarrow NH_4^+ \\ & H & \end{matrix}$$

Ammonia is very soluble in water. Aqueous ammonia is an alkali. It contains hydroxyl ions, OH

$NH_3 + H_2O \rightarrow NH_4^+ + OH^-$

Ammonia also reacts with acids. The products are ammonium salts.

$NH_3 + HCl \rightarrow NH_4^+.Cl^-$

Ammonia is manufactured by the Haber Process. Nitrogen and hydrogen are mixed and compressed. They pass through a catalyst, iron, at 500 °C. As the products cool, ammonia turns to a liquid. It separates from unused gases which are used again. The reaction is exothermic.

reactants
catalyst
temperature
separation

$$N_2(g) + 3H_2(g) \rightarrow 2NH_3(g) \quad \Delta H \text{ is minus}$$

Ammonia is used to make other substances. It and its salts are fertilizers. They supply nitrogen to the soil. Ammonium salts decompose on heating.

## Questions

1. Salt A consists of white crystals. It is heated with slaked lime. A colourless gas, B, is formed. B has a sharp smell. It turns litmus blue. It is very soluble in water giving solution C. Sulphuric acid is added to C. When the solution is neutral it is evaporated. White crystals of solid D remain.

   Name one salt A which gives these results.
   Name the gas B and give its formula.
   What ions are present in solution C?
   Name the white solid D.
   B is made on the large scale from two gases, E and F. Name these gases.
   They are passed through a catalyst. Name the catalyst.
   Explain what the word catalyst means.

2. Ammonium nitrate is a fertilizer. What element does it put into the soil?
   Why do plants need this element?
   Explain two natural ways in which this element gets into soil.
   Ammonium nitrate fertilizer is usually mixed with chalk. Give one reason why.

3. Ammonia is heated with copper(II) oxide. The oxide is reduced to copper. A colourless liquid is formed. It boils at 100 °C. What element does this show to be present in ammonia? Give reasons.

4. In each part, five answers are given. They are labelled A, B, C, D and E. Only one of these answers is correct. Choose the correct answer.

a) A certain gas puts out a lighted splint. It does not affect lime water. It does not burn. The gas is
A carbon dioxide
B hydrogen
C nitrogen
D oxygen
E natural gas

b) All these statements about ammonia are true, except one. Which statement is not true?
A Ammonia turns moist litmus blue
B Ammonia is very soluble in water
C Ammonia has a recognizable smell
D Ammonia reacts with hydrogen chloride
E Ammonia is an ionic (electrovalent) compound

c) Ammonia dissolves in water. The solution is an alkali because
A Ammonia is a covalent compound
B The solution contains hydrogen ions, $H^+$
C The solution contains hydroxyl ions, $OH^-$
D The solution smells of ammonia
E It turns litmus red

d) A food is heated with soda lime. It gives off ammonia. This kind of food is
A a carbohydrate
B a fat
C a protein food
D a mineral salt
E sugar

# *Ammonia and nitric acid*

Ammonia is less dense than air. It rises out of a gas jar. It puts out a lighted splint. It almost burns in the air above the jar. It may burn in oxygen.

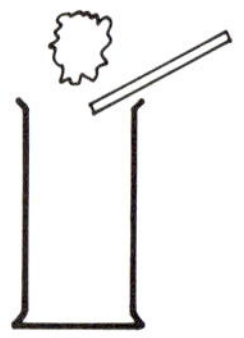

### *Experiment 10.6 Ammonia and oxygen

**Set up the apparatus shown in the diagram. Pass ammonia up the middle tube. Pass oxygen up the other tube. Hold a lighted splint above the middle tube. Reverse the gas connections. Hold a lighted splint above the middle tube again.**

Are the two flames exactly the same?

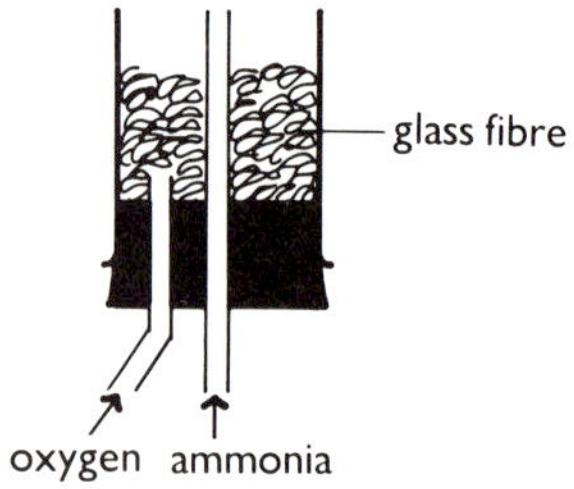


The fibre spreads the oxygen. It surrounds the middle tube. Ammonia burns in it with a yellow flame. Oxygen burns in ammonia. The two flames are alike. This tells us what a flame is.

**A flame is the space in which gases react. The reaction gives heat and light.**

Ammonia does not burn in air. It does burn in pure oxygen. It may react with air if we use a catalyst.

### *Experiment 10.7 Ammonia and air with a catalyst

**Take a flask. Put in a little concentrated aqueous ammonia. Hold a coil of platinum wire above the neck. Put a piece of white paper behind it.**

**Gently heat the coil. Either a) touch it with a small flame or b) pass a current through it. Puff air into the flask to get the maximum effect. Hold a wet litmus paper above the coil. Try a Universal Indicator paper as well.**

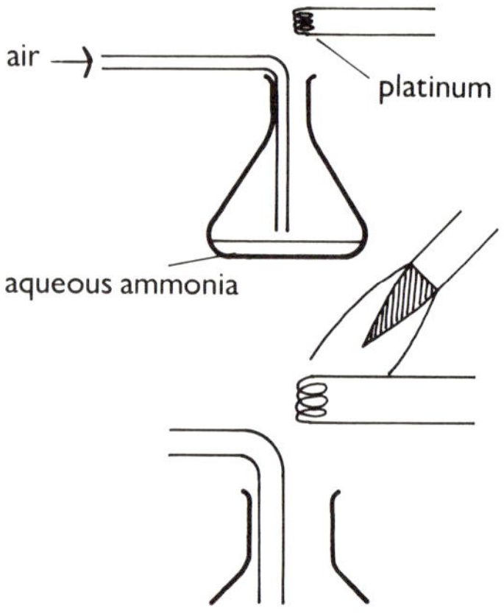


Did you see any new substance?
Did the white paper let you see its colour?
What happens to the indicator papers?
Is there any change in the platinum?
Is there any chemical change?
If so, is it exothermic or endothermic?

The aqueous solution gives ammonia gas. It mixes with the air. The mixture passes over the platinum. This acts as a hot catalyst. The two gases must be in the right proportions, then the products of the reaction can be seen. The white paper makes it easier.

The best results show a brown gas. The litmus paper becomes red. Water and the gas form an acid. The platinum glows red hot. The reaction is exothermic.

Ammonia reacts with the oxygen in the air. Too much ammonia may be present. It can react with the brown gas. No brown gas will be seen. The catalyst may still become hot. Puffing in air alters the ammonia–air proportions. We can get the best results.

In Experiment 10.6 ammonia burns in oxygen. Nitrogen and steam are formed.

$$4NH_3 + 3O_2 \rightarrow 2N_2 + 6H_2O$$

With a catalyst the products are different. The brown gas is nitrogen dioxide. It reacts with water to give an acid solution. It contains two acids.

One is nitric acid, $HNO_3$. The other is nitrous acid, $HNO_2$. Air slowly oxidizes it to nitric acid.

Manufacturing nitric acid.

## The manufacture of nitric acid

The method of Experiment 10.7 is used. Ammonia is mixed with ten times its volume of air. Reaction happens in a converter. The catalyst is wire gauze. This is stretched across the converter.

The gauze is 90% platinum. It is heated electrically. Then heat from the reaction keeps it at about 900 °C. Ammonia and air react to form nitrogen monoxide, NO.

$$4NH_3 + 5O_2 \rightarrow 6H_2O + 4NO \quad \Delta H \text{ is minus}$$

The gases which leave the converter are cooled. Nitrogen monoxide reacts with oxygen from air. The brown gas nitrogen dioxide, $NO_2$, is formed.

$$4NO(g) + 2O_2(g) \rightarrow 4NO_2(g)$$

It is mixed with more air and dissolved in water. Only nitric acid is formed in solution.

$$4NO_2(g) + 2H_2O(l) + O_2(g) \rightarrow 4HNO_3(aq)$$

In solution its ions are $H^+$ and $NO_3^-$ .

Nitric acid has many important uses. So have its salts. They are called nitrates. They all contain the nitrate ion, $NO_3^-$. They all dissolve in water.

*Grace: I'm making nitric acid. Get the catalyst.*
*George: I got the cat a list. He can't read it though.*

# Nitric acid and nitrates

Sodium nitrate is found in nature. Large amounts once existed in Chile. It was used to manufacture nitric acid, before the ammonia method was used. It is also a well known fertilizer.

### *Experiment 10.8  To make nitric acid

**All the apparatus must be made of glass. Put a teaspoonful of sodium nitrate crystals in the flask. Cover them with concentrated sulphuric acid. Gently heat the mixture. Collect any liquid in a cooled test tube.**

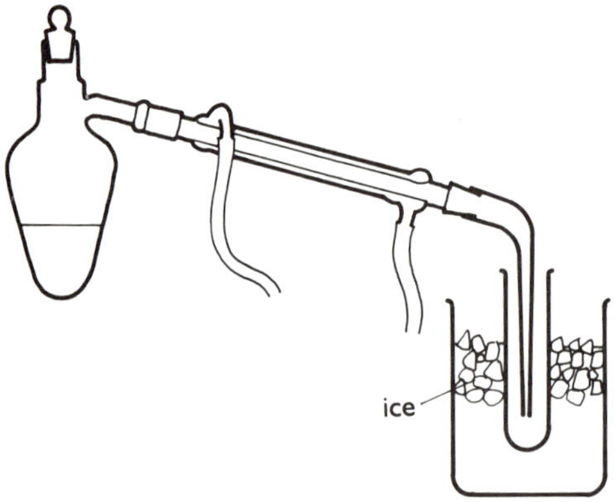


**Use it for three tests. Do these in a fume cupboard. Hold a white screen behind them.**

**a) Add a little of the liquid to copper in a test tube.**
**b) Heat some of the liquid in a crucible. When it boils drop in a red hot piece of charcoal.**
**c) Heat a small pile of sawdust on a tin lid. Add drops of the liquid to it using a dropper.**

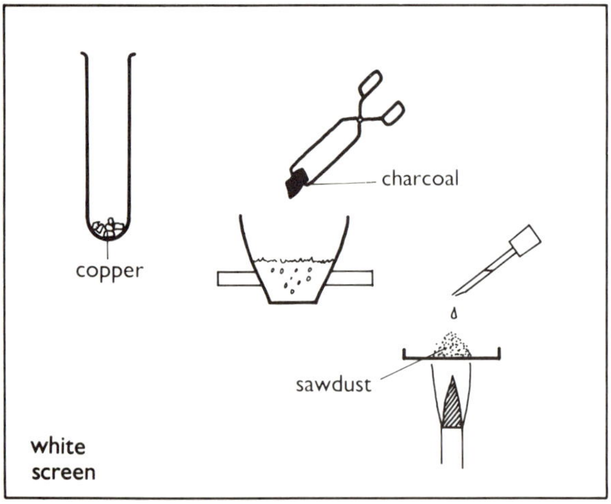


What new substance is formed in every test?
Are carbon and copper very reactive elements?
Does copper react with other acids?
Do non-metals such as carbon usually react with acids?

Sodium nitrate and sulphuric acid react. Drops of oily liquid form in the condenser. They collect in the test tube. This is colourless nitric acid. Some brown gas may also form. It dissolves in the nitric acid. It gives the acid a yellow colour.

Copper and carbon are not reactive. Both react vigorously with nitric acid. Sawdust may burst into flame. All three give brown nitrogen dioxide gas. The acid is losing oxygen.

$$4HNO_3 \rightarrow 2H_2O + 4NO_2 + O_2$$

Nitric acid is able to oxidize. It oxidizes charcoal to carbon dioxide. Sawdust burns in oxygen from the acid. Copper may be oxidized to copper(II) oxide. This can then react with the acid to form a salt.

You can see why corks and rubber stoppers are not used. They would react with the nitric acid formed. Another all-glass apparatus is shown. It can be used instead of flask and condenser.

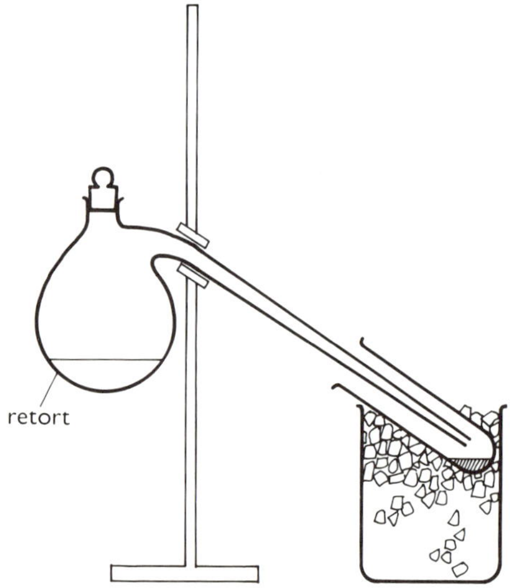


Nitric acid is an oxidant as well as an acid.

## Experiment 10.9 Dilute nitric acid and nitrates

Into separate test tubes put
a) magnesium ribbon, pieces of copper, zinc lumps;
b) black copper(II) oxide, zinc oxide;
c) copper(II) carbonate, marble, sodium carbonate.

To each of the eight substances add dilute nitric acid. If there is no change with cold acid, heat gently. Test any gas with lighted splint and with damp litmus paper.

Do any of the metals give off hydrogen?
Which substances give the gas carbon dioxide?
Are any of the products coloured?
Is brown nitrogen dioxide a product of reaction?
Is any unknown gas formed?

Magnesium and cold dilute acid give hydrogen. The mixture becomes very hot. Copper reacts when heated. So does zinc. A colourless gas is formed. It is not hydrogen. It becomes brown at the mouth of the tube.

Copper compounds give blue solutions. They contain copper(II) nitrate. Other nitrates have no colour. There are four ways of manufacturing nitrates.

dilute nitric acid } + metal → nitrate + hydrogen or other gases
+ metal oxide → nitrate + water
+ metal carbonate → nitrate + water + carbon dioxide

The fourth method uses alkali and acid.

*Grace: What does a policeman on night duty earn?*
*George: What does he earn?*
*Grace: Copper nitrate!*

## Experiment 10.10 To make sodium nitrate crystals

Use the method of Experiment 6.10. Use dilute nitric acid in the burette. Add it to sodium hydroxide solution. Keep the crystals for later use.

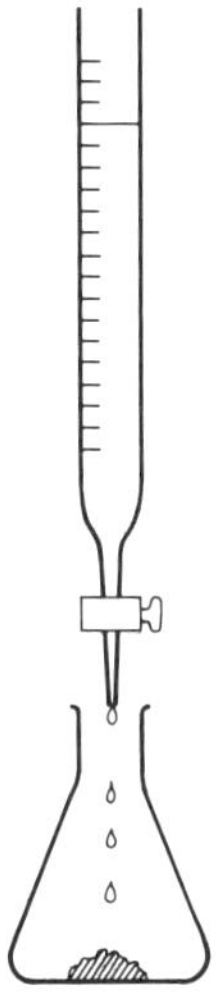

We need a test to recognize a nitrate.

## Experiment 10.11 The brown ring test

**Put solutions of several nitrates in separate test tubes. Include very dilute nitric acid. Add to each iron(II) sulphate solution. Tilt each tube. Pour in concentrated sulphuric acid. Let it run to the bottom.**

What result is the same in every test tube?

The sulphuric acid runs to the bottom. It forms a separate layer. A brown ring forms above the acid. It proves a nitrate is present.

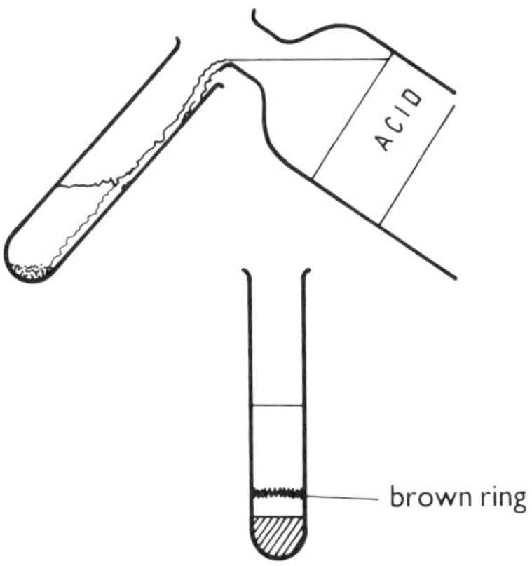

# Heating nitrates

## Experiment 10.12 To heat sodium nitrate

**a) Use the crystals from Experiment 10.10. Put them in a small test tube. Hold it in a holder. Heat gently and then strongly. Test any gas with a lighted and then a glowing splint.**

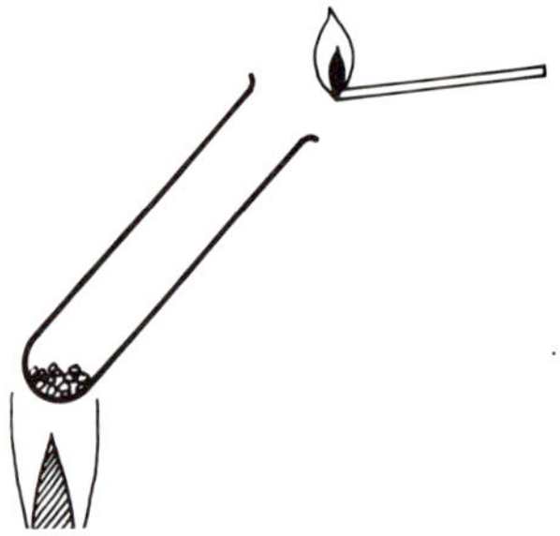

Are the crystals easy to melt?
What result suggests that a gas is given off?
Do the splints show what this gas is?
Did you see other changes during the heating?
Is sodium nitrate easy or hard to decompose?

**b) Heat and test other nitrates in the same way. Some contain water of crystallization. Genly heat to drive this off as steam. Then heat the solid nitrate. Compare results for potassium, magnesium and copper nitrates.**

Sodium nitrate is not easy to melt. It needs strong heating. Very strong heating is needed to decompose it. Bubbles appear. The gas is oxygen. The liquid becomes pale yellow. It cools to an off-white solid, sodium nitrite, $NaNO_2$. It is a salt of nitrous acid.

Does potassium nitrate decompose in the same way?
Is it harder or easier to decompose?
Is potassium above sodium in the Activity Series?

Copper nitrate crystals give steam.
What gas is seen when the nitrate decomposes?
Does the gas contain oxygen?
A black powder is left after heating. What is it?
Is the nitrate easy to decompose?
Which needs stronger heating, magnesium or copper nitrate?

Potassium nitrate and sodium nitrate decompose in the same way. Both need very strong heating. Potassium nitrate is less easy. Copper is low in the Activity Series. Its nitrate is easy to decompose. Black copper oxide forms. Brown nitrogen dioxide is seen. It is mixed with oxygen. Magnesium nitrate gives the same gases.

***c) Heat a little lead nitrate in the apparatus shown. Pass the gases through the cooled tube. Collect any gas which comes through. Test it with a glowing splint.**

What substance remains in the tube?

Nitrogen dioxide condenses to a liquid in the cold tube. Oxygen bubbles through the water. The other product is solid lead(II) oxide.

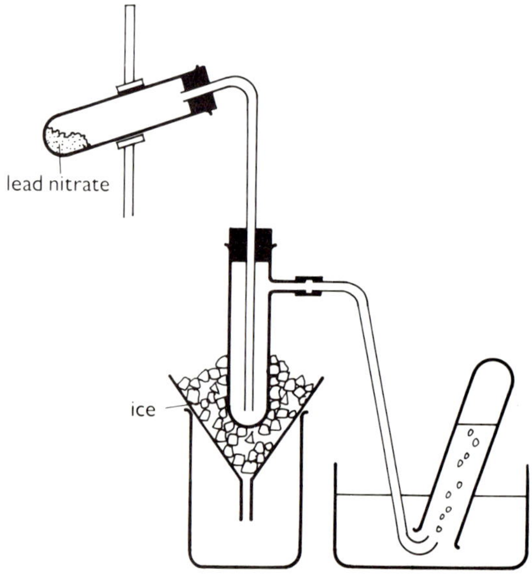

Heat decomposes nitrates. Nitrates of active metals form the nitrite and oxygen.

$$2NaNO_3 \rightarrow 2NaNO_2 + O_2$$

Other nitrates split up more easily. Nitrogen and oxygen are formed.

$$2Pb(NO_3)_2 \rightarrow 2PbO + 4NO_2 + O_2$$

The solid metal oxide is the other product. Mercury and silver oxides decompose too.

$$Hg(NO_3)_2 \rightarrow Hg + 2NO_2 + O_2$$

The final product from these nitrates is the metal.

## The uses of nitric acid

About three million tonnes of nitric acid are made in Britain every year. Most of it is used to make nitrates. They are important fertilizers. Nitrates provide plants with nitrogen. Ammonium nitrate is a fertilizer and an explosive. Potassium nitrate is used in making gunpowder. Sodium nitrate is used as a fertilizer.

Nitric acid reacts with carbon compounds. It adds nitro groups, $-NO_2$. This change needs concentrated sulphuric acid as well. They react with the cellulose in cotton. The result is gun cotton. They react with methylbenzene (toluene). The result is TNT.

Both substances are explosives. An explosion is a very fast reaction. It is over in a fraction of a second. The products are gases. Heat is given out in large quantities. The hot gases exert a huge pressure. They make room for themselves. Things around them are 'blown up'. Most explosions must be started. Detonators and heat can do this.

## Summary

Ammonia burns in oxygen. With a catalyst it also reacts with oxygen in air. Nitrogen monoxide forms. On cooling this reacts with oxygen. Brown nitrogen dioxide is formed. This gas dissolves in water. The solution contains two acids. One is nitric acid $HNO_3$. The other is nitrous acid, $HNO_2$. Oxygen from air oxidizes $HNO_2$ to $HNO_3$.

These changes are used to manufacture nitric acid. Ammonia is mixed with large amounts of air. The mixture passes through platinum gauze at 900 °C. The nitrogen dioxide is mixed with more air. It is then dissolved in water. Nitric acid is the product.

The salts of nitric acid are nitrates. They are made from the acid by four normal methods. They can be recognized by the 'brown ring' test. All nitrates decompose on heating. They do so in three main ways.

Nitrates of active metals give the nitrite and oxygen. Other nitrates give nitrogen dioxide and oxygen. Most of them leave a residue of the oxide. Some decompose to leave the metal itself.

Nitric acid oxidizes. It gives up oxygen. Brown nitrogen dioxide is one product. This shows that oxidation is taking place. The acid can react with the less active metals. Copper gives copper(II) nitrate.

Nitric acid is very important. It is used to make nitrate fertilizers. These provide nitrogen. It is also used to make explosives such as TNT.

## Questions on nitrogen and carbon chemistry

1. Nitrogen can be made from air. The apparatus for doing it is shown.

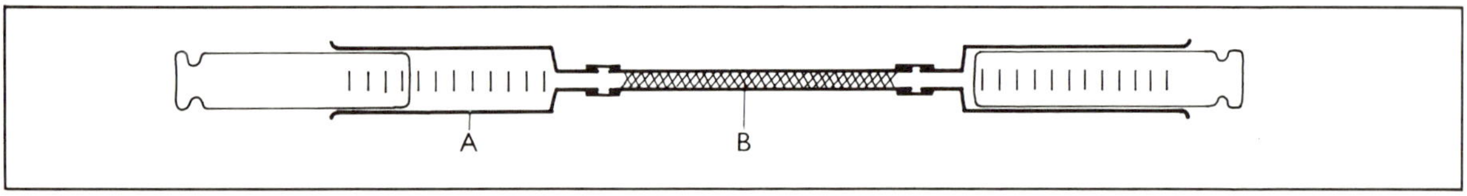


A contains 100 $cm^3$ of air. The substance in B is heated. The air is pushed through it several times. At the end the volume of gas left in A is 79 $cm^3$. It is tested.

a) Name vessel A.
b) What is the substance in B?
c) What colour is it at the start?
d) What colour does it become when heated?
e) What gas does it take out of the air?
f) What is the percentage of this gas in air?
g) Name the chief gas left in A at the end.
h) Name another gas present in small amounts.
j) What do these gases do to a lighted splint?

2. A powdered food is heated with soda lime. It blackens. Smoky vapour comes off. This smells like smelling salts. It turns red litmus blue. Mixed with hydrogen chloride it gives white smoke. This smoke settles as white crystals.

a) What is the black substance likely to be?
b) Is the food a carbohydrate, a fat or a protein?
c) Name one foodstuff which would give these results.
d) What do the tests with litmus show?
e) Only one common gas gives these test results. What is it?
f) Give the formula of this gas.
g) What ions in solution turn litmus blue?
h) Name the substance in the white crystals. Write an equation for the reaction which gives them.

3. Ammonia is made on a large scale by this reaction

$$\underset{\text{substance A}}{N_2(g)} + \underset{\text{substance B}}{3H_2(g)} \rightleftharpoons 2NH_3(g) \quad \Delta H \text{ is } -$$

a) Name substances A and B.
b) What does the sign $\rightleftharpoons$ mean?
c) $\Delta H$ is $-$. Is the reaction exothermic?
d) How does heat affect the speed of a reaction?
e) What is a catalyst?
f) Which substance is a catalyst for this reaction?
g) What does (g) mean in the equation?
h) What volume of B reacts with 10 $cm^3$ of A?
j) Why are A and B compressed before reaction?
k) As the products cool what happens to the ammonia?

4. A platinum coil is made red hot. It is put into the flask as shown. It continues to glow red hot. Brown gas is formed.

a) What two substances are reacting?
b) For what reason is platinum used?
c) Why does it stay red hot?
d) What is the name of the brown gas?
e) What is its formula?
f) What effect will the brown gas have on litmus?
g) What substance forms in water when the brown gas dissolves?
h) What substance is made on the large scale by these reactions?

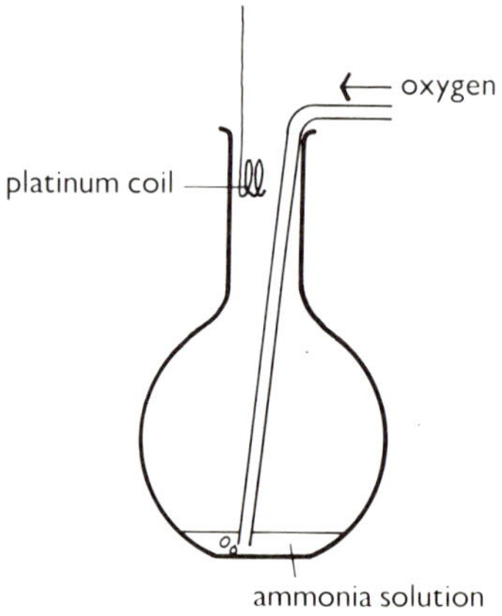


5. Give one important use of each of the following substances.

a) ammonia,
b) ammonium chloride,
c) ammonium sulphate,
d) nitric acid,
e) ammonium nitrate,
f) potassium nitrate.

6. Nitrates are made from nitric acid. Name the substance you would add to the acid to make
 a) sodium nitrate,
 b) ammonium nitrate,
 c) copper(II) nitrate,
 d) magnesium nitrate.

7. Nitrates decompose on heating in three ways:
 a) to form a nitrite and oxygen
 b) to form a metal oxide, nitrogen dioxide and oxygen.
 c) to form a metal, nitrogen dioxide and oxygen.
 In which way, a), b), or c) do these nitrates decompose:
 i) lead nitrate,
 ii) copper nitrate,
 iii) potassium nitrate?
 Explain how you would separate the two gases formed in b).

8. Choose the best answer in each case:
 a) The percentage of nitrogen in air is
 A 0.03%  B 1%  C 21%  D 78%  E 98%
 b) The formula of nitric acid is
 A $NO_2$  B NO  C $HNO_2$  D $HNO_3$  E $NH_3$
 c) Soil in a garden has just been limed with calcium hydroxide. It would be wrong to add one of the following fertilizers because it would react with the lime. Which one?
 A sodium nitrate
 B potassium nitrate
 C ammonium sulphate
 D sodium chloride
 E chalk
 d) Esters are formed by the reaction between
 A acid and alkali
 B alcohol and oxidizing agent
 C sugar and water with yeast present
 D alcohol and organic acid
 E monomer molecules of the same substance
 e) The formula of ethane is
 A $CH_4$, B $C_2H_4$, C $C_4H_{10}$, D $C_2H_6$, E $C_2H_2$

9. Give the name of each compound shown below as a formula:

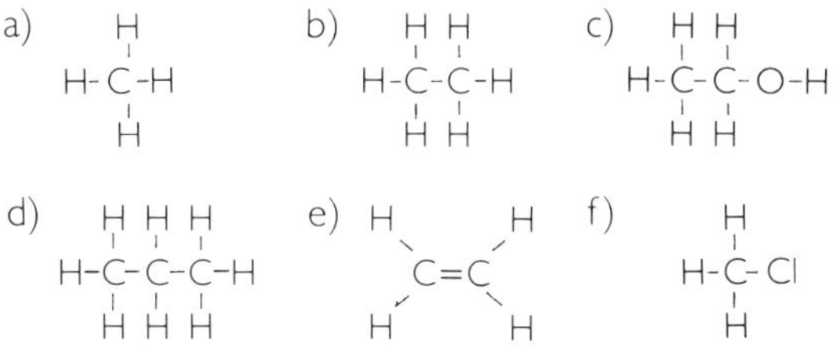

 i) Which formula contains a double bond?
 ii) Which of the six is an alcohol?
 iii) Three of the six substances belong to the same family or homologous series. Which ones?
 iv) Substance e) is shaken with bromine water. What would you see? Use this reaction to explain 'addition reaction' and 'unsaturated compound'.
 v) Use the formulae a) and f) to explain what is meant by a substitution reaction.
 vi) Which of the six substances can be used to form an ester?

10. Describe how you would make a small sample of
 a) soap, b) detergent in the laboratory.
 Explain why hard water affects soap. Does a detergent affect hard water in the same way?

11. Crude oil is distilled in a refinery. It takes place in a tall tower. Liquids are piped off at different heights up the tower. Explain how the method works. Use the words 'fraction', 'bubble caps', 'boiling point', 'gasoline'.

12. $CH_4 + 2O_2 \rightarrow CO_2 + 2H_2O \; \Delta H = -888$ kJ per mole
 Using the equation answer the following questions:
 a) Name the substance with formula $CH_4$.
 b) Is it an alkane or an alkene?
 c) How many molecules of oxygen does one molecule of $CH_4$ react with?
 d) What are the products of reaction?
 e) Is the reaction exothermic or endothermic?
 f) What does $\Delta H$ stand for?
 g) What does kJ stand for?
 h) What is one mole of $CH_4$? ($C = 12, H = 1$)
 i) Draw a structural formula for $CH_4$.
 j) Is it saturated or unsaturated?

13. Explain each of the following terms:
 a) monomer,
 b) polymer,
 c) isomers,
 d) homologous series,
 e) enzyme,
 f) fermentation.
 Give one example of each in your explanation.

14. The formula of propanol is $C_3H_7OH$. Draw two different structural formula for this formula. Name the two propanols they represent. What is this effect called?

# Fertilizers

Human beings need food. It gives us energy. It provides us with growth. Our bodies use it for repair and replacement of body tissue.

We grow plants and breed animals to use as food. The animals eat plants too. So all our food supply depends on plants. We need to grow them well.

How big is a carrot seed? How big is the carrot it grows into? Where does all the extra stuff come from?

### What do plants need for growth?

Plants need carbon, hydrogen and oxygen. They get them by taking in carbon dioxide and water. Using energy from sunlight they make sugar. The sugar is built up into starch and cellulose. These become the stem, roots and leaves of the plant. This process is called photosynthesis. Only a water shortage will stop photosynthesis.

Plants must have nitrogen, phosphorus and potassium. From nitrogen plants build protein. Potassium helps them to do this. Phosphorus promotes general growth. Most plants use compounds of the three elements.

Plants must also have compounds of calcium, sulphur and magnesium. Tiny amounts of other elements are needed. They are called 'trace elements'. Among them are iron, copper and manganese.

People and animals rely on plants for food.

### How does the plant crop get trace elements?

Plants use compounds of all these elements. They are present in most soils. They dissolve in water. The plants take them in through their roots.

In nature, plants grow, seed and die. They decay and break down into compost. This contains all the substances the plants took in. They pass back into the soil. The next lot of plants can use them.

The crops we grow are eaten. Human beings and animals use them as food. The soil loses some compounds. Manure puts some of them back but not all. The soil becomes poorer. It will not grow such good crops. Decayed vegetable matter (humus) is also needed.

Chemists can manufacture the compounds. They can be added to the soil. They are called fertilizers. They must dissolve in water in the soil. Then they make up for those lost. Fertilizers do not supply humus.

The common nitrogen fertilizers are nitrates and ammonium salts. Others are liquid ammonia and urea. Urea, $CO(NH_2)_2$, is made from ammonia.

Phosphates, salts of phosphoric(V) acid, supply phosphorus. The calcium salt occurs in nature. It is called 'phosphate rock'. It does not dissolve well. Sulphuric acid converts it into 'superphosphate'. This dissolves well, so that plant roots can take it in.

Potassium chloride, nitrate and sulphate supply potassium. Most fertilizers we buy are mixtures. They contain compounds of the three main elements. Some trace elements are there as well.

Moving bags of fertilizer in a warehouse using a robot machine.

## The Third World

Over 4000 million people live on the earth. One in eight of them is near to starving. Over half of them are without one kind of food or another. This is called malnutrition. People who suffer from it need our help. Most of them live in poorer countries. These people are often called 'The Third World'.

Richer countries can help in three main ways.
They can increase the world food supply.
They can ensure that it is shared out more fairly.
They can teach poorer people how to improve their crops.

Their crops fail for three main reasons. They suffer from water shortage or poor soil. The plants die of disease. Crops are eaten by pests. The growing plants may be eaten. Pests may also eat the crops after harvesting.

Sinking wells and building dams will help. Dams collect water in the rainy season. They store it for times of drought. Better types of seed and livestock help. They give bigger food yields. The use of fertilizers improves crops still more.

Chemical substances can prevent crop disease. Others can destroy the pests which eat the crops. Chemical sprays save crops. They can also have harmful effects. They may harm people. They kill useful insects.

Third World crops can fail because of water shortage.

Crops are sometimes destroyed by pests. These maize plants have been damaged by locusts.

# *How fast is a reaction?*

In a chemical change substances react. They are the reactants. Their atoms and molecules form new substances. These are called the products.

reactants → products

Many reactions are very slow. A piece of iron may take years to rust. Some reactions are very fast. An acid and alkali react the instant they meet. We prefer to slow down reactions like iron rusting. It is useful to be able to speed up many others.

The speed of a reaction is called its **rate**. We can measure it. We often measure the rates of other changes. How? We find out how some quantity alters. What is your rate of spending? How much money did you start with? How much has gone? In how many days?

| | |
|---|---|
| at 8 a.m. on Monday | 80p |
| at 8 a.m. on Friday | 20p |
| money spent | 60p |
| time taken | 4 days |
| rate of spending | $\frac{60}{4}$ |
| rate = 15p per day | |

A bucket has a hole in it. How fast does it leak?

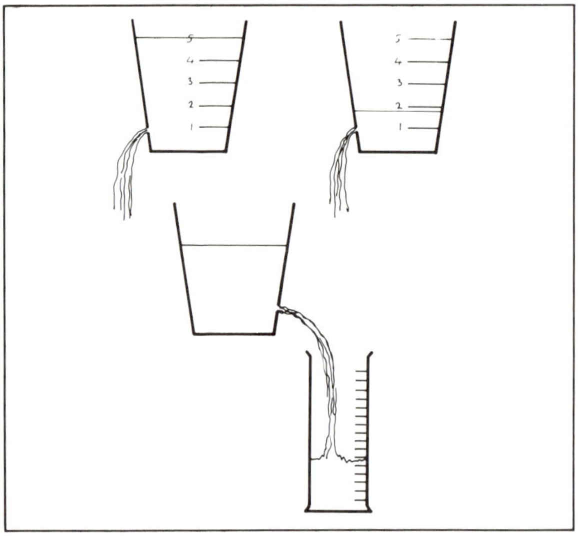


*Method 1.* Mark the bucket in litres. Fill it. Start a stop watch. Note the water level every minute. Work out rate of leaking in litres per minute. How fast is a reaction? Measure one reactant. Some will be used up. At intervals note how much is left. **Rate of reaction** will be in **moles** used per **second**.

*Method 2* is better. Fill the bucket. Note the time. Catch the leaking water. At intervals note the amount collected. Water is a product of the leak. A reaction forms products. Collect and measure one of them. Rate will be in **moles** formed per **second**.

Some factors alter the rate of reaction. Method 2 can show this. Collect the product in every case. Compare the amounts formed in the same time.

### Experiment 11.1 The effect of size when a solid reacts

Measure exactly 20 cm$^3$ of 2 M hydrochloric acid. Put it in a conical flask. Fit a stopper and delivery tube. Select large marble lumps of about the same size. Take 20 g of them. Pour them into the flask.

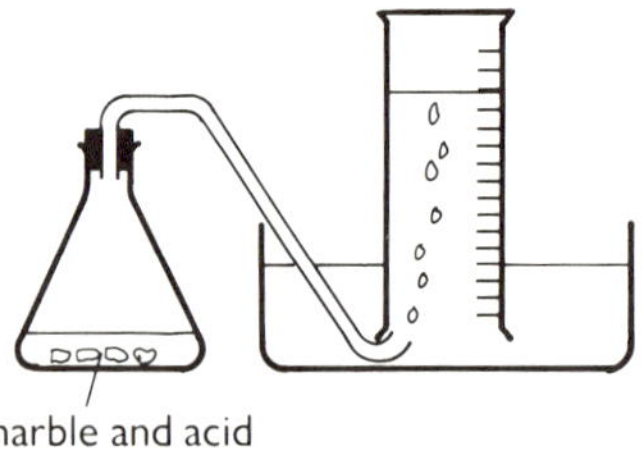


Stopper it at once. At the same moment start a stop watch. Collect the gas product in a measuring cylinder. Note the volume of gas every 30 seconds.

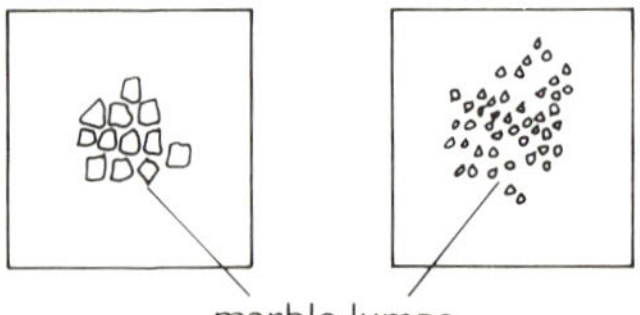


Take more of the marble lumps. Break them into smaller pieces. Take 20 g of these. With them do the same experiment again. Plot both sets of results as a graph.

One product of the reaction is carbon dioxide. The graph shows my results. Times are on the horizontal axis. From the graph we can get the volumes of gas formed after 30 seconds. Use *your* graph if you can.

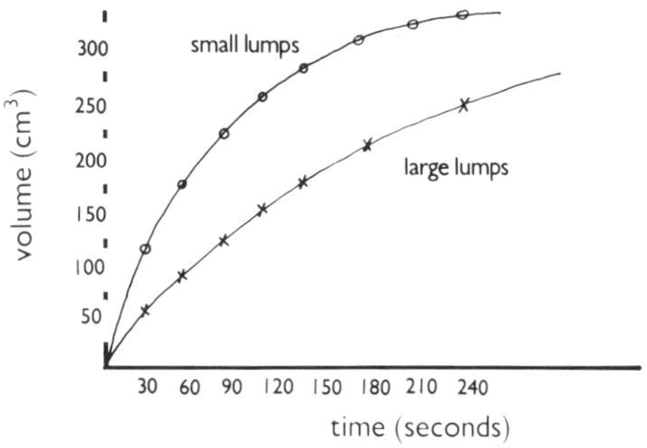


What volume did the large lumps give after 30 seconds?
What volume did the small lumps give after 30 seconds?
Which lumps give the faster reaction?
Can you explain why?

Acid and marble react only where they meet. This is at the marble surface. The smaller lumps give gas more quickly. With them rate of reaction is greater.

The drawing shows why. Cutting a large lump gives a greater surface. More marble and acid will meet.

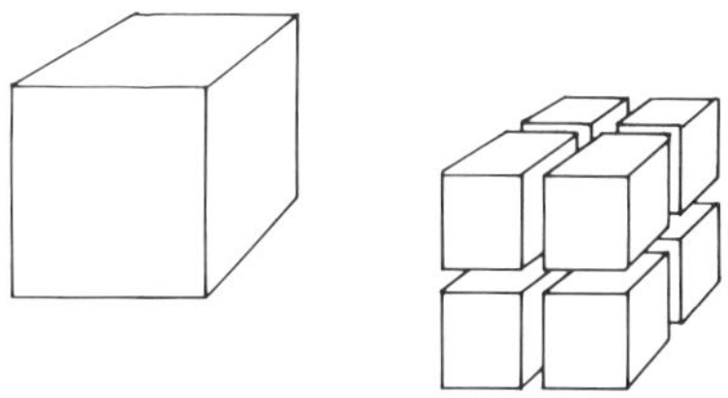

## Catalysts

A catalyst is a substance added to a reaction to alter its rate. It is still there at the end.

### Experiment 11.2 The action of catalysts

**Colour 10-volume hydrogen peroxide with Universal Indicator. Add drops of alkali until the colour is green. The hydrogen peroxide is then neutral.**

**a) Half fill four test tubes with the neutral solution. Stand them in water in a beaker. To tube 1 add dilute acid. To tube 2 add the same volume of alkali solution. Add the same volume of water to 3.**

**Heat the beaker. Watch the tubes. Compare how fast gas forms in them. Add to 4 a pinch of manganese(IV) oxide. Test the gas given off with a glowing splint.**

What gas does the reaction give?
How fast is this product formed in tube 3?
Is the rate faster in acid solution in tube 1?
Does alkali increase the rate in tube 2?
Does manganese(IV) oxide act as a catalyst?

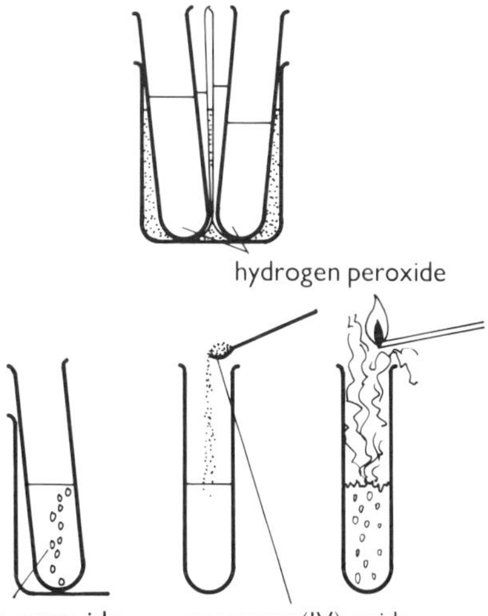


**b) Half fill six tubes with hydrogen peroxide. Add different amounts of manganese(IV) oxide to three. Try other metal oxide powders in the other three.**

Does the amount of catalyst used make a difference?
Are any other oxides catalysts for this reaction?

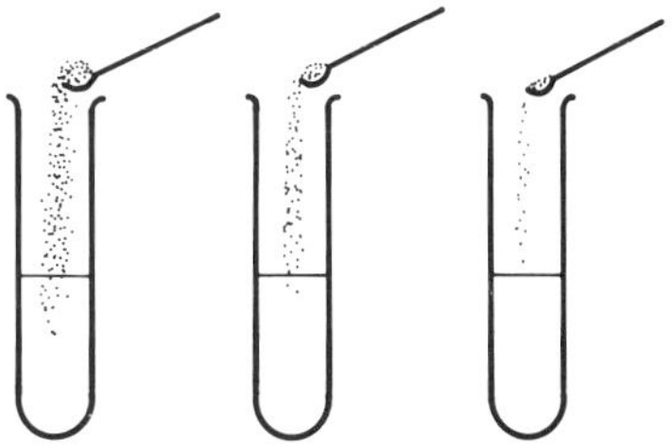

Tube 3 is a control experiment. The neutral hydrogen peroxide in it decomposes. It gives oxygen. It does so faster when hot. The solution has no possible catalyst in it. Its reaction is normal. Manganese(IV) oxide and alkali increase this rate. They are catalysts for this reaction. In acid no gas forms. Acid decreases the rate.

# Concentration and temperature

Marble and acid form a gas. We *collect* it. The results show best on a graph. Hydrogen peroxide also gives a gas. We can *see* how fast it is formed. So we are able to compare rates of reaction.

Then we can show which factors alter the rate. In hydrogen peroxide acid does. It decreases the rate. It is called a **negative catalyst**.

Metal oxides are catalysts for this reaction. Manganese(IV) oxide is much the best. The more catalyst used the greater its effect.

Experiment 11.2 also shows the effect of heat. Gas comes off faster. The rate is increased. We watered down the solution in test tube 3. Will this alter the rate of reaction?

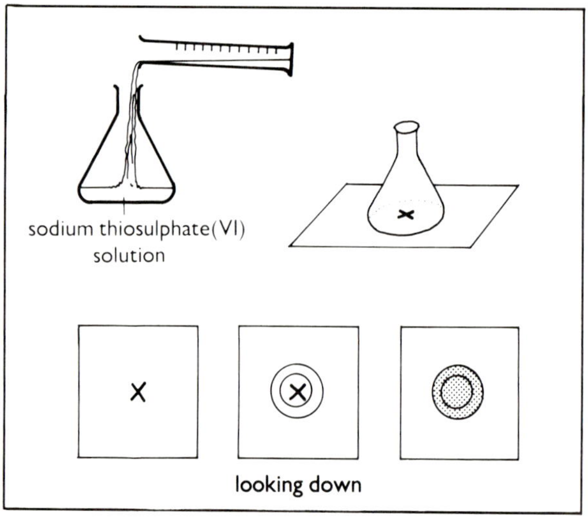


**Experiment 11.3 The effect of concentration.**

**Take 100 cm$^3$ of distilled water. Add a pinch of sodium hydrogencarbonate. Put in 12 g of sodium thiosulphate(VI). Stir to dissolve the crystals.**

**Draw a pencil cross on paper. Measure 20 cm$^3$ of the sodium thiosulphate(VI) solution. Put it in a small conical flask. Stand it over the cross. In a measuring cylinder put 20 cm$^3$ of 0.5 M nitric acid. Pour it into the flask.**

**At the same moment start a stop watch. Swirl the solution in the flask. Look down through it at the pencil cross. When it disappears, stop the watch.**

**Take a second flask. In it put 10 cm$^3$ of thiosulphate(VI) solution. Add 10 cm$^3$ of distilled water. Pour in 20 cm$^3$ of the 0.5 M nitric acid. Start the stop watch at the same time. Swirl the solution. Find the time taken to blot out the pencil cross.**

What product appears in the mixture?
Why does the pencil cross disappear?
In which flask is rate of reaction greater?

| | |
|---|---|
| time for first flask | 23 secs. |
| time for 2nd flask | 47 secs. |

Acid and thiosulphate(VI) react. One product is sulphur. It blots out the cross. It does this in both flasks. It needs the same amount of sulphur each time. The mixture in the second flask takes twice as long. The rate has been halved. The solution in this flask was weaker. Its concentration was halved. The greater the concentration the greater the rate.

## Experiment 11.4 The effect of temperature

Take two flasks. Put 5 $cm^3$ of thiosulphate(VI) solution in each. Add 15 $cm^3$ of distilled water. Use the first one to do Experiment 11.3. Take the temperature of the solution. Heat the other solution to about 40 °C. Do the experiment. Take the temperature.

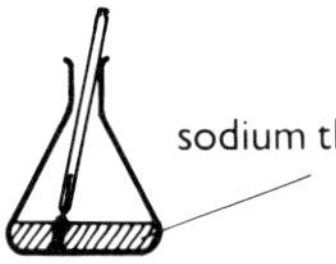

sodium thiosulphate(VI) solution

What time should you expect for the first flask?

Here are some results.

| Temperature | 20 °C | 30 °C | 40 °C |
|---|---|---|---|
| Time taken in seconds | 36 | 18 | ? |

Is reaction faster at higher temperatures?
What time would you expect at 40 °C?

The first temperature was 20 °C. This was the temperature of the reactants. They produce sulphur. They need only thirty-six seconds to produce enough sulphur to blot out the cross.

Then the reactants were at 30 °C. They produce the same amount of sulphur. They take only eighteen seconds. They do it twice as fast. The rate of reaction is twice as great.

We can alter the rate of reaction in four ways.

1 We can alter the temperature. A rise in temperature increases the rate. A rise of 10 °C often doubles it.

2 We can find a catalyst. Most of them increase the rate. Some, called negative catalysts, decrease it.

3 Small lumps of solid react faster than larger ones.

4 Liquids and gases react. Rate depends on concentration. The greater the concentration the greater the rate.

*George drives the mower, grass falls in it.*
*To fill the box takes just a minute.*
*By crazy driving Willie reckons*
*To fill this box in thirty seconds.*
*This is a simple way of showing,*
*Who has the greater rate of mowing.*

## Summary

Reactions vary from very slow to very fast. The speed of a reaction is called its rate. We can measure it in moles per second. We can also compare rates of reaction. The best method is to use one of the products formed. By comparing rates we show that:

a) Small lumps of solid react faster than large ones.
b) A catalyst can be used to increase the rate. Negative catalysts decrease it.
c) A rise in temperature increases reaction rate. A 10 °C rise often roughly doubles the rate.
d) Concentration affects liquid and gas reactions. The higher the concentration the greater the rate.

## Question

20 g of metal lumps react with 20 $cm^3$ of 2 M acid. Hydrogen is formed. The total volume is measured every minute. The results are shown below.

Draw a graph of these results. Plot time on the horizontal axis. On the graph sketch the results you would expect if

a) the temperature was about 10 °C higher;
b) 20 $cm^3$ of M acid were used instead;
c) 20 g of smaller lumps were used in the same acid at the same temperature.
d) The last two volumes shown in the results are the same. Why is this?

| Time from start of reaction (mins) | 1 | 2 | 3 | 4 | 6 | 8 | 10 | 12 | 16 | 19 |
|---|---|---|---|---|---|---|---|---|---|---|
| Volume of gas formed ($cm^3$) | 48 | 87 | 118 | 142 | 172 | 203 | 220 | 231 | 240 | 240 |

# Metals

A metal is easy to recognize. It has metallic lustre. If not, it can be polished up. A metal conducts electric current and heat. Most metals have a high melting point. Most have high densities.

These are physical properties. In Book 1 we tested some reactions of metals. We used the results to put the metals in order. The list is called the Activity Series. The most active metal is at the top. The least active comes last. The Series included hydrogen.

Try some of these tests again. Remember, * means 'for teachers only'.

### Experiment 12.1 Metals and air

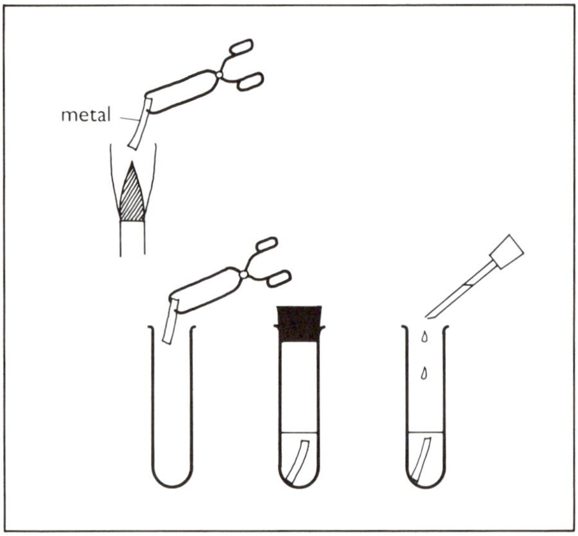


**a) Use a bunsen with its hole half open. Hold a strip of metal in the flame. Use copper, zinc, aluminium, magnesium, tin, iron and platinum.**

***b) Hold a tiny piece of sodium in tongs. Put it in the flame. Use calcium too. Let the product cool.**

**Drop each cold product from a) and b) into a test tube. Shake it with distilled water. Add Universal indicator. If the product does not dissolve, add dilute hydrochloric acid. Heat if necessary.**

Which metals burn?
What are the products?
Do these products form alkalis in water?
Which metals form new products without burning?
Do these products give alkalis in water?
Do the products dissolve in dilute acid?

Some metals burn in air. They form oxides. These oxides dissolve in water. They react to form alkalis. The alkalis are metal hydroxides. Less active metals do not burn. Many become coated with an oxide. These oxides do not react with water. They do react with acids.

Put the metals in order of how well they react with air.

### Experiment 12.2 Metals and acid

**Use the same metals as in Experiment 12.1a). Drop each into dilute hydrochloric acid. Warm if needed. Test any gas. Put the metals in order again.**

Is the order the same as in Experiment 12.1?
Which reactions give heat?
Does this help to place the metals in order?

Magnesium reacts at once. The mixture becomes very hot. The metal disappears. Hydrogen is given off. Less active metals give less heat. Some need heat to start the reaction. Copper and platinum do not react.

## Experiment 12.3 Metals with water or steam

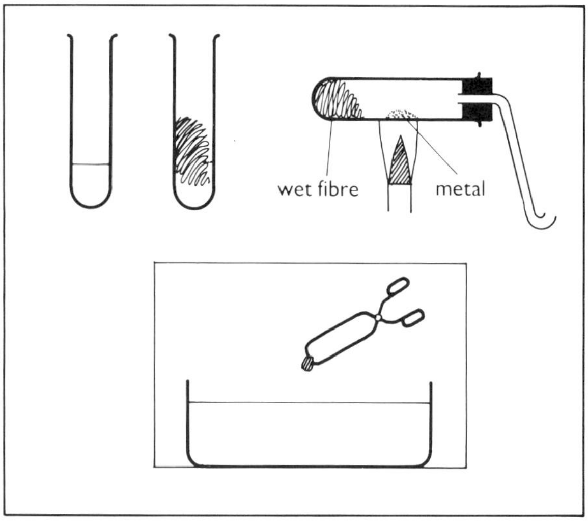


**Put a 2 cm depth of water in a test tube. Push into it some rocksill fibre. Set it up as shown. Put a small pile of metal powder in the tube. Heat it. Collect and test the gas. Use copper, iron and zinc.**

***Use small piles of magnesium and aluminium.**

***Put safety screens round a trough of water. Drop in a small freshly cut piece of sodium. Drop a piece of calcium into a beaker of water. Collect the gas. Test both solutions for alkali.**

Which metals react with cold water?
Which metals burn in steam?
Which do not burn but become red hot?
Write word equations for all reactions.

Sodium and calcium react vigorously with water. Magnesium burns violently in steam. It also reacts slowly with water. Aluminium burns in steam. Zinc and iron glow red hot. The gas is hydrogen. Typical equations are

calcium + water → calcium hydroxide + hydrogen
zinc + steam → zinc oxide + hydrogen
Both reactions are exothermic. $\Delta H$ for each is minus.

Metals which react are turning into their ions. A full equation shows how. It gives in detail each ion formed.

Magnesium burns in air. White magnesium oxide forms.

$$Mg(2.8.2.) + O(2.6.) \rightarrow Mg^{2+}(2.8.) + O^{2-}(2.8.)$$

We may not need all this detail. If not, we write

$$2Mg + O_2 \rightarrow 2MgO$$

We can treat other reactions in the same way.

calcium + water → calcium hydroxide + hydrogen

$$Ca\,(2.8.8.2.) + 2H_2O \rightarrow Ca^{2+}\,(2.8.8.) + 2OH^- + H_2$$

With less detail:

$$Ca + 2H_2O \rightarrow Ca\,(OH)_2 + H_2$$

sodium
calcium
magnesium
aluminium
zinc
iron
tin
(lead)
hydrogen
copper
platinum

Metals react with air, acid, water and steam. Each puts the metals in order. The order is roughly the same in each case. Copper reacts only with air. It cannot take oxygen from steam. In Book 1 we heated copper(II) oxide in hydrogen.

copper oxide + hydrogen → copper + steam

$$CuO + H_2 \rightarrow Cu + H_2O$$

*My name is William Henry Lamb.*
*It says exactly who I am.*
*Unless I need to be official*
*I may use only one initial.*
*With those who know me well its silly*
*To use more detailed names than Willie.*

*copper(II) oxide,* $Cu^{2+}.O^{2-}$

*CuO*

*copper oxide*

# *Metal versus metal again*

Elements fall into two classes, or groups. An element is either a metal or a non-metal. Its properties decide which. Putting things into classes is called classification.

All metals have some similar properties. But some are more active than others. We place them in order of how active they are. This is a second kind of classification. The list is the Activity Series. We can use it to predict results.

People who do football pools predict. Before the games they say what the results may be. Magnesium is more active than copper. Suppose we mix magnesium with copper oxide. Will they react?

## Experiment 12.4 Metal versus metal

***a) Dry magnesium powder and copper(II) oxide in an oven. Mix small amounts of them in a crucible. Stand the crucible on a pipe clay triangle on a tripod. Stand the tripod on tiles. Put safety screens around it. Light a bunsen burner under the crucible.**

Did you predict that the two substances would react?

The reaction is almost explosive. Nothing is left in the crucible. We can only guess what is formed.

***b) Put some of the magnesium and copper oxide in another crucible. Mix in magnesium oxide. Heat the crucible. Let it cool. Scrape the contents into a beaker. Add dilute acid. Heat to dissolve the white oxide. Filter.**

What substance is left in the beaker?
Write a word equation for the crucible reaction.

Adding magnesium oxide makes the reaction less vigorous. The products are not blown out of the crucible. Acid dissolves magnesium oxide. We can see the other product. We can prove that it is copper.

magnesium + copper oxide → magnesium oxide + copper

$$Mg + CuO \rightarrow MgO + Cu$$

We could predict this result. Magnesium is much higher in the Series than copper. It is much more active. It can take oxygen from copper oxide. It will do so vigorously.

c) **Mix copper(II) oxide with iron powder. Put a small pile of the mixture in a porcelain boat. Wear eyeshields. Heat the mixture gently and then strongly. Heat iron with other oxides in the same way. Use zinc oxide, a lead oxide and aluminium oxide. Try to predict each result before you begin.**

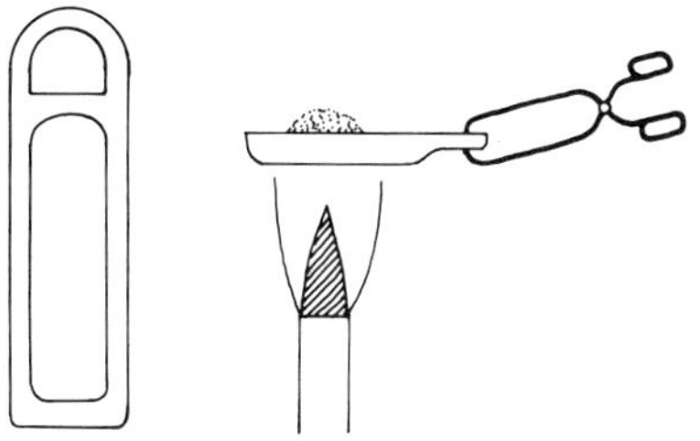

Which mixtures glow when they are heated?
Is the glow a sign of a chemical change?
Which mixtures show no change?
Did you predict each result correctly?

Iron is above copper in the Series. It is more active. It will take oxygen from copper oxide. Taking away oxygen is reduction. Iron reduces lead oxide. It does not affect zinc and aluminium oxides.

iron + copper(II) oxide → iron oxide + copper

Iron has 'displaced' copper. Can it do this with other copper compounds. What other copper compound could we try?

## Experiment 12.5 Displacement reactions

**Clean pieces of iron, copper and zinc with emery paper. Dip iron into copper(II) sulphate solution. Dip zinc into lead(II) nitrate solution. Put the copper into silver nitrate solution. After a few minutes take them out. Observe the results.**

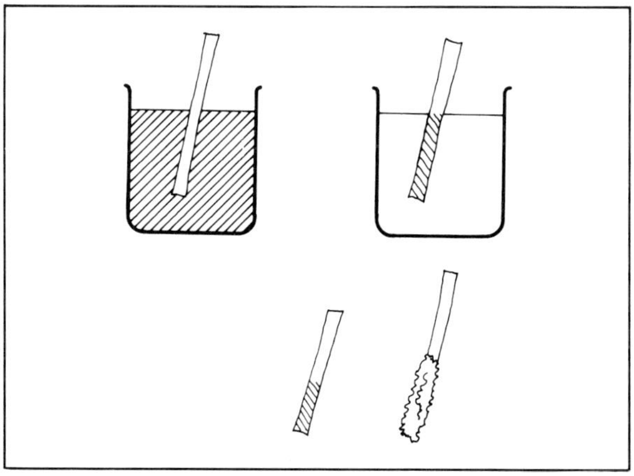

What metal forms on the copper foil?
Where should silver appear in the Activity Series?
What forms on the surface of the zinc?
Does iron always displace copper?

Each metal becomes coated. Copper appears on the iron. Crystals of shiny lead appear on the zinc. A white metal is formed on the copper. This is silver. Silver comes below copper in the Series.

## Oxidation and reduction

Using simple formulae

$Mg + CuO \rightarrow MgO + Cu$

Magnesium gains oxygen. $Mg \rightarrow MgO$ is oxidation. Copper oxide loses oxygen. $CuO \rightarrow Cu$ is reduction.

We can write the equation to show the ions.

$Mg + Cu^{2+}.O^{2-} \rightarrow Mg^{2+}.O^{2-} + Cu$

By gaining oxygen a magnesium atom turns into an ion. Mg(2.8.2.) loses 2 electrons to become $Mg^{2+}$(2.8.). Gaining oxygen is the same as losing electrons.

$Cu^{2+}.O^{2-} \rightarrow Cu$ is a copper atom turning into an ion. To do this it gains two electrons from magnesium. Losing oxygen = gaining electrons.

**Oxidation is gaining oxygen or losing electrons.**
**Reduction is losing oxygen or gaining electrons.**

If one substance gains oxygen another must lose it. If one substance loses electrons another gains them. Oxidation and reduction always happen in the same reaction. The change is reduction *and* oxidation. It is called a **redox reaction**.

# The extraction of metals

Metal compounds are found in the earth. They are called ores. Getting the metal from an ore is called extraction. There are many methods of doing it.

Mining bauxite.

Most ores are oxides, sulphides or carbonates. They are mixed with rock and other substances. This makes extraction much harder. The first step is to get rid of as much of the rock and impurities as we can. This process is called refining the ore. It makes the ore much purer.

Ores are metal compounds. They contain ions of the metal. Extraction turns them into atoms. In this change the ions gain electrons. It is reduction. Some ores are easy to reduce. Some are difficult.

The Activity Series tells us which. The top metals react vigorously. Changing their atoms to ions is easy. So the reverse change will be difficult. Ores of the top metals are hard to reduce to the metal.

Metals lower down react less easily. Turning their atoms into ions is harder. Then their ores will be easier to reduce. Extracting these metals is much easier.

The least active metals are copper, silver and gold. They are easy to extract. They are also found as the metals themselves. They occur 'native'. So they were known and used very early in history.

Metals are extracted in large amounts. The simple method is to reduce the oxide. The best substance for doing this is carbon. Coke is the form of carbon usually used. It is cheap. It is easily made from coal. It turns into carbon oxides as it reduces the ore. These oxides escape as gas.

Many metal ores *are* oxides. Sulphide and carbonate ores can be turned into oxide. They are strongly heated in air, or 'roasted'. One zinc ore is zinc carbonate, calamine. Another is zinc sulphide or zinc blende. Both are roasted.

$ZnCO_3 \rightarrow ZnO + CO_2$

$2ZnS + 3O_2 \rightarrow 2ZnO + 2SO_2$ (sulphur dioxide)

The metal oxide is mixed with coke and heated. The temperature needed varies. For metals high in the Activity Series it is very high. It can be over 2000 °C.

Manufacturing coke.

**High temperatures** are very costly to produce
need special furnaces to stand the heat
make it hard to separate the products

For active metals we need a different method. They are extracted by electrolysis. A suitable compound is melted. A current is passed through it. Metal ions move to the cathode. It is the negatively charged electrode. It provides the ions with electrons. The metal is formed. The cathode reaction is reduction.

calcium chloride
$Ca^{2+}\ 2Cl^-$

at the cathode
$Ca^{2+} + 2e \rightarrow Ca$ (metal)

Why is a melted compound used? Why not a solution? The cathode reaction is the same for both. Remember we are extracting 'top' metals. They are very active and would react with water at the cathode.

The table shows the methods of extraction. The metals are in Series order. You can see how method links up with position.

| Metal | Ore used | Reduction of oxide by carbon | Actual method used |
|---|---|---|---|
| Potassium<br>Sodium<br>Calcium<br>Magnesium | chloride<br>chloride<br>carbonate<br>carbonate | Temperature needed for this reduction is much too high. Magnesium has been made this way. | Electrolysis of the molten chloride. Calcium and magnesium chlorides are made from their carbonates. |
| Aluminium | oxide | Temperature too high. Aluminium reacts with carbon. | Electrolysis of the oxide dissolved in a molten aluminium salt. |
| Zinc<br>Iron<br>Tin<br>Lead<br>Copper | sulphide<br>oxide<br>oxide<br>sulphide<br>sulphide | The temperature for reduction is below 1000 °C. For copper oxide it is below 100 °C | Sulphide ores are roasted to give the oxide. This is mixed with coke. The mixture is heated. |
| Silver<br>Mercury<br>Gold | sulphide<br>sulphide<br>native | Reduction by coke is not needed. | Extraction with cyanide.<br>Heating the ore→metal.<br>Extraction with cyanide. |

# *The Periodic Table*

On page 56 we compared chlorine, bromine and iodine. Their reactions are very much alike. They belong to a chemical family called the halogens. Look at their relative atomic masses.

| Cl | | Br | | I |
|---|---|---|---|---|
| 35 | | 80 | | 127 |
| | 45 | | 47 | |

Lithium, sodium and potassium are very much alike. They belong to a family too. They are alkali metals. Their relative atomic masses differ by equal amounts.

| Li | | Na | | K |
|---|---|---|---|---|
| 7 | | 23 | | 39 |
| | 16 | | 16 | |

Dobereiner was the first to notice this. He said that properties and relative atomic mass were connected. In 1865, about sixty elements were known. Newlands put them in order of atomic mass. Similar elements came at regular intervals. Newlands said they were like notes in a scale. The first and second doh are not the same note. But they are very much alike.

*doh* re me fah sol lah te *doh*

In 1869 a Russian took the idea further. His name was Mendeleef. He put the elements in order of relative atomic mass. The smallest one came first.

H Li Be B C N O F Na Mg Al Si P S Cl K Ca....

He built the list into a table. It is called the Periodic Table.

| | | | | | | |
|---|---|---|---|---|---|---|
| H | | | | | | |
| Li | Be | B | C | N | O | F |
| Na | Mg | Al | Si | P | S | Cl |
| K | Ca | .. | .. | | | |

On page 158 there is a modern Periodic Table. It has in it 104 known elements. They include the noble gases. These were unknown in 1869.

Each element is shown in the Table by its symbol. Those in black are of the more common elements. The atomic number is shown above the symbol. The name of the element is in small print. Below this is the relative atomic mass.

| | |
|---|---|
| 20 | atomic number |
| Ca | symbol |
| Calcium | name |
| 40 | relative atomic mass |

The vertical lines of elements are called groups. They are labelled with Roman numbers. Each group contains a chemical family.

The horizontal rows are called periods. They are numbered from 1 to 8. Metals are on the left-hand side of a period. Non-metals are found on the right.

| GROUPS | I | II | III | IV | V | VI | VII | O |
|---|---|---|---|---|---|---|---|---|
| Period 1 | H | | | | | | | He |
| Period 2 | Li | Be | B | C | N | O | F | Ne |
| Period 3 | Na | Mg | Al | Si | P | S | Cl | Ar |
| Period 4 | K | Ca | .. | .. | | | | |

Mendeleef had many problems. We shall deal with two of them. We shall use the modern Table.

In 1869 many elements had yet to be discovered. Suppose silicon, Si, had been one of them. Without it the list becomes

H He Li Be B C N O F Ne Na Mg Al P S Cl Ar K

The Periodic Table then becomes:

| I | II | III | IV | V | VI | VII | O |
|---|---|---|---|---|---|---|---|
| H | | | | | | | He |
| Li | Be | B | C | N | O | F | Ne |
| Na | Mg | Al | *P* | *S* | *Cl* | *Ar* | K |
| | | | | | | | noble gases |

This looks wrong. It puts phosphorus under carbon. Sulphur appears in Group V under nitrogen. Argon, a noble gas appears in the halogen family. The metal potassium is in Group O with the noble gases.

Mendeleef avoided this by leaving a gap. He said that an element would be discovered to fill the gap. He predicted its properties. He also described its compounds in detail.

| II | III | IV | V | VI |
|---|---|---|---|---|
| Be | B | C | N | O |
| Mg | Al | .. | P | S |

Each element for which he left a gap was discovered. Its properties were found to match Mendeleef's predictions. Its compounds were as he had said they would be.

The second problem came at element 21. Element 20 is calcium. It fits well in Group II with beryllium and magnesium.

| | I | II | III | IV | V | | |
|---|---|---|---|---|---|---|---|
| Period 4 | K | Ca | 21 | 22 | 23 | .. | .. |

Element 21 is scandium. It fits fairly well in Group III. The next nine elements fit less and less well. The metal manganese, for example, comes in the halogen group VII.

| | I | II | III | IV | V | VI | VII |
|---|---|---|---|---|---|---|---|
| Period 3 | Na | Mg | Al | Si | P | S | Cl |
| Period 4 | K | Ca | Sc | Ti | V | Cr | Mn |

It is simpler to see this in the modern Table. Take out the elements from scandium to zinc. This brings us to element 31, gallium, Ga. It fits well in Group III. Those which follow it fit well too. The period ends with krypton, Kr. This noble gas is in its right group, Group O.

| I | II | III | IV | V | VI | VII | O |
|---|---|---|---|---|---|---|---|
| K | Ca | .. | .. | .. | .. | .. | .. |
| .. | .. | Ga | Ge | As | Se | Br | Kr |

Element 20 is in its right group. So are the elements from 31 to 36. The ten elements in between are all metals. They are alike in many ways. They have coloured compounds. Each forms more than one ion. They act as catalysts.

| II | | | | | VIII | | | | | | III |
|---|---|---|---|---|---|---|---|---|---|---|---|
| Ca | Sc | Ti | V | Cr | Mn | Fe | Co | Ni | Cu | Zn | Ga |
| 20 | Transition metals | | | | | | | | | | 31 |

They are called the transition metals. The modern Table puts them in a separate group. It is Group VIII. It lies between Groups II and III.

# *Modern ideas and the Periodic Table*

From 1896 onwards, experiments 'opened up' the atom. They showed that every atom has a nucleus. The nucleus contains protons. The number of protons is called the atomic number of the element. It turns out to be the position of the element in the Periodic Table. It is also the number of electrons in the atom.

Electrons are in shells. The outside shell is important.

When an atom reacts the outside shell loses or gains electrons.
the ions formed attract each other.

or the outside shell shares electrons with other atoms.
covalent bonds hold the atoms together.

How does this fit in with the Periodic Table?

Periods differ in length. Period 1 contains hydrogen and helium, a noble gas. Helium has two electrons. They fill the first shell.

| | | |
|---|---|---|
| Period 1 | H | He |
| Electrons | 1 | 2 |

Period 2 has eight elements. It ends, like Period 1 with a noble gas, neon. The outside shell of each atom is the second shell. It is full when it has eight electrons.

| | | | | |
|---|---|---|---|---|
| Period 2 | Li | Be............................ | F | Ne |
| Electron structure | 2.1 | 2.2 | 2.7 | 2.8 |

Sodium is the first element in Period 3. Its electron structure is 2.8.1. The last element in Period 1 is argon. It is a noble gas, structure 2.8.8.

Period 4 begins with potassium, 2.8.8.1. Its outside shell has one electron. So have the atoms of sodium and lithium. This is why all three react in the same way.

| Group I | | II | |
|---|---|---|---|
| Hydrogen | 1 | | |
| Lithium | 2.1 | Beryllium | 2.2 |
| Sodium | 2.8.1 | Magnesium | 2.8.2 |
| Potassium | 2.8.8.1 | Calcium | 2.8.8.2 |

Li 2.1 $\rightarrow Li^+$ + 1 electron
Na 2.8.1 $\rightarrow Na^+$ + 1 electron
K 2.8.8.1 $\rightarrow K^+$ + 1 electron

Calcium is next. Its structure is 2.8.8.2. It reacts like magnesium 2.8.2 and beryllium 2.2.

The third shell is not filled by eight electrons. Scandium follows calcium. It has one more electron in its atom. This extra electron is not in the fourth shell. The structure of scandium is 2.8.**9**.2.

| Calcium | Scandium |
|---|---|
| Element 20 | Element 21 |
| Structure 2.8.8.2 | 2.8.9.2 |

The next nine elements fill the third shell. Titanium, element 22, has the structure 2.8.10.2, Vanadium 2.8.11.2, . . . Iron 2.8.14.2. The last one is the metal zinc, 2.8.18.2. These are the transition metals. Most have two electrons in the outside shell. They are metals.

Iron Fe 2.8.14.2

Fe 2.8.14.2 $\rightarrow Fe^{2+}$ + 2e
2.8.14

## Summary

Metals and non-metals differ in properties. Most metals have metallic lustre, high density and high melting point. They all conduct electric current and heat. These are physical properties.

Some metals burn in air. Others only tarnish. The result is an oxide. If it dissolves in water the oxide forms an alkali. Alkalis put hydroxyl, $OH^-$, ions into solution. The solution turns litmus blue.

Very active metals react with cold water. Alkali forms in solution. Reaction is exothermic. Many heated metals react with steam. The metal oxide forms. Hydrogen is formed in both cases.

All the reactions are examples of oxidation and reduction. $Mg \rightarrow MgO$ is oxidation (oxygen added). It is also $Mg \rightarrow Mg^{2+}$. The atom loses electrons. Oxidation is gaining oxygen and losing electrons. Reduction is losing oxygen or gaining electrons. They happen at the same time in redox reactions.

More active metals can displace less active ones. They are displaced from oxides and other compounds. All these reactions place a metal in the Activity Series. So do its reactions with acids.

Extraction means making a metal from its ores. Very active metals are difficult to extract. They are made by electrolysis of a molten salt. Less active metals are easier to extract. Their oxides are reduced by heating with coke. Very inactive metals occur 'native'. They were used early in history.

Mendeleef listed elements in order of relative atomic mass. He started with hydrogen. The result is called the Periodic Table. Vertical lines are called groups. Each contains a chemical family. Horizontal lines are called periods. They begin with an alkali metal and end with a noble gas.

Later periods contain a Group VIII. It contains transition metals. They include iron and copper. The Periodic Table is explained by the electron structures of the elements.

## Questions

1. Sodium, aluminium, iron, tin, copper, gold. These metals are in order of activity. The most active chemically comes first. Read each statement below. Is it true or false? Say why you think so.
   a) Sodium is extracted by electrolysis.
   b) Iron oxide is reduced by heating it with tin.
   c) Gold is likely to occur 'native'.
   d) Tin is made by reducing its oxide with coke.
   e) Aluminium reduces copper oxide to copper.
   f) Iron in copper sulphate solution becomes coated with a layer of copper.

2. Use the equation to answer the questions below.
   zinc oxide + carbon → zinc + carbon monoxide
   $ZnO + C \rightarrow Zn + CO$
   a) Which substance is being oxidized?
   b) In this case what does oxidation mean?
   c) Which substance is being reduced?
   d) What is the reducing agent or reductant?
   e) What name is given to this type of reaction?
   f) What substance is manufactured by this reaction?

3. Look at Group I of the Period Table. Find answers to fill the gaps below.

   All the elements are metals except ______. They are called the ______ metals. The outside shell of each atom contains ______ electron(s). They lose this electron to form ______ ions. The sodium ion is written ______. All the metals react with water to form the gas ______. The water then turns litmus ______. It contains an ______. The most reactive metal in the list is ______

*Uncle Dick and Auntie Mabel*
*Learnt the Periodic Table,*
*To teach Willie, George and also Grace*
*How the elements fit into place.*
*Arranging all the elements*
*Shows chemistry is common sense.*

# Group I – the alkali metals

We shall study only sodium and its compounds. Some of the work will not be new. Use it as revision.

The other alkali metals are very much like sodium. Those below it are more active than sodium. Activity increases as we pass down the group. The compounds of the group members are like those of sodium.

Group I

| | |
|---|---|
| lithium | Li |
| sodium | Na |
| potassium | K |
| rubidium | Rb |
| caesium | Cs |
| francium | Fr |

Sodium chloride is mined as rock salt. It is also present in sea water. The pure substance is made by crystallization. The crystals are cubic. The crystal lattice contains ions. The ions are not free to move. So solid salt is not a conductor.

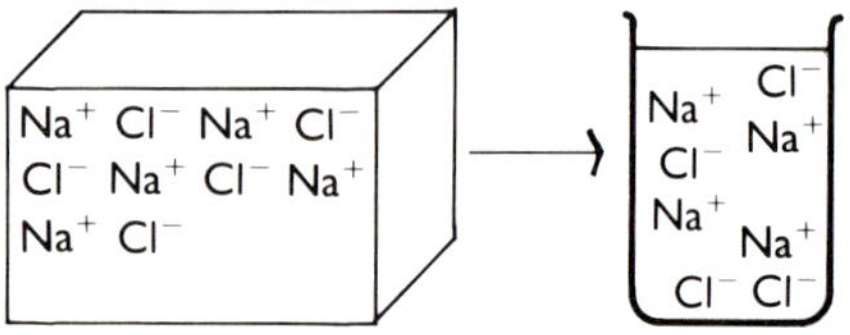


Sodium chloride melts at about 800 °C. The ions can move in the liquid. It can be electrolysed. The anode is a graphite cylinder. It is surrounded by an iron ring. This acts as the cathode of the cell. Molten sodium chloride contains $Na^+$ and $Cl^-$ ions.

At the anode $2Cl^- \rightarrow Cl_2 + 2e$
Chlorine is liberated. It does not react with the graphite.
At the cathode $2Na^+ + 2e \rightarrow 2Na$
Liquid sodium rises through the molten salt. If it mixes with chlorine they react. Steel gauze keeps them apart.

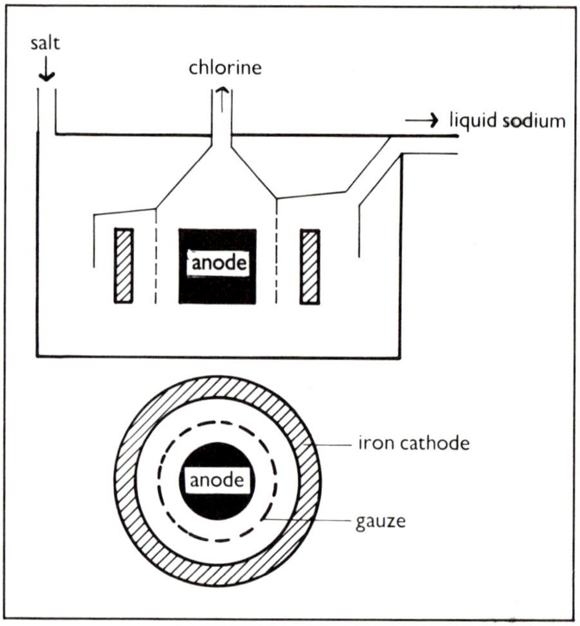


Sodium is a useful metal. It is used in sodium vapour lamps. These give a bright orange-yellow light. It is used to make sodium cyanide. This is used in extracting gold. Sodium is used as conductor in atomic reactors.

### Experiment 12.6 Alkali metals and flame tests

**Put sodium compounds on watch glasses. Clean a flame test wire. Dip it in hydrochloric acid. Pick up a few crystals of a compound on the wet end. Hold them in the edge of a blue bunsen flame. Test all the others. Test the chlorides of other alkali metals.**

What flame colour do sodium compounds give?
Is the colour caused by the metal in the compound?
List the colours given by other alkali metal salts.

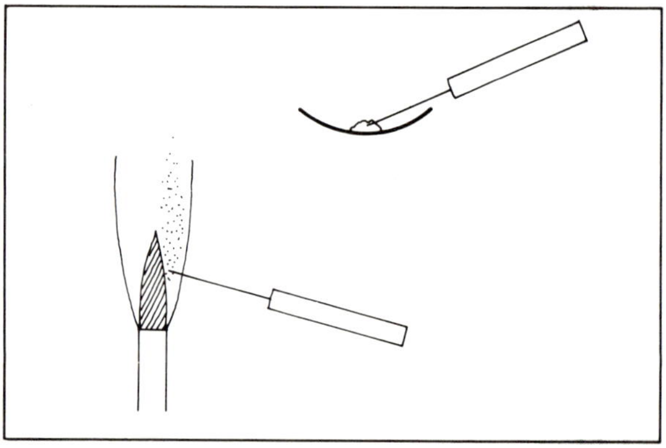

## Sodium hydroxide

### Experiment 12.7 Properties of sodium hydroxide

**1. Put a sodium hydroxide pellet on a watch glass. Let it stand in air for as long as possible.**

**2. Add four pellets to distilled water in a test tube. Stir the liquid to make them dissolve. Take the temperature before and after dissolving.**

**3. Make separate solutions of salts. Use sulphates of magnesium, zinc, iron(II), copper(II) and aluminium. Add sodium hydroxide solution to each. Add a little at a time until there is no further change.**

**4. Warm ammonium chloride crystals with sodium hydroxide solution. Hold a moist litmus paper in the mouth of the tube. Smell the gas with GREAT CARE!**

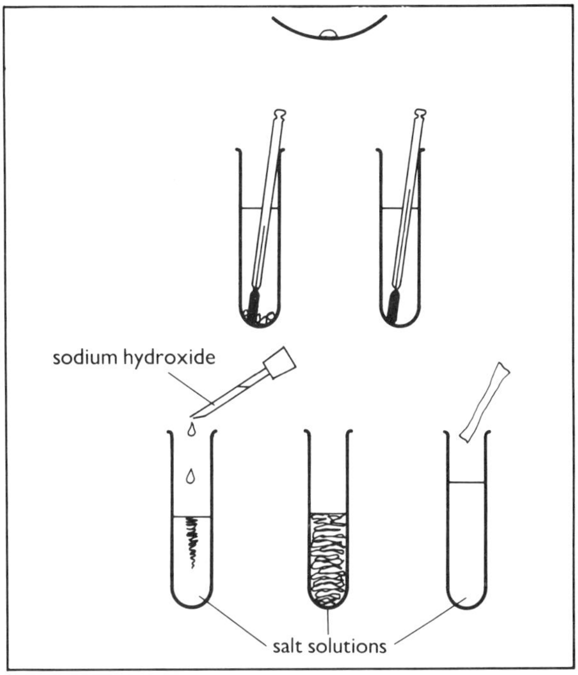


The solid alkali is deliquescent. It takes water vapour from the air. It slowly dissolves in water. When it dissolves heat is produced.

What are the precipitates formed?
Which of them dissolve in extra alkali?
What is the gas formed from ammonium chloride?

Sodium hydroxide + iron(II) sulphate can only form iron(II) hydroxide + sodium sulphate. All sodium salts are soluble. The ppt is green iron(II) hydroxide. Zinc and aluminium hydroxides dissolve in alkali.

$Fe^{2+}(aq) + 2OH^{-}(aq)^{-} \rightarrow Fe(OH)_2(s)$

All ammonium salts react with alkali. Ammonia forms. It has a pungent smell and turns litmus blue.

### Experiment 12.8 Electrolysis of brine

**Use a voltameter as in Experiment 4.2. Add Universal Indicator to brine. Fill the voltameter with it. Collect any gases formed at the electrodes.**

What gas forms at the cathode?
What happens to the indicator round the cathode?
What gas forms at the anode?
What happens to the indicator round the anode?

At the cathode hydrogen appears. The indicator becomes violet. Alkali has been formed. It is mixed with unused brine.
At the anode chlorine appears. It is used up by bleaching the indicator.

| Alkali metal | Colour of flame |
|---|---|
| lithium | scarlet |
| sodium | orange-yellow |
| potassium | lilac |

# Other sodium compounds

Sodium hydroxide is called 'caustic soda'. Sodium carbonate is 'washing soda'. Baking soda is sodium hydrogencarbonate. The last two often give a gas when they react or are heated. What gas is it likely to be?

**Experiment 12.9 To compare washing soda and baking soda**

**a) To both solids add dilute hydrochloric acid. Test any gas with lime water. Evaporate one of the solutions. What shape are the crystals formed?**

**b) Heat a little of each solid in a dry test tube. Test any gas with lime water. Let the tubes cool. Add dilute hydrochloric acid. Again test for a gas.**

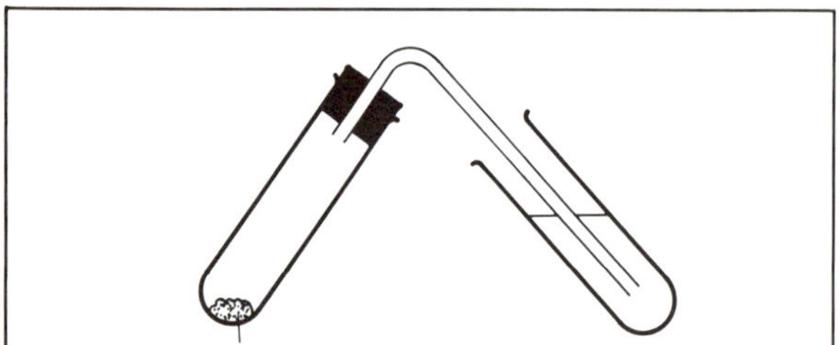


Both react with acid to form carbon dioxide. The crystals are cubic. They are sodium chloride.
Both give steam when heated. One gives carbon dioxide as well. Is it washing or baking soda?
After heating a solid is left in each tube. Does hydrochloric acid tell us what the solids are?

**c) Shake each solid in distilled water. Do these three tests on samples of each solution.**
**i) Add drops of Universal Indicator.**
**ii) Heat each solution. Test any gas. Let the solutions cool. Add dilute acid to each of them.**
**iii) Take solutions of the sulphates of magnesium, copper and zinc. Add sodium carbonate solution only.**

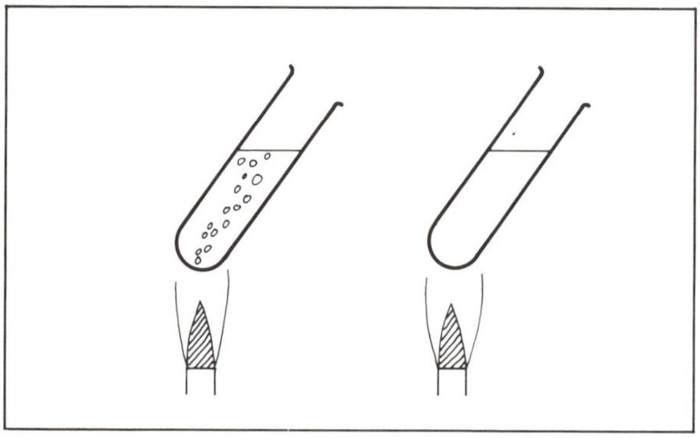

What is the pH of each solution?
Which solution, when heated, gives carbon dioxide?
After heating what does this solution contain?
What are the precipitates formed in test iii)?

Sodium carbonate gives an alkaline solution, pH 10+. It reacts with acids. The effervescence is carbon dioxide. The substance left in solution is a salt, sodium chloride.

The heated crystals give steam. They are losing water of crystallization. We know the carbonate is not changed. It still gives off carbon dioxide with acids. The ppts in iii) are carbonates of metals.

Sodium hydrogencarbonate is not very soluble. The pH of the solution is about 7. It reacts with acids to form carbon dioxide and a solution of a salt, sodium chloride.

Gentle heating decomposes the solid. Water and carbon dioxide are given off. The solid left in the tube reacts with acids. The effervescence is carbon dioxide. The solid must be sodium carbonate. The solution also decomposes when gently heated.

baking soda heated

↓

sodium carbonate + carbon dioxide + water

## The manufacture of sodium hydroxide

Brine is sodium chloride solution. Experiment 12.6 is electrolysis of brine. Sodium hydroxide forms round the cathode. It is mixed with unused brine. It would be difficult to separate them. The manufacture uses this method. It avoids the separation difficulty.

Brine is fed into the cell. Chlorine appears at the graphite anodes. It leaves through B. The cathode is mercury. Sodium forms there and dissolves in the mercury. The liquid is called sodium amalgam. It runs down the sloping floor.

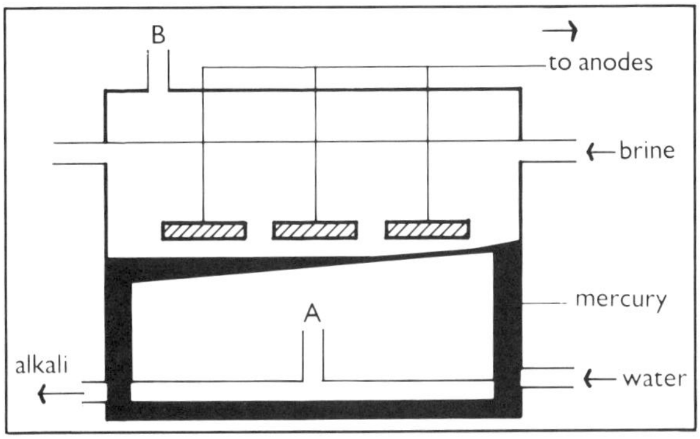


It passes out of the cell into water. Sodium reacts with water. One product is hydrogen. It leaves through A. The other product is sodium hydroxide solution. It is evaporated. Pure mercury passes back into the cell.

Sodium hydroxide is used in making soap, rayon and paper. It is needed to make pure aluminium oxide. This is used in extracting aluminium. Sodium hydroxide solution reacts with chlorine to form household bleach.

## The manufacture of sodium carbonate

Sodium carbonate is also made from brine. Concentrated brine solution is sprayed down a tower. Ammonia is passed in. It dissolves. The liquid is sprayed down a second tower. The liquid is saturated with carbon dioxide. Bubble caps ensure that both gases mix and dissolve.

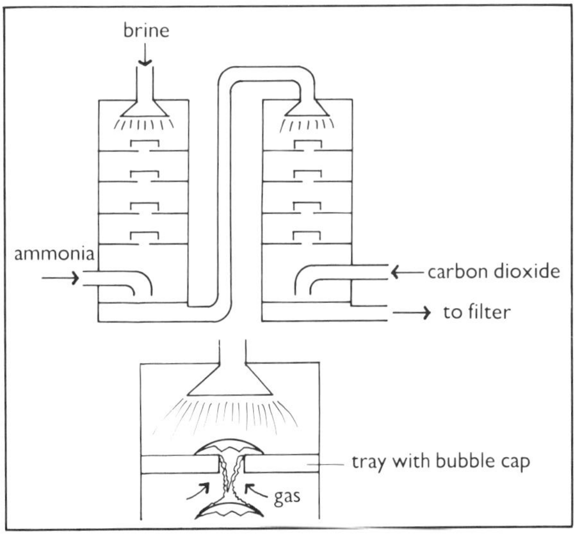


A precipitate appears. It is sodium hydrogencarbonate. It is filtered off and heated. The filtrate is ammonium chloride solution. Ammonia is recovered from it. The ammonium chloride is heated with slaked lime.

Heating the ppt gives sodium carbonate and carbon dioxide. This gas is used again. The carbon dioxide needed is made by heating limestone. This also gives lime used to regain ammonia. Nothing is lost.

Sodium carbonate is used in making soap, rayon, glass and paint.

Baking soda is the sodium hydrogencarbonate ppt. In baking, it can be mixed with dough. When heated in the oven it gives carbon dioxide. Baking powder is baking soda mixed with acid. The acid is solid and weak. The two give carbon dioxide. In both cases this 'raises' the dough. The gas bubbles make it light and porous.

Baking soda is used in fire extinguishers. It is mixed with a foaming agent. They react and give carbon dioxide. The fire is put out when it is covered with the carbon dioxide foam.

# *Group II – the alkaline earth metals*

Limestone, chalk and marble are calcium carbonate. Dolomite is a rock containing magnesium carbonate and calcium carbonate. We have used both elements and their compounds. The drawings will remind you of experiments to do again.

| | | |
|---|---|---|
| beryllium | Be | 2.2 |
| magnesium | Mg | 2.8.2 |
| calcium | Ca | 2.8.2 |
| strontium | Sr | 2.8.18.8.2 |
| barium | Ba | 2.8.18.18.8.2 |
| radium | Ra | |

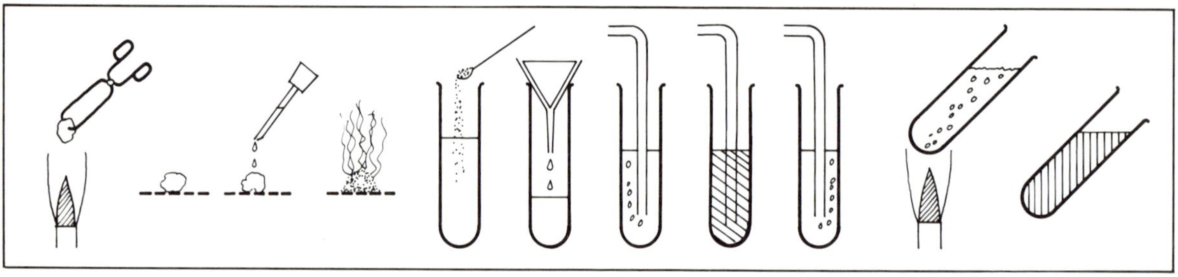

a) Heat chalk or marble. Let it cool. Add drops of cold water. Shake the powder with water. Filter. Test the solution with litmus paper. Pass carbon dioxide through it. Heat the final solution.

b) Burn magnesium in air. Burn calcium. Dip a flame test wire in hydrochloric acid. Do a flame test on each product. Shake some of each product in water. Test the solution with litmus paper.

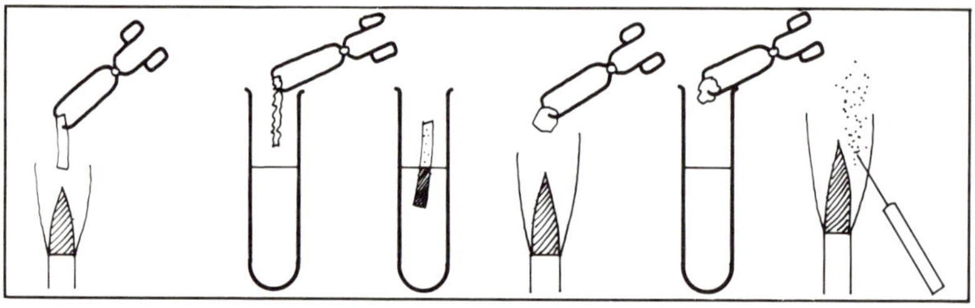

c) Heat magnesium in water. Drop calcium into water. Collect the gas. Test it with a lighted splint. Test the two solutions with litmus. Which is the more active metal? Write equations.

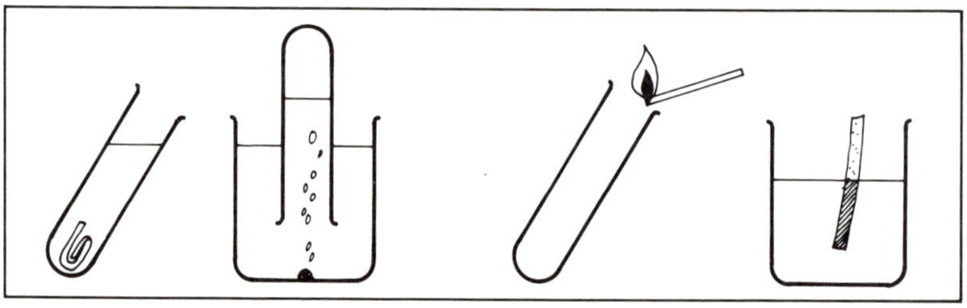

d) Add dilute hydrochloric acid to marble. Collect a gas jar of gas. Put burning magnesium into it. Try to dissolve the product in dilute acid. Which part does not dissolve in the acid? Do a flame test on the solution in the flask.

Look at the position of strontium in the Group. Elements in a group are alike. Each metal is more active than those above it.

What compound is the common strontium ore likely to be?
What is the formula of its carbonate?
Will it decompose on heating?
If so, is it harder to decompose than chalk?
Do strontium oxide and water react?
Is strontium hydroxide an alkali?
Does strontium metal react with water?
Will strontium burn in air?
What is the formula of strontium oxide?
Write down the formula of the strontium ion.

## Questions on Groups I and II

1. Write this out. Fill in the spaces.

   The apparatus below is used for ______. It is called a ______. It contains brine which is sodium ______ solution. Universal Indicator in brine is coloured ______. This shows that the solution is ______. Electrode A is the ______. The gas set free at A is ______. Electrode B is the ______. The gas set free at B is ______. The indicator round the ______ becomes violet. This colour shows an ______. Its name is sodium ______. It is manufactured by the electrolysis of ______. It is used in making ______.

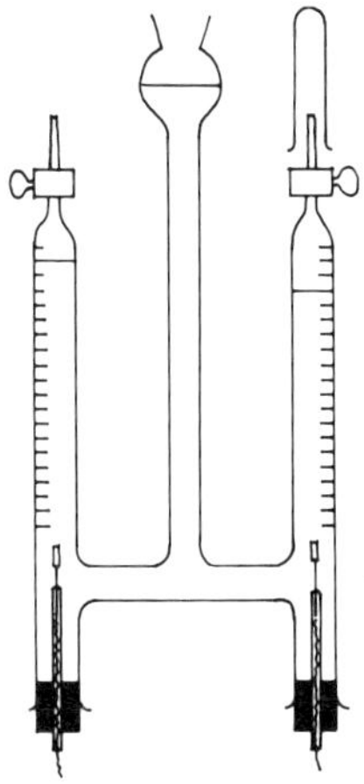


2. What is the chemical name of a) washing soda, b) baking soda?
   Both are made by the Solvay Process. Name the two main raw materials used in this method.
   What other substance is needed?
   How is this other substance got back at the end?
   A precipitate of sodium hydrogencarbonate is formed. Is it insoluble in water?
   How is it used to make sodium carbonate?
   Give two important uses of this carbonate.
   Give two uses of baking soda other than baking.

3. What is the everyday name of sodium chloride?
   What is its formula?
   What two ions are there in its crystals?
   If sodium chloride contains ions why is the solid a non-conductor?
   Why is the molten salt a conductor?
   When it is electrolysed, what forms at a) the cathode, b) the anode?
   Electrolysis of sodium chloride solution gives three products. What are they?
   Why does the industrial method use a mercury cathode?

4. Substance A is a shiny white solid. It is strongly heated. It loses mass or weight. It becomes a dull white solid B. Drops of water are added to B when it is cold. It crumbles to a white powder C. Steam is given off. C is shaken with water and filtered. The clear filtrate turns litmus blue. Carbon dioxide is blown through it. It becomes first 'milky' and then clear. Heating the clear liquid makes it 'milky' again.

   What substance could the shiny white solid A be?
   Explain why A loses mass or weight on heating?
   What is the name of the dull white solid B?
   How do we know that B reacts with water?
   What is the new substance formed, the powder C?
   What kind of substance does litmus show C to be?
   Why does carbon dioxide make the solution of C 'milky'?
   The milky solution becomes clear. Which kind of hardness does it contain?
   What does hard water mean?

**Answers**
carbonate
$SrCO_3$
Yes
harder
Yes
Yes
Yes
Yes
SrO
$Sr^{2+}$

# *Aluminium – a Group III metal*

Aluminium compounds are part of many rocks and clay. The main ore is bauxite. This is aluminium oxide, $Al_2O_3$. There is plenty of it. Yet finding a way to extract the metal proved to be difficult.

Carbon will reduce the oxide. But it needs high temperature. Carbon also reacts with the metal. Electrolysis could be used. It needs a liquid which contains aluminium ions. What about molten aluminium oxide? It melts at about 2000 °C. This is too hot for use. The oxide does not dissolve in water. What about the chloride? Aluminium chloride is odd. It melts easily but the liquid does not conduct.

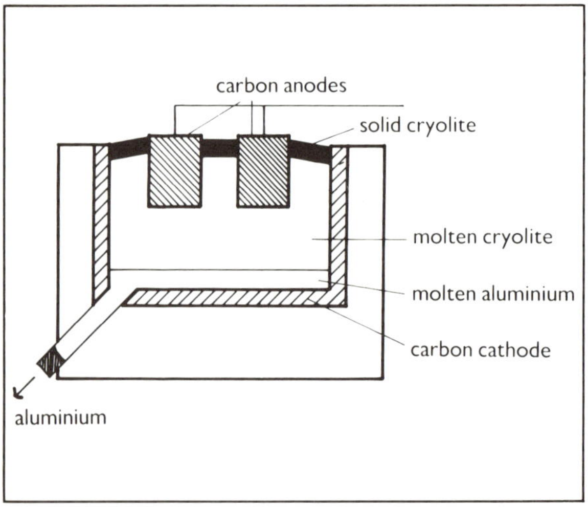


Another aluminium ore is cryolite. It is sodium aluminium fluoride. It is made pure and melted. Pure oxide is made from bauxite. It is dissolved in molten cryolite at 900 °C. The cell is lined with carbon. This lining acts as the cathode.

Aluminium is set free. At 900 °C it is a liquid. It is run out as pure metal. Oxygen forms at the carbon anodes. The anodes burn away and must be replaced.

Aluminium is an attractive metal. It keeps its metallic lustre. Its density is low for a metal. Aluminium is a good conductor. It is strong. It forms alloys with other metals. These are strong and light.

| I | II | III | IV | V |
| --- | --- | --- | --- | --- |
| Na | Mg | Al | Si | P |
| | | 2.8.3 | | |

$$Al\,(2.8.3) \longrightarrow Al^{3+} + 3e$$

**Experiment 12.10 Chemical properties of aluminium**

a) Add aluminium foil to the three common dilute acids. Add foil to sodium hydroxide solution. If nothing happens, warm the mixtures. Test any gases formed.

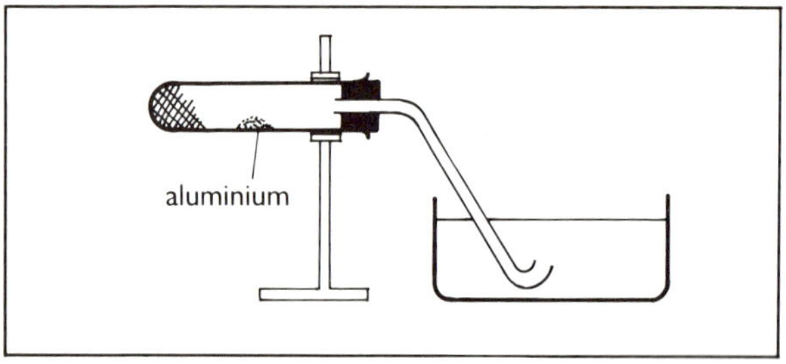


*b) Pass steam over heated aluminium powder as in Experiment 10.3.

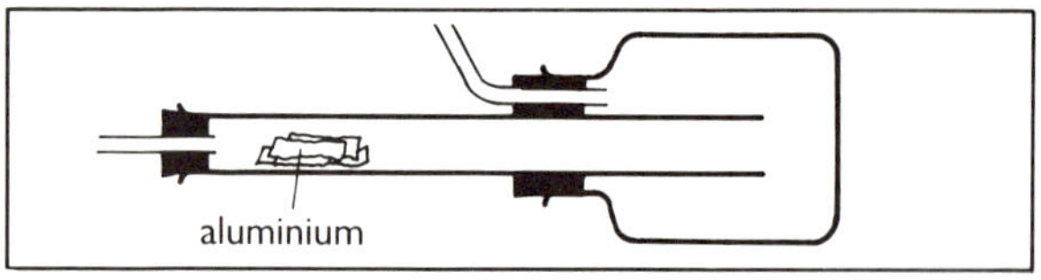


*c) Pass chlorine or hydrogen chloride over heated aluminium foil. Use the apparatus of Experiment 6.14.

d) Hold a strip of aluminium foil in the bunsen flame.

*e) Put a drop of dilute hydrochloric acid on a piece of foil. Add a tiny drop of mercury. Rub the mixture over the foil with a rod. Let it stand.

*f) Repeat the Thermit reaction (Book 1, page 72).

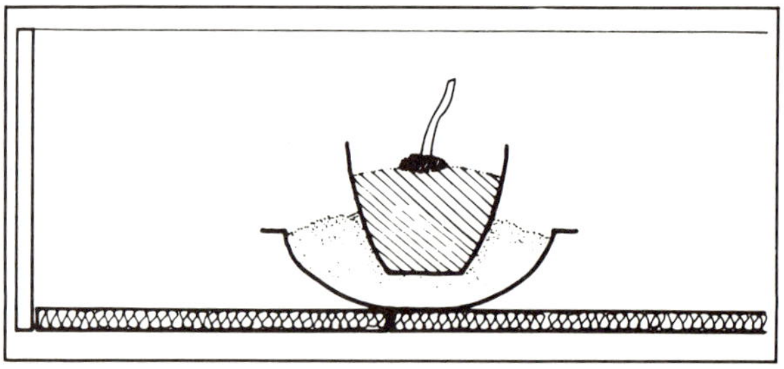

You have used some of these tests before.
Do they show aluminium to be an active metal?
With which substance does it *not react*?

With acids and alkalis the metal gives hydrogen. It reduces steam. It reduces oxides of other metals. Yet it does not easily burn. It appears not to tarnish in air. It does not react with nitric acid.

It reacts with chlorine and hydrogen chloride. Both form the same chloride. It is a covalent solid, formula $Al_2Cl_6$. Aluminium is very active. It only *appears* to be unreactive.

Aluminium does tarnish in air. A layer of oxide forms on the surface. This layer is very thin. The shiny surface of the metal shows through it. So the metal appears not to change. The layer of oxide protects the metal.

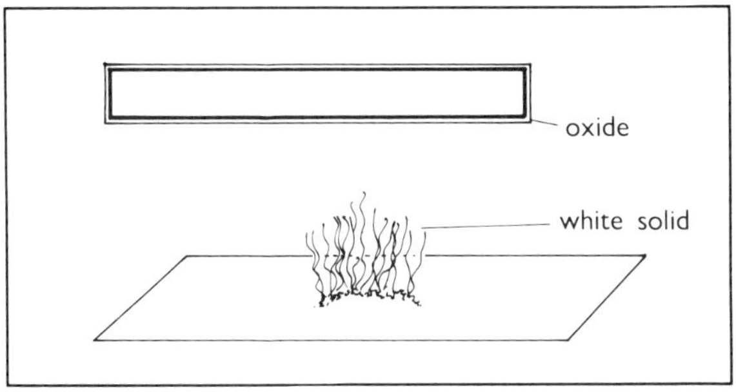


Substances can reach the metal only by dissolving the oxide. This may take time. The reaction is slow to start because of this. It then becomes vigorous. Hydrochloric acid reacts with the oxide. Mercury dissolves the exposed metal. Air can get at it. The white solid oxide 'grows' quickly on the surface.

Aluminium has many uses from food containers to speed boats.

## Experiment 12.11 Aluminium compounds and the $Al^{3+}$ ion

**Add aqueous ammonia to aluminium sulphate solution. Divide the mixture into three parts.**
**a) To one part add a drop of litmus solution. Shake the mixture. Centrifuge or filter it.**
**b) To the second add dilute acid.**
**c) To the third part add sodium hydroxide solution.**
**Add drops of the alkali to aluminium sulphate solution.**

Ammonia gives a white jelly-like ppt.
What is it?
What happens to the litmus?

Manufacturing blocks of aluminium.

The sulphate contains aluminium ions. Alkalis give hydroxyl ions, $OH^-$. The jelly-like ppt is aluminium hydroxide. It reacts with acids. It also reacts with alkalis. This is why sodium hydroxide dissolves it. It acts as a base with acids. It acts as an acid with strong alkalis.

$$Al^{3+}(aq) + 3OH^-(aq) \rightarrow Al(OH)_3(s)$$

Litmus makes the mixture blue. The filtrate is colourless. The ppt has absorbed the litmus dye. Aluminium oxide does this too. The protective layer on the metal is oxide.

Aluminium and its alloys have an enormous number of uses. They are strong and light. They are used for making cars, aircraft, ships, trains, cooking vessels, bottle tops, cans, building materials and many more.

The oxide layer on the metal can be made thicker. The metal is used as an anode. The cell contains dilute sulphuric acid. Oxygen forms at the anode. Oxygen reacts with aluminium. More oxide forms. The process is called 'anodizing'. Aluminium panels can be coloured. The oxide layer on the metal absorbs dyes.

Aluminium is used in packaging. Its lightness and the oxide layer make it ideal 'silver' paper.

# *Iron – a transition element*

The transition elements are metals.
They all have the physical properties of a metal. Can you write these down?

II VIII III
Ca Sc Ti V Cr Mn Fe Co Ni Cu Zn Ga
2.8.14.2

Iron is silvery grey. It has metallic lustre.
Why does it rarely look like this?
Pure iron is fairly hard but not brittle.

Will the bulb light up when we switch on?
What property of iron does this show?

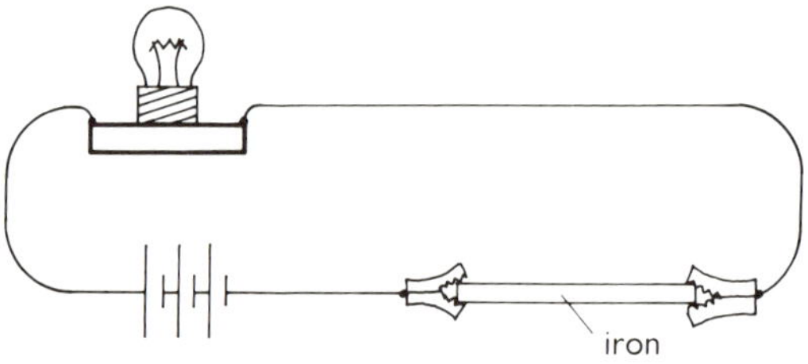


Will the balance show 0.1 g, 1 g or 8 g?
What property of iron does this show?

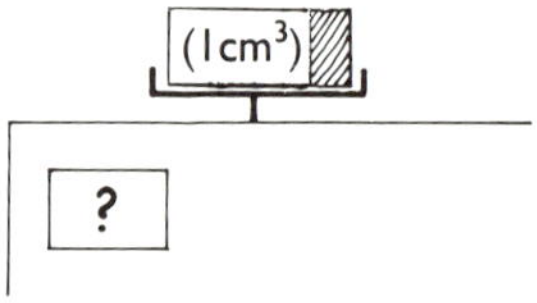


Which is the most likely melting point of iron:
0°C, 200°C or 1500°C?

**Experiment 12.12 The chemical properties of iron**

**Put a little iron filings in a test tube. Add some dilute sulphuric acid. Let the mixture stand. Warm it gently if nothing happens. Test any gas. When the reaction has almost stopped, filter.**

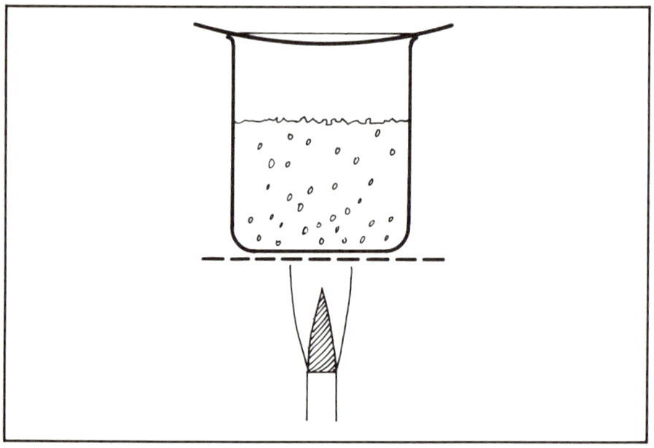

**Add a few drops of dilute sulphuric acid to the filtrate. Evaporate some of it to form crystals. Divide the rest into four. Test each part with one of the following:**
**a) aqueous ammonia,**
**b) sodium hydroxide solution,**
**c) potassium manganate(VII) solution made acid with dilute sulphuric acid,**
**d) hydrogen peroxide.**

**Add aqueous ammonia to the final solutions in c) and d).**

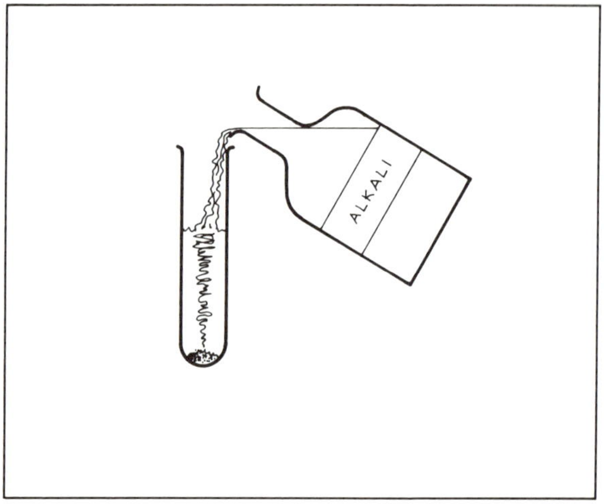


The filter takes out iron. Is the filtrate coloured?
Does the filtrate give coloured crystals?
The filtrate gives a ppt with alkalis. What colour is it?
Potassium manganate(VII) solution oxidizes the filtrate.
How do we know that it does?
Alkali is added after oxidation. What colour is the ppt?

Iron reacts with the acid. The gas formed is hydrogen. Metal and acid give a salt. The filtrate is pale green. It gives green crystals. They are iron(II) sulphate, $FeSO_4.7H_2O$. They contain water of crystallization.

The electron structure of iron is 2.8.14.2. An iron atom loses two electrons from its outside shell. It loses them to hydrogen ions from the acid. The iron(II) ion formed is $Fe^{2+}$.

$$Fe(s) + 2H^{+}(aq) \rightarrow Fe^{2+}(aq) + H_2(g)$$

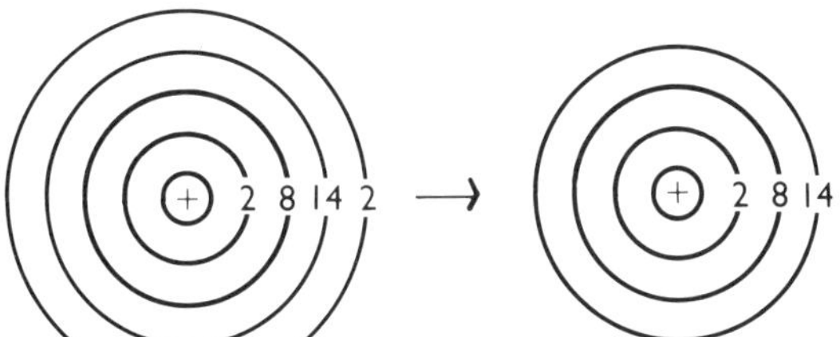


Alkali provides hydroxyl ions, $OH^-$. They react with $Fe^{2+}$. The grey green ppt is iron(II) hydroxide.

$$Fe^{2+}(aq) + 2OH^{-}(aq) \rightarrow Fe(OH)_2(s)$$

$Fe^{2+}$ 2.8.14. does not have noble gas structure. It can lose one more electron to form $Fe^{3+}$. This is the iron(III) ion. Loss of electrons is oxidation.

$$Fe^{2+} - e \rightarrow Fe^{3+}$$

We know that potassium manganate(VII) oxidizes iron(II). It shows this by becoming colourless. Iron(III) sulphate forms in solution. It also gives a ppt with alkali. The colour of this ppt is rusty brown.

$$Fe^{3+}(aq) + 3OH^{-}(aq) \rightarrow Fe(OH)_3(s)$$

Iron has two different ions. It has two sets of compounds. Alkali added to a solution shows which one. Iron(II) compounds give a grey green ppt. Iron(III) compounds give a brown ppt.

## *Experiment 12.13 The two chlorides of iron

**Set up the apparatus as shown in a fume cupboard. Put iron wool in the tube. Pass hydrogen chloride through it. Heat the iron gently and then strongly.**

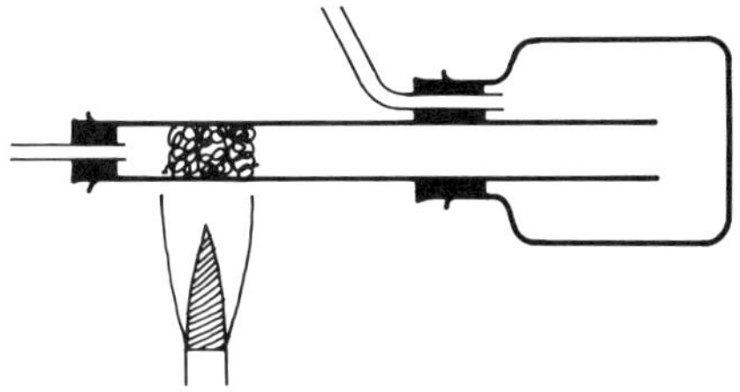

**Set up the apparatus a second time. This time pass chlorine over the heated iron. In each case a solid collects in the bottle. Dissolve each separately in water. Take a sample of each solution. Add aqueous ammonia to it.**

**Take a second sample of each solution. To the one from hydrogen chloride add acidified potassium manganate(VII) solution. To the other add sulphuric acid and zinc. Leave it to stand. After five minutes pour off the solution. Add aqueous ammonia to both liquids.**

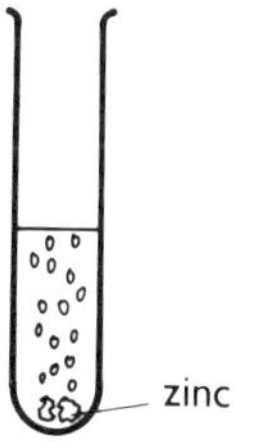


Do the two solids formed appear to be different?
Do they both dissolve in water?
What colour is each of the solutions?
Which of them contains iron(II) chloride?
Does potassium manganate(VII) solution oxidize it to iron(III)?
Chlorine gives iron(III) chloride. How do we know?
What do zinc and acid do to iron(III) chloride?

$Fe + 2HCl \rightarrow H_2 + FeCl_2$ iron(II) chloride
ppt with alkali is grey green
$2Fe + 3Cl_2 \rightarrow 2FeCl_3$ iron(III) chloride
ppt with alkali is rusty brown

Potassium manganate(VII) oxidizes iron(II) to iron(III). Hydrogen from zinc and acid reduces iron(III) to iron(II).

# Other iron compounds

## Experiment 12.14 The three oxides of iron

**a) Heat iron(II) oxalate powder. Put a lighted splint at the mouth of the test tube. Pour the hot powder out of the tube. Let it fall from a height on to white paper. Rub the powder over the paper.**

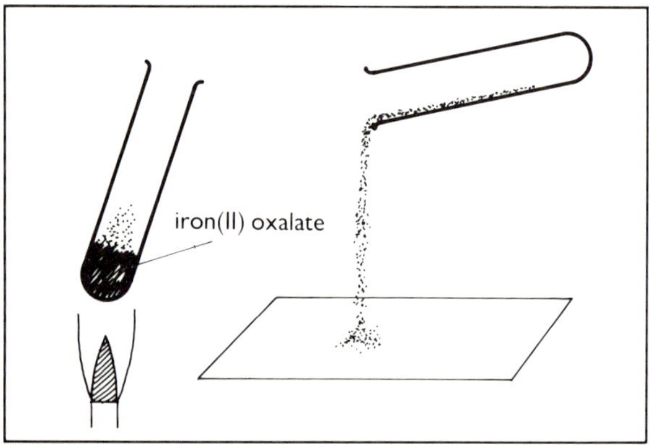


**b) Set up the apparatus. Clean some iron wire. Put it with iron powder in the tube. Heat it so that steam passes over it. Test the gas. Examine the iron.**

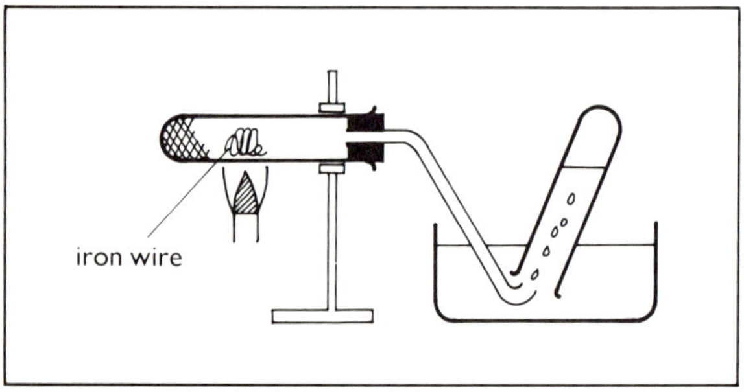


What is the colour of iron(II) oxalate?
How do you know that it gives off gas?
What colour is the powder which remains?
What happens as it falls through the air?
What colour is the powder on the paper?
Steam passes over the heated iron in the tube. What is the colour of the solid which remains?

Yellow iron(II) oxalate 'boils'. The gas given off burns. The black powder formed is iron(II) oxide. It glows white hot as it falls. This heat must come from a reaction. The oxide combines with oxygen from air. The powder on the paper is brown iron(III) oxide, $Fe_2O_3$.

Iron is silvery grey. It reacts with steam to give hydrogen. The substance left is blue-black. It is magnetic iron oxide, $Fe_3O_4$.

**c) Rub iron wire with emery paper. Hold it in the bunsen flame. Drop iron filings through the flame. Catch the product on white paper.**

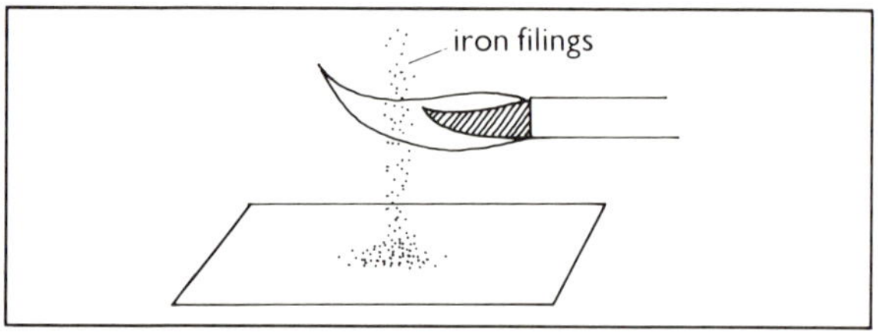


Which oxide is it?

Iron has three oxides. Iron(II) oxide is FeO. It is oxidized by air. The product is iron(III) oxide. The formula $Fe_2O_3$ shows oxygen added to FeO. Heating iron forms the third oxide $Fe_3O_4$. It is blue-black. It behaves as the other two combined, $FeO.Fe_2O_3$.

Most metals tarnish in air. Iron shows it most. Its tarnish is red-brown rust. Everyday life shows that rusting needs water. What else does it need?

## Experiment 12.15 Does rusting use air?

**Wet the inside of a test tube. Sprinkle iron filings inside it. Turn it upside down in water. Measure the height of air in the tube. Leave it for a few days. Measure the height of the air again. Take out the tube. Test the air in it with a lighted splint.**

What percentage of the air is used up?
What happens to the lighted splint?
What gas is used up during rusting?

These are some results:
first height of air = 14 cm
height after rusting = 11 cm

The volume of air is roughly proportional to height. 3 cm used out of 14 cm is about 21%. The lighted splint goes out. Both show that rusting uses oxygen. Can you guess what iron compound rust might be?

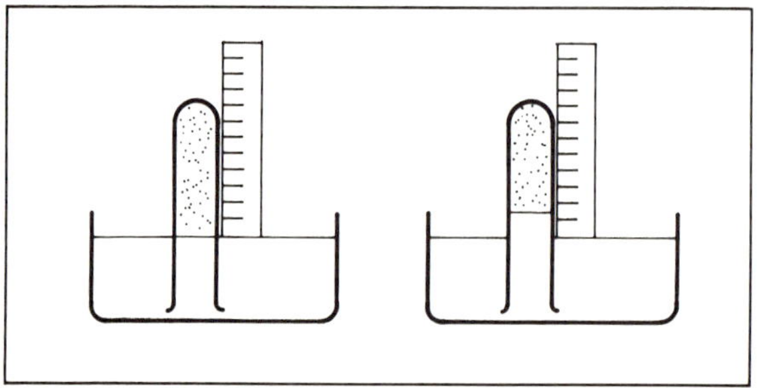

## Experiment 12.16 Are other substances needed for rusting?

Clean some nails with emery paper. Set them up in test tubes as shown. Leave them for several days.

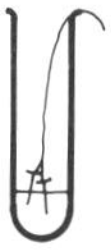

This tube contains water and air (carbon dioxide and oxygen). It is a control.

This tube contains anhydrous calcium chloride. It takes out water from the air in the tube.

Boil some water in this tube. Pass carbon dioxide through it for a few minutes. Stopper the tube.

This tube contains sodium hydroxide solution. It removes any carbon dioxide.

Fill the tube with water. Boil the water for two minutes. Lower the nails into the water. Stopper it with no air inside.

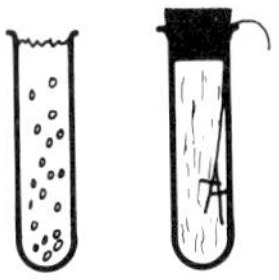

In which tubes do the nails not rust?
Which substances have been taken out of these tubes?
What substances are needed if iron is to rust?

Rusting needs water, oxygen and carbon dioxide. They oxidize iron to iron(III) oxide. This is 'rusty-brown'. A layer of oxide protects aluminium. Rust does *not* protect iron. The layer of rust flakes off. This exposes iron underneath. The iron turns into a heap of iron(III) oxide.

Rusting can be prevented or slowed down. Iron must be kept away from water and air. It can be painted. It can be coated with another metal. Chromium, tin, nickel and zinc are all used. The seal must be perfect. Cracks allow water and air to get in. They rust the iron. This is true of painted iron. The other metals, except zinc, are not changed.

*Iron cranes and ships all must,*
*Like any iron, turn to rust.*
*So paint them all with loving care*
*To keep out water and the air,*
*Or oxidation at the dockside*
*Will turn them into iron oxide.*

### Summary

Iron has two sets of compounds. This is because it forms two different ions. They are iron(II). $Fe^{2+}$, and iron(III), $Fe^{3+}$. Its compounds are coloured. Oxidization is

$$Fe^{2+} + e \rightarrow Fe^{3+}$$

The reverse change is reduction. Both ions in solution give a ppt with alkali. Iron(II) hydroxide is grey green. Iron(III) hydroxide is rusty-brown. Alkali shows which ions are present in solution. Iron has three oxides.

Iron is important. So are its alloys. They are the steels. They rust unless they are protected.

# Iron and steel

There are four main ores of iron. Two are oxides. Haematite is iron(III) oxide. Magnetite is $Fe_3O_4$. There are also sulphide and carbonate ores. These are roasted in air. They give iron(III) oxide.

Iron is extracted from the oxide. It is mixed with coke and limestone. The mixture is fed into the top of a blast furnace. This is a steel tower about 30 metres high. It is lined with firebrick.

The 'blast' is air mixed with oxygen. It is heated to 900 °C and blown into the furnace. The air tubes are called tuyeres (twyers). The coke burns in the oxygen. This reaction is exothermic. The furnace temperature rises to about 1900 °C.

$$C + O_2 \rightarrow CO_2$$

The carbon dioxide rises through the mixture. Coke reacts with it. Carbon monoxide is formed. This reaction is endothermic. The temperature falls.

$$CO_2(g) + C(s) \rightarrow 2CO(g)$$

The monoxide is a gas. It reduces iron(III) oxide to iron. This melts and runs down through the furnace. It is a liquid so substances dissolve in it. Impure liquid iron falls to the bottom.

$$Fe_2O_3(s) + 3CO(g) \rightarrow 2Fe(l) + 3CO_2(g)$$

The high temperature decomposes limestone. Calcium oxide, quicklime, forms.

$$CaCO_3 \rightarrow CaO(s) + CO_2(g)$$

Quicklime reacts with impurities in the iron ore. For example, sand forms calcium silicate. The result is liquid slag. This runs down the furnace. Slag floats on the molten iron. Both slag and iron are tapped off.

Mixture fed in at the top keeps the furnace full. The process need only stop for repairs. Waste gas leaves at the top. It is piped off and burnt. The heat is used to heat the blast. The slag is used in the building industry.

The impure iron contains up to 4% carbon. It may contain other elements such as phosphorus. These make it harder but more brittle. They are removed from the iron before turning it into steel.

A blast furnace.

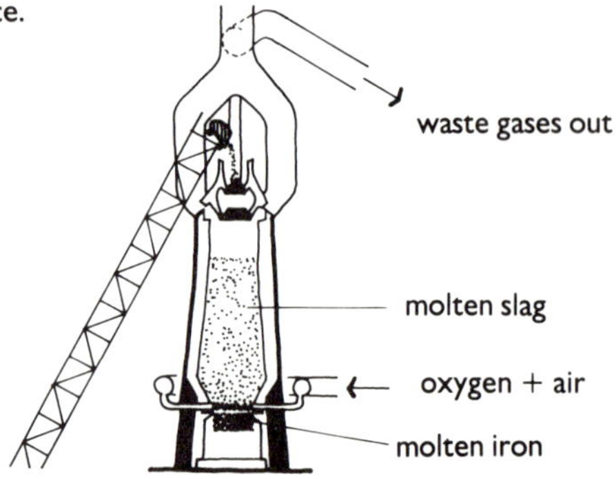

Tapping iron from a furnace.

There are two main methods of doing this. Both use the molten metal from the furnace. Some impurities are burnt out. Some react with basic oxides such as quicklime.

1. The Open Hearth method uses an open hearth furnace which is a shallow basin. The furnace is lined with fire brick. The molten iron is put in. Ore and scrap iron are added. Lime is the basic oxide used. The total charge may be 500 tonnes.

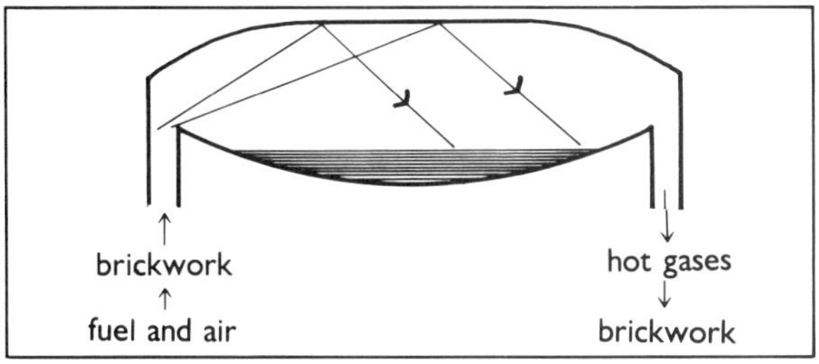


Liquid and gas fuel are burnt at one end. The flame is deflected by the roof. It heats the charge. Carbon is burnt out of the iron. Other impurities react with the lime. The slag floats on the iron.

Hot gases pass out through brickwork. They heat it. The flow of fuel and air is reversed. It is made much hotter by the brickwork. The iron becomes pure.

2. The Basic Oxygen method uses a converter.

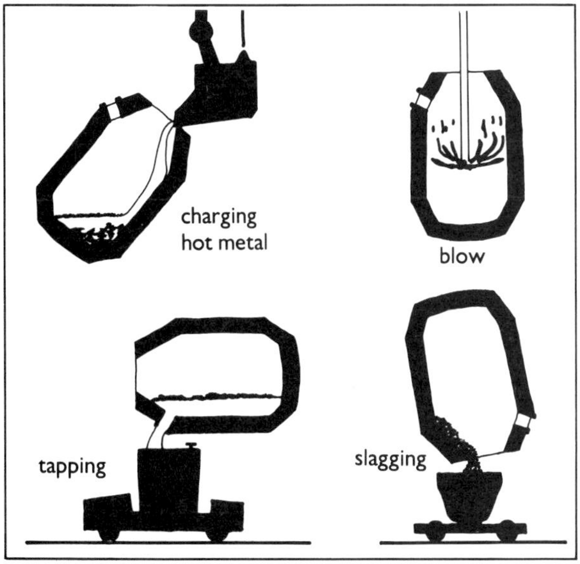

**Pouring hot metal into a basic oxygen furnace.**

This is a steel vessel lined with fire brick. It holds about 300 tonnes of molten iron. Scrap iron and lime are added. Oxygen under pressure is blown in. It passes through a water cooled tube called a lance.

Lime removes impurites. Carbon is burnt out. A slag forms. It floats on the pure iron. In both methods this iron is turned into steel. Other elements are dissolved in it to give alloys. The amounts are decided by the properties needed.

Ordinary steels are alloys of carbon and iron. The carbon content varies from 0.2 to 1.5%. Special steels contain other metals. Steel for magnets will contain cobalt. Stainless steel contains nickel and chromium. They are examples of the fourteen million tonnes of steel manufactured in Britain every year.

A third method of making steel is the electric arc method. The furnace is charged with ore, scrap iron and lime. Heat comes from an electric arc. Pure steel is formed. It has the correct amount of carbon. The steel is poured out as a liquid.

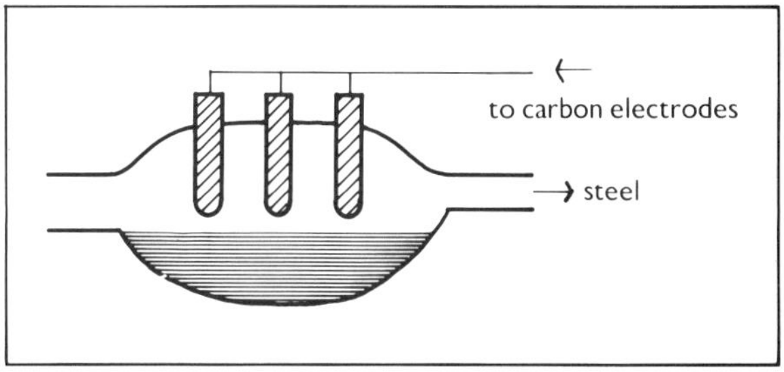

# Questions

Questions 1 to 6: elements may be placed in the following groups:
A Alkali metals, B Noble gases, C Group II metals, D Halogens, E Transition metals. In which group would you place an element:

1. whose molecule contains two atoms?
2. whose atom has the electron configuration 2.8.8?
3. whose atom easily loses one electron?
4. whose ions give coloured solutions?
5. whose atom forms two different positive ions?
6. whose atom forms the ion, $X^{2+}$, only?

Questions 7 to 12: the following are sets of three elements: A (Cl, Br, I), B (He, Ne, Ar), C (Li, Na, K), D (Na, Mg, Al), E (Be, Mg, Ca).
Which set

7. forms few if any compounds?
8. has the electron configurations 2.8.1, 2.8.2, 2.8.3?
9. contains alkali metals?
10. contains halogens?
11. contains elements from more than one group of the Periodic Table?
12. has atoms with an outside shell of 7 electrons?

Questions 13 and 14: electrical conductivity is the result of movement of particles. Which of the particles below move when:

13. a metal conducts a current?
14. a salt solution conducts?
    A atoms, B electrons, C protons, D ions, E neutrons.

Questions 15 to 20: five terms used in electrolysis are:
A electrolyte, B cathode, C anode, D anion, E cation.
Select the correct one for:

15. the liquid through which the current passes,
16. a negatively charged ion,
17. the positive electrode,
18. the electrode at which metals and hydrogen appear,
19. a positively charged ion,
20. the electrode at which oxygen often appears.

21. A good conductor of electric current is
    A hydrogen chloride
    B a solution of hydrogen chloride in water
    C a solution of hydrogen chloride in methylbenzene
    D pure water
    E methylbenzene.

22. A sodium ion differs from a sodium atom in having
    A one less proton
    B one less electron
    C one more proton
    D one more electron
    E one more neutron.

23. An aqueous solution of copper sulphate is electrolysed. Both electrodes are platinum. The products could be

| | at the positive anode | at the negative cathode |
|---|---|---|
| A | copper | sulphate |
| B | hydrogen | copper |
| C | oxygen | copper |
| D | hydrogen | oxygen |
| E | oxygen | hydrogen |

Questions 24 to 36: each question has four statements. One or more of them is correct. Decide which are the correct ones. Then write down as the answer
A if only 1, 2 and 3 are correct,
B if only 1 and 3 are correct,
C if only 2 and 4 are correct,
D if only 4 is correct,
E if another statement or group of statments is correct.

24. The rate of reaction between calcium carbonate and dilute hydrochloric acid is increased by
    1 using powdered chalk instead of lumps
    2 raising the temperature
    3 increasing the concentration of the acid
    4 using a larger flask to hold the mixture.

25. The nucleus of a large atom contains
    1 electrons only
    2 protons only
    3 neutrons only
    4 protons and neutrons.

26. The element rubidium, Rb, comes below sodium and potassium in Group I of the Periodic Table. You would expect it to
    1 react vigorously with water
    2 have a very high density
    3 to form the ion $Rb^+$
    4 not tarnish in air.

27. Oxidation is
    1 the loss of oxygen by a substance
    2 the gain of oxygen by a substance
    3 the gain of electrons
    4 the loss of electrons.

28. The change from a metal atom to its ion, $Mg \rightarrow Mg^{2+}$, is an example of
  1 reduction
  2 oxidation
  3 extraction
  4 ionization.

29. Which statements about nitrogen are true?
  1 its molecule contains two atoms
  2 it burns readily in air
  3 it reacts with hydrogen to form ammonia
  4 it is 21% of the air around us.

30. The gas methane
  1 has the formula $CH_4$
  2 burns in air forming carbon dioxide and water
  3 is the chief compound in 'natural' gas
  4 has two isomers.

31. Which gases have a relative molecular mass of 28 if $H = 1, C = 12, N = 14, O = 16$?
  1 carbon monoxide, CO
  2 nitrogen
  3 ethene, $C_2H_4$
  4 oxygen.

32. Acids
  1 can be neutralized by bases
  2 in water have a pH between 0 and 6
  3 contain hydrogen which gives $H^+$ ions in solution
  4 react with non-metals to give hydrogen.

33. Two different substances have the formula $C_4H_{10}$. The two substances are called
  1 isotopes
  2 polymers
  3 carbohydrates
  4 isomers.

34. A metal is below aluminium in the Activity Series. It is above iron. It would be expected to
  1 react with cold water
  2 react when heated in steam
  3 reduce aluminium oxide to the metal
  4 displace hydrogen from dilute acids.

35. Ethanol
  1 has the formula $C_2H_5OH$
  2 reacts with acids to form esters
  3 decomposes to form ethene and water
  4 puts hydroxyl ions, $OH^-$, into solution in water.

36. Polymers are made by
  1 small molecules of the same substance reacting
  2 large molecules decomposing
  3 monomers reacting to form a giant molecule
  4 fermentation of sugar solution.

37. Describe an experiment to determine the heat of reaction of an acid with a metal. How can the results of such experiments be used to put metals in order of activity? What is this order called?

38. Describe how you could set up a simple cell. Use the metals copper and zinc and any solutions you need. Which electrode is negative? How would you measure the voltage the cell gives? Why does the voltage fall away during use? How does a dry cell prevent this effect?

39. The apparatus shown contains 20 g of marble chips.

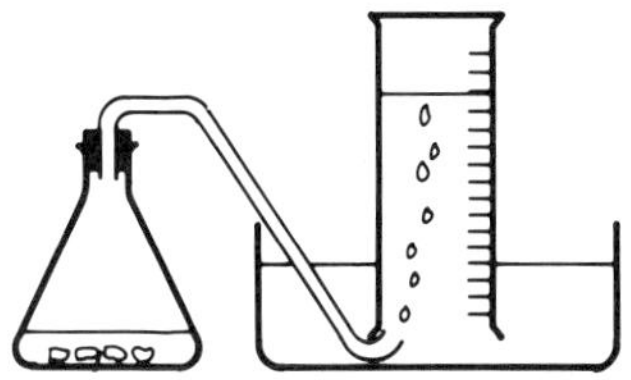

50 $cm^3$ of M hydrochloric acid is added. The temperature of the acid is 16 °C. The gas given off is collected. The volumes of gas are shown:
volume collected after one minute is 40 $cm^3$
volume collected after two minutes is 70 $cm^3$

a) What volume of gas is collected in the second minute?
b) Why is it less than the volume collected in the first minute?
c) Would it be even less in the third minute?

The experiment is repeated with 20 g of smaller lumps of marble. 50 $cm^3$ of M acid at 16 °C is used.

d) Will the gas collected in one minute be greater or less than 40 $cm^3$? Explain why.

The experiment is repeated with the acid at 32 °C.

e) Will the gas collected in one minute be greater or less than 40 $cm^3$? Say what you think the volume will be?

The experiment is repeated with 50 $cm^3$ of 0.5 M acid.

f) Will the volume be less or more in the first minute? Say what you think the volume will be.

# Periodic Table

| | | | | | | | | | | | | | | | | | | |
|---|---|---|---|---|---|---|---|---|---|---|---|---|---|---|---|---|---|---|
| 1 | 1 H Hydrogen 1 | | | | | | | | | | | | | | | | | 2 He Helium 4 |
| 2 | 3 Li Lithium 7 | 4 Be Beryllium 9 | | | | | | | | | | | 5 B Boron 11 | 6 C Carbon 12 | 7 N Nitrogen 14 | 8 O Oxygen 16 | 9 F Fluorine 19 | 10 Ne Neon 20 |
| 3 | 11 Na Sodium 23 | 12 Mg Magnesium 24 | | | | | | | | | | | 13 Al Aluminium 27 | 14 Si Silicon 28 | 15 P Phosphorus 31 | 16 S Sulphur 32 | 17 Cl Chlorine 35·5 | 18 Ar Argon 40 |
| 4 | 19 K Potassium 39 | 20 Ca Calcium 40 | 21 Sc Scandium | 22 Ti Titanium | 23 V Vanadium | 24 Cr Chromium 52 | 25 Mn Manganese 55 | 26 Fe Iron 56 | 27 Co Cobalt 59 | 28 Ni Nickel 59 | 29 Cu Copper 63·5 | 30 Zn Zinc 65 | 31 Ga Gallium | 32 Ge Germanium | 33 As Arsenic 75 | 34 Se Selenium | 35 Br Bromine 80 | 36 Kr Krypton 84 |
| 5 | 37 Rb Rubidium | 38 Sr Strontium 88 | 39 Y Yttrium | 40 Zr Zirconium | 41 Nb Niobium | 42 Mo Molybdenum | 43 Tc Technetium | 44 Ru Ruthenium | 45 Rh Rhodium | 46 Pd Palladium | 47 Ag Silver 108 | 48 Cd Cadmium 112 | 49 In Indium | 50 Sn Tin 119 | 51 Sb Antimony 122 | 52 Te Tellurium | 53 I Iodine 127 | 54 Xe Xenon 131 |
| 6 | 55 Cs Caesium | 56 Ba Barium 137 | 57* La Lanthanum | 72 Hf Hafnium | 73 Ta Tantalum | 74 W Tungsten | 75 Re Rhenium | 76 Os Osmium | 77 Ir Iridium | 78 Pt Platinum 195 | 79 Au Gold 197 | 80 Hg Mercury 201 | 81 Tl Thallium | 82 Pb Lead 207 | 83 Bi Bismuth 209 | 84 Po Polonium | 85 At Astatine | 86 Rn Radon |
| 7 | 87 Fr Francium | 88 Ra Radium | 89† Ac Actinium | | | | | | | | | | | | | | | |

*58–71 Lanthanum series
†90–103 Actinium series

# Glossary

The glossary is a list of important words or terms. The first number refers to the first page on which it is mentioned. Other page numbers refer to important uses.

**Acid:** A substance which forms hydrogen ions, $H^+$, in water/72
**Activity Series:** The metals listed in order of how well they react/78, 134
**Addition reaction:** Two or more substances react to form one product/96
**Alkali:** A substance which puts hydroxyl ions, $OH^-$, into water/72
**Alkali metal:** A Group I metal/138, 142
**Alkaline earth metal:** A Group II metal/138, 146
**Allotropy:** The existence of allotropes of the same element/9, 86
**Anion** A negative ion. It moves to the anode during electrolysis/36
**Anode:** A positively-charged electrode /32
**Atomic number:** The number of protons in the nucleus of an atom/41
**Atomic structure:** The way smaller particles are arranged in an atom/41
**Avogadro's Constant Number:** L = 602 000 000 000 000 000 000 000 000/19
**α-rays (alpha radiation):** A stream of positively-charged helium ions/40
**β-rays (beta radiation):** A stream of electrons/40
**Catalyst:** A substance which alters the rate of reaction. It is still there at the end of the reaction/23
**Cathode:** A negatively-charged electrode/32
**Cation:** A positive ion attracted to the cathode/36
**Carbon chemistry:** The branch of chemistry dealing with carbon compounds/86
**Cell:** A device for turning chemical energy into electrical energy/80
**Condensation reaction:** A reaction between two molecules forming a bigger one and a smaller one such as water/102, 104
**Covalent bond:** A shared pair of electrons joining two atoms/68
**Covalent compound:** A compound held together by covalent bonds/68, 70
**Dehydration:** The removal of water from a substance. It is also the removal of hydrogen and oxygen in the same proportions as in water/27
**Displacement reaction:** A reaction in which one element replaces another/78
**Double bond:** Two covalent bonds joining the same atoms/91, 96
**Electrode:** The conductor which a current enters or leaves by/32
**Electrolysis:** Current passing through a liquid forming new substances at the electrodes/32, 50
**Electrolyte:** The liquid used in electrolysis/32
**Electron:** Negatively-charged particle, with a mass about $\frac{1}{2000}$ of an H atom/40, 62
**Electron shell:** Group of electrons round the nucleus of an atom/42, 62
**e.m.f.:** The electric pressure (in volts) which causes current to pass/82
**Endothermic reaction:** A reaction during which heat is taken in/74
**Exothermic reaction:** A reaction during which heat is given out/74
**Formula:** A way of showing the atoms in a molecule/19

**$\gamma$-rays (gamma radiation):** A stream of rays similar to X-rays/40
**Half-life:** The time taken for half a radioactive element to disintegrate/45
**Heat of reaction ($\Delta H$):** The heat change when moles react according to the equation for the reaction/74
**Heat of combustion:** Heat of reaction for combustion/75
**Heat of displacement:** Heat of reaction for displacement/78
**Heat of neutralization:** Heat of reaction for neutralization/76
**Hydrogen ion:** The ion $H^+$ which makes a solution acid/72
**Hydroxyl ion:** The ion $OH^-$ which makes a solution alkaline/72
**Ion:** A charged atom or group of atoms/36
**Ionic bond:** Attraction between ions of opposite charge/65
**Ionic compound:** A compound held together by ionic bonds/65, 71
**Isomers:** Substances with the same molecular formula but different structural formulae/89, 94
**Joule:** The unit of energy. 1000 joules = 1 **kilojoule**/74
**Mass number:** The number of protons and neutrons in the nucleus of an atom/41
**Molar solution:** 1 mole of solute in 1000 $cm^3$ of solution/20
**Mole:** Avogadro's Number of atoms, molecules, ions or electrons/19
**Monomer:** A compound with small molecules which polymerize/102
**Neutron:** Particle with no charge and mass of 1 atomic mass unit/41
**Nucleus:** The tiny centre of an atom/40
**Nuclear reaction:** A change in the nucleus of an atom/45
**Oxidation:** Addition of oxygen to a substance or loss of electrons/22, 53, 135
**Periodic Table:** The elements arranged in order of atomic number/138
**pH:** A number showing the concentration of hydrogen ions/73
**pH range:** The numbers from 0 to 14 which measure pH/73
**Plastic:** A substance, usually a polymer, which can be moulded/102, 108
**Polymer:** The substance formed by small molecules combining/102, 108
**Primary cell:** An electric cell which cannot be re-charged/81, 82
**Properties:** The appearance and behaviour of a substance/7
**Proton:** Positively-charged particle with mass of one unit/41
**Radioactivity:** Radiation from the breakdown of atomic nuclei/40, 44
**Rate of reaction:** The speed of a chemical change/128
**Redox reaction:** A reaction in which reduction and oxidation happen/135
**Reduction:** The loss of oxygen from a substance or the gain of electrons/22, 135
**Relative atomic mass:** The numbers which compare the masses of atoms of the elements. They are written H = 1, O = 16 etc./18
**Saturated compound:** A compound which only reacts by substitution/87
**Secondary cell:** A cell which can be re-charged/82
**Structural formula:** A formula which shows how atoms are joined in a molecule/88
**Substitution reaction:** A reaction in which atoms are replaced by others/87
**Unsaturated compound:** A compound which reacts by addition/97